TO ERIKA AND DAVID

CONTENTS

PREFACE
ABOUT COMMUNICATING WHEN WE SPEAK

☐ YOU AS A MEDIUM

Communicating When We Speak was selected for this book's title because by itself the term *communication* has come to mean many things. We wanted our readers to know that this book is not about computers, or telephones, or newspapers, or television, or radio waves. It's about people who speak to each other, in private or public.

The title is also intended to let you know that communicating consists of some things which we may not include here. We are not concerned with written communication, however important it may be and however many years of school are devoted to learning its skills. Too few years have been dedicated to learning about our spoken communication; too little is known about how to speak and, especially, about how to listen.

Something you have learned—whether or not you know the work of Marshall McLuhan and others—is that any message you want to get across will be affected by the medium you use to convey it. McLuhan's way of saying this was familiarly expressed as "the medium is the message," but earlier writers had tried to make us aware that we cannot separate what is being said from the structure and process of the medium through which it is expressed. Just as Benjamin Lee Whorf (coupled with Edward Sapir, Alfred Korzybski, and others) wrote that the nature of our language determines the thought processes we use, so did other social commentators (such as George Herbert Mead, Carl Hovland, and Buckminster Fuller) tell us about the medium-bound nature of some kinds of communication.

When you stand to talk to others, certain things happen which don't happen when you hand someone a note, or listen to the radio, or watch a movie, or read a newspaper. Only in human speech (and its extensions and preservations such as television or films) can we shade our meanings by inflections, tones, voice, and body control. Only in human speech can we relate to each other so immediately and change our signals so quickly. Only in human speech can we call up the richness of unrehearsed joy, sudden sorrow, or unexpected surprise in a flowing stream of relationships with others.

This book is about communicating when we speak. We deal with the limitations of our speaking as well as the richness of its potential. There are limits to what we can do in speaking, as there are in any medium. Listening to radio, for example, limits our perceptions to the medium of sound, but television adds vision to it.

The printed page is a purely visual medium, although—as in all media—surrounding characteristics help determine how printing will affect a reader. For example, in a culture where books are primarily religious writings, the appearance of something so trivial as a comic book might inspire awe, just because it was in printed form and therefore likely to be religious.

Another example of how religion can affect communication occurs in cultures that adhere to the teachings of Mohammed, when a camera is used to produce a "forbidden" human figure in graphic representation. Photography as a medium of communication is thus restricted by the norms and prevailing practices of the followers of Islam. To point a camera at someone who believes in this taboo is to court danger; even the possession of a camera is sometimes considered sinful, and looking at photographs of people is held to be distasteful.

Primitive people who experienced tape recording for the first time feared that the machine had stolen the human voice and would not give it back. In such a situation, effective communication requires more than a mechanical knowledge of how to operate a tape recorder; some understanding of how the machine relates to the human participant is needed.

In our attitudes about speaking and the act of speech making we also have developed some taboos and norms which can affect how we approach speaking. We hope in this book to introduce you to the spoken communicative act as an exciting and vital medium—one that offers tremendous potential for relating with others, for getting the job done, and for expressing ourselves as both medium and message.

You are already accustomed to the fact that you can speak; that others speak; and that in speaking with others some things seem to happen. Speaking ranges in form and substance and formality and function over a wide spectrum of types and styles. You've been speaking most of your life, and it is not therefore surprising to discover that you have more experience at it than you might think. Now that you have begun reading a book about speaking, you will find out that you knew how to speak all the time; but maybe you can also learn to do some of it better.

Information about what you can expect from this book and how it is put together will be useful to you. And we'll say some things about public speaking/communication and how we think people learn. These latter points may be of less use to you, except as warnings about our biases as authors. No author can be perfectly neutral about a subject all the time, and we want to acquaint you with some of our biases. You should know where we stand so that you can choose your response to items in this book. You'll learn more about communicating—and we'll feel more honest—if we start by admitting that we have a point of view, and you have your own.

What you will get from this book will depend a lot on what you are after in reading it. It's designed to (1) introduce you to basic information about speaking with others; (2) guide you in practical speaking opportunities; (3) give you a better understanding of how your public utterances can be improved through knowledge about communication; and (4) help you evaluate the effectiveness of your speaking and the speaking of others.

The book is written as a beginning course in practical speaking with others. "Others" may include one other person or a large formal audience. This is not an exhaustive study of human communication. Rather it is a guide to your understanding and involvement in the natural and frequent (for most of us) activity of speaking. We hope this approach will give you enjoyment as well as insight—pleasure as well as information—some fun in the experience of learning about your speech.

We hope this book will increase your curiosity about communicating. If you choose, a whole world of study is available involving the science and art of communicating. Principles of logical argument are refinements you can become deeply involved in; or you can study in depth about linguistic systems, communication models, speech avoidance, voice and diction, oral interpretation of written literature, speech pathologies, or specialized speech making and famous or little-known speakers.

To spur your involvement, we have drawn together some traditional ideas about public speaking with some more recent emphases of interpersonal communication. Systems for learning about speaking which have succeeded for years are joined by some innovative systems which have helped students learn to communicate better. In addition to information about speaking, this book includes things to do which will help you see how to improve your speaking. Our main objective is to present information about speech and then give you a chance to try the things we've written about. This plan reflects our bias—our point of view—about how people learn. We believe people learn better when they are given data plus the chance to do something with the data. That's why we have included "Applications" as a frequent invitation to look at communication; why we have suggested activities and exercises; and why we have tried to relate your real-life experiences to that mystical and challenging situation when you face a public audience.

A second bias must be mentioned. We believe that the growing field of communication (sometimes referred to as "interpersonal communication" or "communication behavior") need not be divided from public speaking or regarded suspiciously by rhetoricians. Public speaking as a science/art is historically very old. Indeed, classical rhetoric examines the same principles used today in speech making. Although Quintillian never heard of radio, and Aristotle had no vision of television, the principles of how people influence each other are firmly planted in behaviors which humans show to each other regardless of mechanical or technological inventions. Teaching of speaking gained great prominence in the societies where the politician or legal advocate needed a significant ability to inform or persuade. Speaking to entertain others dates back to the primitive story-tellers who orally reported and recited tales of warriors, wise men, fools, and great events. Our enjoyment of others, day by day, is related to how we keep in touch; how we communicate; how we share information, ideas, plans; how we learn about each other by talking together about our past experiences, present problems, and future dreams.

We see, then, no dichotomy between public speaking and communicating. These are not separable activities or processes, and certainly not competing opposites. In this book we have demonstrated their interrelatedness, their logical association, and—most importantly—the necessity of treating the speech act as a dynamic part of our lives.

☐ INTRODUCTION TO THE SECOND EDITION

This second edition of *Communicating When We Speak* has been produced with major changes; all designed to make the text more effective for the student and the teacher. Changes were suggested by excellent and thoughtful reviewers and by many teachers (including, of course, the authors) who used the book in the classroom and workshops.

Interfacing public speaking as a traditional learning experience with interpersonal communication is still the primary purpose of the book. Both the content and methods of learning have been updated; and new exercises supplement successful exercises from the first edition. A new look at self-concept is added to emphasize the personal relationship between the speaker and an audience. The section on mass communication (and media) has been moved to the final chapter at the request of many teachers who find it very useful as a consumer-oriented wrap-up for their courses. The very long portions in the early part of the text on language and symbols have been divided and some new material added.

Because this is a text of "doing" as well as "reading about," the thrust for early and consistent experiential involvement has been sharpened and extended. "Applications" now replace the "What's Happening?" items from the earlier edition to perform the essential function of bringing students in touch with speaking situations, analyses, and action.

The text's format, having undergone extensive simplification and revision, will link even more closely the *activities* with *content* and the *experiences* with *examples*.

☐ ACKNOWLEDGMENTS

This second edition of *Communicating* has been guided by Alison Meersschaert and the thoughtful reviews from teachers who used the text in its first edition. In producing both editions it has been a pleasure working with the McGraw-Hill staff and editors.

We've enjoyed it from the time the initial concept for this book was first relayed to us by Rob Fry, through the patient guidance of Bob Weber, the editorial sharpening by Aline Wolff, and the editing and production efforts of Jim Belser. Work on the manuscript was aided by the Tolela and Munoz friends, and the typing was translated from rough, rough copy by Pearl Hyman.

Our main debt, however, is to our many friends and colleagues in the communication field who have assured us that this kind of text—a bridge between "interpersonal" and "public speaking" based on student activities—is vitally needed and will be useful in, what is to us, the most exciting and challenging discipline in today's exciting and challenging world.

Gail E. Myers
Michele Tolela Myers

PART ONE

It is important to realize that although you have been communicating all your life, you stand to gain much by developing and sharpening your understanding of what you actually <u>do</u> when you engage in so basic an activity. Simply because you have spoken English or Spanish all your life does not make you a Hemingway or a Cervantes. Being a lifelong communicator does not necessarily guarantee your effectiveness in communicative encounters.

Our purpose in this first part is to have you take a look at the basic elements which make up and affect your communicating. In Chapter 1 we will explore a variety of communication perspectives and define the scope of your communication — intrapersonal, interpersonal, and a-personal. After examining the functions communication serves, we will present basic postulates about communication and define the components of communication.

In Chapter 2, we will discuss <u>you</u>, the source of your communication. You need to learn how your perceptual proc-

THE ELEMENTS
OF YOUR
COMMUNICATION

esses affect what you communicate about and how the way you see yourself and feel about yourself largely determines the roles you choose to play, and hence your communicating. How your audience sees you also plays a crucial part in how you will be heard and how your communicative messages will be received.

Chapter 3 will introduce you to a study of language and symbols, the essential tools of your communicating. It will also emphasize that nonverbal communication is an integral part of communicating.

Chapter 4 will examine your audiences and introduce you to a variety of systems to analyze them effectively.

Finally, Chapter 5 will describe the variety of speaking situations you ·may encounter; we will discuss how you need to adjust your communicating to the setting in which you find yourself.

CHAPTER 1
COMMUNICATION PERSPECTIVES

He talked, and as he talked
  Wallpaper came alive;
Suddenly ghosts walked
  And four doors were five.
            — Mark Van Doren

Sometimes a neighbor whom we have disliked a lifetime for his arrogance and conceit lets fall a single commonplace remark that shows us another side, another man, really; a man uncertain, and puzzled, and in the dark like ourselves.
            — Willa Cather

I know that one is able to win people far more by the spoken than by the written word, and that every great movement on this globe owes its rise to the great speakers and not to the great writers.
            — Adolf Hitler

An infant babbles; a father coos and smiles. A child reaches up and pulls on her mother's dress; the mother, without appearing to notice, takes the child's hand in hers as they continue walking. A telephone rings; letters are in the mailbox; the President makes a speech on television to his "fellow Americans"; a professor lectures in an auditorium; a teacher talks to two students in the hall; a small group of students chat casually over a cup of coffee at the university cafeteria. A job interview; a planning committee meeting; a campaign speech in favor of a political candidate; a strike; ringing a doorbell to sell Girl Scout cookies or to raise money for the local symphony; selling a car; accepting a date; asking for a date; silence; holding hands.

These activities and many more, as diverse as they may first appear, have common elements. These common elements stem from the very basic fact that speech-communication activities are essentially *symbolic* activities. An infant babbling and a President addressing a nation over electronic media are not as far apart as they may seem. Both are senders of communicative messages, both will get a response of some kind from the receiver(s) of their message, and both will be affected in some way by the outcomes of their communicative encounter, whatever its length.

You have been communicating in one way or another since you were born. Even before you developed the language of adults, you communicated with them. Your earliest needs for food or attention were met because you made noises or motions which indicated that you—the communicator—wanted to give a message to an audience—your parents.

You still do the same thing. When you feel a need to be heard, you let others know it. Whether ordering a cup of coffee, asking a clerk in the post office for a stamp, or saying "hi" to a friend on the street, you are practicing communication. And you cannot avoid it. You may be asked for directions to another part of the city or be called on to debate the rights of certain citizens to vote. You may give speeches, reports, or lectures, or you may lead discussions of major issues before a large audience. You may have a heated argument with friends at lunch; you may preside at convocations, special ceremonies, rallies, awards presentations, or meetings of an action group.

☐ APPLICATIONS

Throughout this book there are exercises and applications that you may want to use as a supplement to your experience. Developing your understanding of the communication process will involve not only reading about it but also doing something about it. The Applications are the "doing" part.

Not all these exercises will be necessary to gain insights into the communication process as it relates to your behaviors. Some are designed to be applied to specific parts of a chapter. Others are more general in their relations to communication. Some will be assigned as individual exercises, and some will be assigned to be accomplished in groups. Your normal channels of communication in class—talking with other students and with the instructor—will be used in most of these applications as you discuss with others or develop a speaking assignment for the class.

The "cases" or anecdotes presented are followed by some questions or suggestions on how to trigger discussion about the case. Most of the incidents can be related to your own communication experiences, or you can speculate on how these stories can affect you and others around you.

Some other exercises will ask you to begin immediately in this first chapter to prepare for your ultimate speaking assignments in the course. You will begin to determine how your own communication affects others, how others affect you. Some practice at these communication behaviors will be valuable to you as practical applications of the reading material presented in the chapter.

☐ THE SCOPE OF YOUR COMMUNICATION

Although all the speech-communication activities discussed in the beginning of this chapter are bound by common elements which we will describe later in this chapter, they differ in their *scope*. While silent contemplation, for example, is a form of *intrapersonal* communication, asking someone for a date involves at least one other human being and thus revolves around the establishment and/or maintenance of an *interpersonal* relationship.

Interpersonal communication includes *dyadic* situations—two people exchanging ideas, information, feelings—in an informal context, a date for example, or a formal context, such as a job interview.

Interpersonal communication also includes small-group situations where from three to fifteen people engage in communication activities to achieve a common purpose, to identify and solve a problem, to make a decision, or simply to socialize informally.

When the scope of communication activities enlarges, we deal with *a-personal* communication. A-personal communication comprises *public communication*, those situations in which one person addresses a fairly large group of people, face-to-face, but not as spontaneous interacting participants. A-personal communication also includes *mass communication* which is generated through the print or electronic media (newspapers, radio, television) and which reaches very large groups of people.

The diagram in Figure 1-1 may help you visualize the scope of communication activities.

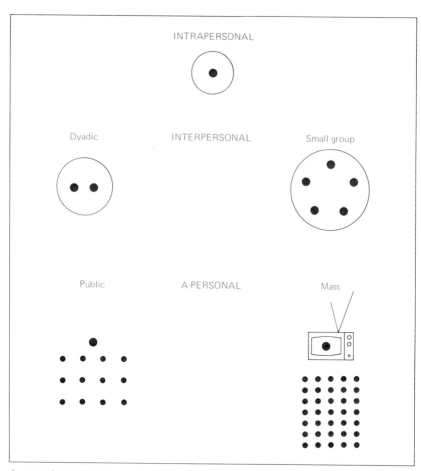

Scope of speech-communication activities.

☐ THE FUNCTIONS OF YOUR COMMUNICATION

While the scope of your speech-communication activities may vary, all communication activities perform certain common functions. Basically we communicate because we need to.

The Need to Communicate

Man's need to communicate is undeniable. We must communicate to get things done. People need words, signs, motions—some kind of signals—to accomplish tasks. Modern human beings are interdependent. We do very little alone. We need one another to perform the work that keeps us alive. Communication springs from this basic need. No one of us can exist in today's society without some form of communication with others. Even carrying out the urge to be alone is a significant form of communication because it demands that others get the message and respect our wish for solitude.

Most of our needs in this world—to eat, drink, and have shelter; to have friends; to go places, hear things, watch events, and read things—are met by means of communication. Most things that happen to us are made more simple or more complicated by the way our communication works.

Our communication thus serves many functions. The following summary of these functions is based on McCroskey and Wheeless's discussion of some general postulates about communication.[1]

---

[1] James C. McCroskey and Lawrence R. Wheeless, *Introduction to Human Communication*, Allyn and Bacon, Boston, 1976, pp. 21–23.

Modern human beings are interdependent. *(Jim Jowers/Nancy Palmer Photo Agency.)*

THE AFFINITY OR SOCIAL FUNCTION

Without interaction with others we shrivel up and die. We all need to interact, to be wanted, to love, to show feelings. We need social relationships and intimacy, and we communicate in order to relate to other people. Our messages indicate the existence or absence of attraction, similarity, and commonality we perceive among people. Our ability to develop and maintain social and intimate relationships is in direct relationship with our communication skills. Although the affinity or social function of communication is more clearly related to the interpersonal range of our communication, it is also applicable to our public communication.

THE INFORMATION AND UNDERSTANDING FUNCTION

Much of our communication—intrapersonal, interpersonal, and a-personal—is designed to increase our store of information and thus our understanding about ourselves and the world in which we live. We exchange information with one another informally ("What did the Vikings score last night?") or in more formal settings ("The square of the hypotenuse is equal to the sum of the squares of the other two sides of a right triangle").

THE INFLUENCE FUNCTION

Much of our communication is designed to change people's attitudes, beliefs, opinions, and actions. We persuade a friend to go to a movie with us, a consumer to buy a certain kind of soap, a voter to support a political candidate, a parent to let us have the family car on Saturday night, a youngster not to drop out of high school. Naturally, communication initiated by others influences us.

THE DECISION FUNCTION

Communication is often preliminary to making decisions. Deciding to get up in the morning, what clothes to wear, what, if anything, to have for breakfast, whether to go to college, what classes to take, what to major in, what groups to join, what ideas to support, all imply communication activities. Unless a decision is a spontaneous emotional reaction, it involves sharing and processing information.

THE NEED TO COMMUNICATE: APPLICATIONS

GETTING YOUR PAPER

You are new in town and want the local newspaper delivered to your apartment. You check the telephone book and phone the newspaper office, getting the circulation desk. You are told that the newsboy will be notified of your order and that you can expect to receive the paper the next day. Three days pass, but you find no paper outside your apartment door. You call the newspaper office again to complain. After a long wait, the person at the circulation desk gives you the newsboy's name and telephone number. You call and get the boy's mother on the phone. When you explain your problem, she promises to have the boy call you. Three hours later, while you are eating your supper, the newsboy calls and insists that he left the paper for you. You ask where. "Right where I leave all the others for that apartment building." It becomes clear that you have been looking for the paper outside your door, while the boy has been leaving it three floors below, near the mailboxes in the entry hall. When you ask him to bring the paper up to your door, he says the building's rules forbid it. Then, you say, he can cancel the order. But he can't; you must phone the newspaper office yourself. Once again in touch with the circulation desk, you learn that the minimum newspaper order is for one week and that you will be billed, even though the paper was not delivered as you instructed.

1   In thinking about this situation, it is important to *avoid placing blame* on anyone. Concentrate on communication effectiveness, not the sins of a delivery boy or the inequities of newspaper policies. Find out in discussion with others whether anyone has been in a similar situation. Do you have any questions about the channels of communication that the newspaper subscriber used? Should he have called the newsboy's home? The newspaper's circulation desk?

2   In one column, list some ways the newsboy might have felt in this situation.

3   In a second column, list the feelings that the person at the circulation desk of the newspaper might have had about your phone call of complaint.

4   What "next move" can the subscriber make? What words from the above lists might describe how people feel in the next communication?

5   Still trying to avoid blaming anyone for this communication difficulty, can you think of any way that this mix-up could have been avoided? What should the newspaper have done? The newsboy? The new subscriber? Try to generate some actions that these parties might have taken to avoid the misunderstandings.

SILENT JUANA

When Juana was eight years old, her family moved from Mexico, where they had always lived, to Uvalde, Texas. She started school and was placed in the first grade of an English-speaking elementary school. There she was handed a book with funny-looking words in it—even the pictures showed unfamiliar things. Everyone seemed unfriendly, cold, and suspicious to Juana, and the teacher seemed to be watching her every minute. She didn't know how to play the games the other children played at recess. Until she met Ramon, a bilingual boy enrolled in the same school, Juana was silent all day. Only with her family did she suddenly become talkative, and then she out-talked them all.

1   In discussing this case, try to avoid (*a*) using stereotypes of the characters in the story, (*b*) acting like a psychiatrist and solving everyone's problems, and (*c*) blaming everybody in the story and society for making this kind of thing happen.
2   Instead, see whether you can locate the sources of Juana's communication difficulty. Are they linguistic? Cultural? Personal? Intellectual? What else? Describe them more fully.
3   What kind of role did Ramon play in Juana's communication environment?
4   What kind of role did the family play in Juana's communication?
5   How would you try to explain to the teacher about Juana's lack of communicativeness?
6   How would you talk to Juana about her perceptions of her communicating and what is expected of her in school? Be specific. It might be helpful to role-play the situation, with one person acting as Juana, another as the teacher, and still another as an outside counselor (not specified in the story, but representing the views of persons discussing this case).

The Desire to Communicate

Supporting the need to communicate in order to stay alive in an interrelated world is the *desire* to communicate. It is a very strong desire. We don't like being left alone for very long, out of touch with others and without stimulation. We develop habits of communicating, such as telephoning a friend at a certain time of day, reading a newspaper regularly, watching a particular television program, or listening to a favorite radio station. We depend on communication throughout the day—from the first jangle of the alarm clock to the last flicker of "The Late-Late Show." In between, we guide ourselves through a maze of symbols, signs, orders, noises, encounters, and thoughts. We seek out and use some of these communications; others are thrust upon us by the environment. When you make an appointment to meet a friend for coffee to talk over a problem, the sounds of your voices are the communication you want—but the clatter of dishes and other typical restaurant noises are likely to intrude on your conversation.

The desire to communicate will vary from one person to another, and certainly from time to time for an individual. Even when you may not want to communicate directly with another person, you are interested in watching and listening to the wealth of communication interchanges around you. You watch drivers argue over bumped fenders in big-city traffic; a 7-foot-tall stranger gets on your bus; a noisy group of small children sit next to you in a restaurant. You spend some of your

The desire to communicate: We don't like being left alone for very long. *(David Strickler/Monkmeyer.)*

communication time just storing up information about events around you so that you can tell a friend about them later—a form of delayed communication. We fulfill our desire to be in touch with our friends by planning our communications with them even while we are surrounded by strangers or witnessing strange events.

Most of us find it difficult to resist answering a ringing telephone. Watch a crowd of people standing around a pay-telephone booth when the phone inside is ringing. There is a considerable compulsion to get the phone answered—or at least to stop its ringing.

Strangers on a bus or in an airplane may begin to converse simply because human beings like to talk. Even if you prefer not to talk in such situations, you are aware of others around you and will usually modify your behavior because of them. For example, if the person next to you on a bus shifts his feet toward yours, you may move yours away. If he looks out the window, you may do likewise, or if the bus jerks, you may look at each other and shake your heads sympathetically. This awareness of others is both communication and *preparation* for communication. Small talk is necessary for good communication because it is an important indication that we want to communicate and that we are preparing to do so if we get encouragement.

The desire to communicate is so strong that we are inclined to invent reasons for communicating if we are forced to do without it. Experiments have been conducted with human subjects placed in rooms where there is no sound or light and where nothing is touching them. People in such situations begin to hallucinate and to think they hear noises, see flashes of light, or feel touches.

THE DESIRE TO COMMUNICATE: APPLICATIONS

THE TELEPHONE PAGE

When Robert Charles heard his name paged at the San Francisco International Airport, he made his way to the nearest telephone, as instructed by the paging message. At the telephone two airport police arrested him. Charles had earlier escaped from a prison work farm in San Jose, California. Acting on a tip, the FBI had arranged for this phone-call trap.

1 What assumption about human nature and communication did the FBI agents make when they set this trap?
2 Discuss other "communication traps." Do salespersons use tricks to get you into a buying mood? Have strangers ever forced you to talk when you didn't feel like it?

TO SPEAK OR NOT TO SPEAK

List three situations in which you *want* to speak (communicate) with others (for example, asking a salesperson for help in locating the right size clothing).

1 _____
2 _____
3 _____

List three situations in which you *do not want* to speak (communicate) with others (for example, being called on in class when you don't know the answer).

1 _____
2 _____
3 _____

When you have listed those six items, be prepared to discuss how you would act in each situation. (For example, when you need help finding clothes of the right size, you will first try to find out who the salesperson is so that you won't ask another customer; then you get the salesperson's attention; then you tell him or her what you are looking for; and then you give him or her a chance to answer you or to direct you to the right part of the store.)

Are there certain things you usually do in situations like these? Do you make use of the same physical moves and language? Do your strategies (the ways you handle yourself) vary with different kinds of situations? Can you predict how you are going to act?

☐ WE STAND ON COMMON GROUND—BASIC COMMUNICATION POSTULATES

By now, you have some fairly well-developed patterns (or habits) of communicating that are uniquely yours. So do other people. Your friends can tell you a lot about how you communicate, and they depend on some kind of regularity in your patterns of communication—not just the words you use, but the kinds of things you like to talk about, the time of day you are most talkative or most quiet, and even any peculiar speech mannerisms you may have. You also depend on your friends to act pretty much the same today as they did yesterday in their communicating—the quiet ones will generally not talk much, and the highly verbal ones will talk a lot; the friend who hates gossip will be rude to a gossiper; the friend who likes cars will usually find some way to get cars into the conversation; and the one who hates politicians will conclude that the country's problems are politically based.

The important thing to remember in considering the process of communication is that we do most of it by choice. The habits and patterns are our own, and we have the opportunity to continue them or change them. By learning about the patterns of communication, we can be better prepared to make choices among the many communication

We learn about communicating by watching others and also by watching how our communication seems to work with them. *(Grant White/Frederic Lewis Photographs.)*

behaviors available to us. What are some common characteristics of communication that form the patterns we use ourselves and see in others?

Communication Is Not Random

Very early in life we begin to mimic the actions of others. That's basically how we learn to speak, to tie our shoes, to eat an ice cream cone, to ask someone we are interested in for a date, to order a cup of coffee, and to throw a ball. We learn about communicating by watching others and also by watching how our communication seems to work with them. We quickly learn to expect their communication to follow certain patterns that we can identify and understand. We have intuitively set up some rules of communication, and we depend on them.

To say that communication is not random implies two closely interrelated ideas: (1) There is a predictable and dependable pattern to communication, and (2) people communicate on purpose.

We have just discussed some of the reasons why we can say there are predictable patterns of communication. We get the limits and ranges of our communication from our own practice and from watching others. We quickly find out which patterns are effective and which are not, depending on our purposes, and we can choose those which are most useful. Thus we choose our communication patterns purposefully, not randomly. There is a reason for most communication you will either observe or participate in. You will not always understand the reason. Even if you do understand the reason, it may not seem terribly important to you. You may listen to two people arguing about whether to go to a movie or stay home and wonder what the fuss is about. You may hear people simply talking about the weather without seeming to reach a very significant level of conversation. However, such discussions are purposive for the relationship of the communicators. Their communication, even if it seems silly to you, is being carried out on purpose. It very likely precedes or follows some other communication of greater importance and could have been predicted if you had enough data about the speakers or if you had followed the long context of their communication relationships closely enough.

The predictability of our communication patterns is related to the fact that we do things on purpose, not at random. There are so many ways people can communicate that it becomes a challenge to learn more of them and to be able to observe those patterns in ourselves and in others. By increasing the predictability of our communicative relationships, we can become more effective communicators. The first step is to practice watching for the order, the arrangement, the purposes, the patterns, and the behaviors of ourselves and others with full confidence that communication is done on purpose—not at random.

COMMUNICATION IS NOT RANDOM: APPLICATION

Observers of the process of resignation of public officials have made a business of analyzing the feelings of, say, a President when a Cabinet member resigns simply on the basis of the farewell statement he receives. Subtle tones of meaning show how the chief official feels about his assistant, and key phrases often indicate the esteem in which others held the departing official.

Adjectives are used to indicate strength of feeling—and a lack of adjectives and sometimes a lack of nouns may indicate displeasure over either the official's work or his resigning. "Regrets" and "appreciation" are nouns. "Regrets" may be modified by "deep," "personal," or "deepest." "Appreciation" may have shades of "sincere," "deep-felt," "special," or "very special." Public statements and letters of announcement to the press usually contain some specific references that highlight the nature of the relationships between the boss and the person resigning. In one recent Cabinet, the Labor Secretary and the Housing and Urban Development officials were sent away with "special regret." An Attorney General had already departed the Cabinet with a bare-bones "gratitude." But one official who had been in disfavor for some time got nothing more than an acknowledgment of his departure, containing neither nouns nor adjectives.

1 Think of some descriptions you use which vary according to how you feel about someone. Imagine you are writing a letter of recommendation for your best friend and for someone you dislike.
2 Discuss the subject of reading too much into such subtle differences in statements. Do we change our language about someone just for variety, or do we really try to shade our meanings about people and events by using slightly different words? Why do we have various words for a single thing?
3 Is formal communication always very easily identified? Do hidden communication effects occur only in informal communication?

Communication Occurs Everywhere, Intentionally or Unintentionally

In order to understand that communication is all around us, we must think in terms of both "formal" and "informal" communication.

It may be easier for us to recognize formal communication. We know, for example, that a commentator on television is trying to communicate. So are a teacher, a politician running for office, a sales representative, a preacher, and a chairperson. But it is more difficult, perhaps, to realize that we communicate all the time, through our passing remarks to friends, our quizzical looks or frowns at the teacher, our waving to someone across the street, our silence at the dinner table, our clothes, and the way we wear our hair. Can you think of any act that is *not* communication?

Your messages can be sent intentionally and may be intentionally received. But consider some of the other possibilities. You may be sending a message to another person unintentionally and that person may be intentionally receiving it, as in the case of someone eavesdropping on a conversation, or of a teacher watching a student's nonverbal behavior in class. Or someone may be intentionally sending you a message which you unintentionally miss, as in the case of a friend who notices you passing by and says ''hi'' but whom you do not see and therefore to whom you do not respond. Another possibility occurs when neither the sender nor the receiver of communication is aware they are exchanging messages. Often our nonverbal behavior (tone of voice, facial expressions, gestures, postures, dress, and so on) constitutes messages sent and received unintentionally. It is impossible not to communicate.

COMMUNICATION OCCURS EVERYWHERE: APPLICATIONS

CON MAN AT WORK

The con act is neatly illustrated by the story of the man who advertised in the newspaper: "Send $1 for my secret to making money." Anyone who sent the money got this reply: "Ask people to send you $1."

Another man in Fort Worth, Texas, concocted a variation on this theme by sending letters to the editors of newspapers in fourteen medium-sized Texas cities. He wrote that if people wanted to add to their good deeds, they could send $5 to him at his home address. He thanked them in advance, particularly those who might send the money anonymously. The man had checked with the post office to see whether what he was doing was legal, and he learned that it did not violate postal regulations. Saying that he thought this was a good way to get some money without hurting anyone, the man added that he wasn't particularly hard up for cash—he simply wanted more than he had.

1   Does this man's appeal simply give information? Is his approach logical and intellectual? Emotional? What basis did the man have for selecting this way to solicit money? What levels of communication are involved here? Are there intellectual considerations? Are skills involved? Feeling?
2   Would you send the man $5 if you had a very small bank account? What if you had several thousand dollars? And if you were a millionaire? How would you be affected by the information if you were told that he lived in an affluent part of the city? If you knew that he was an insurance salesman?
3   Do you think that newspapers should print this kind of letter? What are your feelings about a newspaper editor who decides to run such a letter? About an editor who decides not to?

The Midlife Insurance Company has a large secretarial pool with a fairly relaxed atmosphere where typists and stenographers sit and do their work. They often get a chance to talk to one another between typing or transcribing assignments, and they also enjoy frequent coffee breaks.

Almost three-fourths of the secretaries are white, English-speaking, and between the ages of twenty and thirty. The others are Mexican or Puerto Rican, bilingual, and in the same age range.

One senior secretary complained to the personnel manager that the Spanish-speaking employees spoke Spanish to one another, even though all other secretaries spoke only English. Those in the majority were sure that the others were talking about them in Spanish. They wanted everybody to be ordered to speak English in the office, since that was the "official" language of the company.

1 If you were the personnel manager and received this complaint, what would you do? (Do not *blame* one group or the other; consider instead how to develop a congenial working situation.)

2 Since the National Labor Relations Board (NLRB) would not support the requirement that employees speak a particular language when conversing among themselves, how would you develop understanding between the two groups? Would you invoke NLRB regulations or company policy, or can you think of a better way to handle the matter?

3 Role-play a conversation between the personnel manager, the English-speaking secretary, and another secretary who speaks both Spanish and English.

Communication Occurs on Different Levels

The scope of communication can be described in terms of who is taking part in it (the *range* of communication) and also in terms of what kinds of things are taking place (the *level* of communication). These are interrelated, as shown in Diagram 1. Of the different ranges of communication, the easiest to define is *interpersonal* communication—communication among a few people. Interpersonal communications involve others— giving instructions, taking orders, talking about things, listening, interviewing, selling, sharing feelings, or persuading someone to our point of view. Because these communications involve two or more people, they are different from *intrapersonal* communications, which take place inside ourselves—thinking, worrying, daydreaming, memorizing, or talking to ourselves, for example. We don't usually think our communication actually begins inside our own heads, just as we don't often realize how much of our own personal communication comes from, or belongs to, the third range: *a-personal*, or mass, communication. This is sometimes called *sociocultural* communication because a larger mass of people is

DIAGRAM 1
Scope and Levels of Communication

Scope	Levels		
	Intellectual Level	Skills Level	Emotional Level
Intrapersonal range	Reading, listening, watching Sensory inputs processed Vocabulary recognitions Language acquisitions Data gathering Data storage in brain Planning, worrying	Overcoming accents Training memory Pronunciation practice Organizing data and arguments Solving puzzles Ear and eye training Problem definitions	Self-image development Acquisition of values Expression of needs Artistic listening and watching Concepts of self and others Worrying Anticipating pleasures
Interpersonal range	Giving instructions Reporting observations Taking orders Telling data Logical persuading Debating, arguing Listening to data	Conversational skills Listening skills Interviewing Leading groups or organizations Selling products Movements and gestures Adapting behavior to feedback	Sharing feelings Persuasion concerning values Discussions of artistic expressions Playing music, reading together High-pressure selling Reporting inferences
A-personal public communication (mass communication—sociocultural) range	Public reports Judicial proceedings Parliamentary practices News reporting Law making Documentary productions Nonfiction writing	Political speaking Public addresses Organization of data by speakers and listeners Debating, open forum, discussion techniques Reports, digests, etc.	Mob actions Panic situations Mass movements in society Artistic performances in music, drama, movies, etc. Art exhibits Oral interpretation

This diagram shows behaviors on different levels of communication related to the range of their influence. There are many more examples that you could add to these. Human communication activity can be identified by level and by range for the sake of study, but the reader should be cautioned that some activities will naturally involve several of the levels and will, in their application to real-life communication, cross many of the ranges. You should remember the *process* nature of communication and assume that this diagram is for the sake of "stopping the process to look at it." "These communication acts are not likely to occur in this carefully defined system except in textbooks and diagrams.

The intellectual level: We communicate to exchange information. *(Andrew Sacks/ Editorial Photocolor Archives.)*

involved, either as the originators of the communication or, more often, as the recipients of it. Because it is not directed at a few identifiable people around us, as interpersonal communication is, nor does it take place within ourselves, like intrapersonal communication, a-personal communication takes on some very special characteristics, which we shall consider in the chapter on audiences.

Besides these ranges of communication—intrapersonal, interpersonal, and a-personal—let us consider the levels of communication that we can relate to the levels of learning discussed below. We can identify on those levels many of the things that happen within the scope of our communication. Some examples appear in Diagram 1 as communication behaviors.

INTELLECTUAL LEVEL

One of the most common reasons we communicate is to exchange information—to tell each other things. We spend a great deal of time listening to instructions about how to do things, gathering facts, and asking questions. Thus we learn and acquire new knowledge.

SKILLS LEVEL

We also communicate in order to *practice* communicating, much as a football player increases his skills by playing the game often. The baby who babbles is trying out the sounds that his or her speaking machinery can produce. The baby very quickly develops some sounds better than others and learns which ones are most useful. Simply by practicing these skills he or she learns how to make most of the sounds the adult makes. The skills level relates to communication because it includes such things as the physical ability to produce rising and falling inflections (to indicate questions or statements), to change pitch and volume, and to accent or overcome special speech characteristics that associate us with a certain class, geographic region, or ethnic and linguistic background.

The skills level: We communicate to practice communication. *(Gail Myers.)*

FEELINGS LEVEL

We also communicate to express our feelings and to understand the feelings of others. Even when we are busy exchanging information, we share our feelings. At the same time we offer intellectual material to someone, we are concerned with a variety of things about ourselves and the other person which are part of (but not necessarily included in) what we would usually think of as information. Crying and laughing are two extreme responses which express more about how we feel than about what kind of information we want to share. Opposing emotions like sadness and joy each have their own vocabularies—in terms of both the words used and the other dimensions of communication, such as our gestures and even our posture.

COMMUNICATION OCCURS ON DIFFERENT LEVELS: APPLICATION

THE SOCIAL WORKER

Elmo Jones, aged thirty-two, was new to the small town in Indiana where he was assigned to teach children with learning problems. He came from a larger city, where he had been a junior high school teacher before he received his certificate to teach special classes.

In his class were two sisters—Agnes and Bertha Smith, aged twelve and fourteen—who had reading problems and other learning difficulties. They came to school bruised from the beatings their stepfather gave them; they shook so hard that they could not sit still and were so fearful that they could not concentrate.

One day after both Agnes and Bertha had appeared with blackened eyes and large welts on their arms, Jones tried to learn what had happened. They said that they had been late getting to the car when their stepfather had come for them after school and that he had beaten them. All the students had had to stay for a few minutes after class in order to hear some special announcements, but the girls' stepfather did not consider that an excuse.

Jones went to the principal with his story. He was told that teachers cannot sign a child-abuse report—only superintendents can make such a charge. The principal told Jones that it was a small town and he should not get involved. Jones went to the superintendent and got the same response. In addition, the superintendent told Jones that the girls tended to exaggerate and he should not believe their story.

After that, Jones turned to the county agency for family services. He was told that a caseworker had visited the family after some neighbors had complained about the treatment of the girls. That visit ended when the stepfather pulled a gun on the caseworker and sent her scurrying to her car.

Talking with the school's guidance counselor, Jones found out that other teachers had brought up the subject but were told not to get too involved with students or their problems. "These things happen all the time in our society, and you can't afford to get involved in every sordid thing that comes along," was the guidance counselor's advice to Jones.

After talking with other teachers, Jones decided that he had to go to the local sheriff to make a formal complaint. He was told again that unless the chief officer of the school would sign the complaint, no action could be taken. At this point, he was warned by the sheriff: "You've been talking a lot about these two kids to a lot of people. Seems to me you're just making it harder on them girls if their stepfather finds out about you making such a big fuss all over town."

The feelings level: We communicate to express our feelings and to understand the feelings of others. *(Berne Greene/Editorial Photocolor Archives.)*

Everyone he talked to told Jones to drop the subject. He did, and planned to resign at the end of the term.

1   Try to consider the Smith sisters' problem as a communication consultant, not as a social worker. Again, avoid blaming anyone or getting indignant about the case. Think about the ways in which the communication patterns exhibited here are representative of the stereotypes we hold of (*a*) small towns, (*b*) schools, (*c*) high school administrators, (*d*) young high school teachers, (*e*) small-town sheriff, and (*f*) caseworkers.
2   Do different occupations depend on different kinds of communication patterns? Do certain kinds of people tend to do the same things over and over again when they communicate with others? If you think so, what was the result of this tendency in this case?
3   Would you react to these people as real human beings or as part of your stereotypes? Did they communicate in a predictable way? Can you count on people to communicate in the way you predict? What happens if they don't? Are you alert to differences in patterns? Will you permit others to "step out" of the stereotypes you have of them?
4   What other stereotypes do you have about communicators in your life? Consider (*a*) parents, (*b*) teachers, (*c*) police officers, (*d*) people with crew cuts, (*e*) politicians, (*f*) waiters, (*g*) used-car salespeople, (*h*) bankers, and (*i*) bus drivers. Can you think of others about whom you have stereotypes?

Communication Is Continuous

It is difficult to know exactly when communication starts and when it ends. A discussion between you and someone you've never seen before may seem new, but the patterns which you have adopted and the other person's habits are part of your exchange. Communication comes from your past experience and goes on into the future.

When you meet someone and make small talk about "safe" subjects like the weather, you begin probing each other's background. That includes, of course, learning whether you know some of the same people. If you do have acquaintances in common, then for all practical purposes you invite them into your conversation—even though they may be miles away and long gone. You bring your past to any communication situation: All the people you've known and the places you've been and the things you've done affect who you are and what you will communicate.

When you meet and talk with someone at a party, you both are affected in some way by the encounter, and your future communication has a good chance of being different as a result. Continued contacts with friends shape our communication patterns in many ways, and their communicative habits become part of our lives. A speech-communication act, as simple as a short greeting and as complex as a persuasive speech, appears to be in itself a discrete unit of thought or action limited by a definite beginning and a definite end. These beginnings and endings are not really definite, however; all speech-communication acts have antecedents that stretch into the past and consequences that reach into the future. What you say and how you say it is influenced not only by the demands of the immediate speaking situations but also by all your past experiences and past learnings. Your values, attitudes, beliefs, your communicative skills, your perceptual and assumptive sets, all developed since you were born, are brought to bear in the immediacy of your present communication. And this goes for your listener(s) too. Whether you will even meet in the present depends in large measure on the commonality of your pasts. No communication encounter is an isolated event.

COMMUNICATION IS CONTINUOUS: APPLICATIONS

THE LAWN CYCLE

At a committee meeting held for the purpose of making recommendations for landscaping the new church, Bill (who was not chairing the meeting) opened by asking where the money would come from. Sam, who was presiding, said that wasn't the committee's problem; they were only to recommend plantings. Joe favored roses rather than something like evergreens. Barbara argued that a lawn area would be less expensive and easier to care for than plants. Dave suggested that they seek outside advice, maybe from a landscaping firm. Bill then asked how much that would cost; Joe warned that the committee ought to stay in control so that somebody from the outside wouldn't get plants that nobody wanted. Barbara again asked whether anybody objected to just a lawn. Chairman Sam began to feel that he was on a merry-go-round and that the committee had started another ride around the circle.

1 What communication patterns were established among these people before the meeting started? Can you predict what will happen on the basis of such patterns?

2 By looking at the comments various committee members made, can you say something about each person and guess why he and she made their remarks? Do you expect certain kinds of communication behaviors from certain kinds of people?

3 Assume the roles of these committee members and begin a meeting with Chairman Sam asking for comments. If the entire class makes up the committee, what comments are likely? After a member has made a comment, will he or she make another on the *opposite* side of the argument, or stick with the points he or she made initially?

Don and Jan find themselves near the beer cooler at a party given by a campus group recruiting volunteers for a community action project. They have never met before. They each get a beer and, because of the crowd, find they can't move away from each other. Forced to converse, they talk about the weather for awhile; then the conversation opens up:

Jan: "Say, do you know Mike Merk by any chance?"

Don: "Don't know. Where's he from?"

Jan: "Right here. You look a lot like him."

Don: "No. I'm from Poughkeepsie. No Merks there."

Jan: "Well, there's a girl from Poughkeepsie in our dorm—Suzy Glotz. Know her?"

Don: "Sure, I know ol' Suze—we were in school together."

The following comments in parentheses show Don's and Jan's hidden thoughts as they talk about their common acquaintance:

Jan: "I don't really know her very well. What's she like?" (I think she's a jerk, but what if he really likes her?)

Don: "Well, it's been awhile since I've seen her." (Better play it cool—this girl may be Suzy's roommate or a close friend.)

Jan: "Well . . . was she popular? Did you ever go with her?" (I can learn about this guy if he'll talk about dating Glotz.)

Don: "No. A friend of mine dated her. They didn't seem to get along too well. Broke up after a little while." (That should let her know I'm not very hot on Suzy.)

Jan: "Some of the girls I know seem to think she isn't very bright. Guess your friend thought so, too."

1 This exchange between two strangers (at the beginning) may lead to more communication. Do you think Jan and Don would have reacted this way if someone had introduced them and filled in some details about each?

2 How would you develop this conversation if Suzy Glotz had been present and introduced Don to Jan and stayed with them? What if Suzy had made the introduction and then walked away?

3 Form teams of two, and role-play some situations like this one, in which two people try to learn about each other without committing themselves. (It might be interesting for the characters to make side comments to the class in which they say what they are thinking after they have said something out loud. Or two people could represent each character in the drama—one person would then speak the lines which are heard by all, and the second person would voice the thoughts of the speaker.)

Communication Is a Transactional Process

How you view things affects greatly how you behave in relation to them. So it is with your communication. The way in which you view your communication profoundly affects how you communicate. Much of the time, however, you are not too aware of your philosophy of communication. One of the purposes of reading a book like this one or taking a course in communication is to help you take a look at this philosophy so that you may better understand how you communicate and perhaps better control your communicative behavior.

As the heading above implies, our own view is to see the communicative act as a transaction. The means we believe that communication involves a complex interrelationship of many variables or changing things; of special importance are the changing roles and behaviors of the participants: speaker-listener and listener-speaker.

Admittedly, there are many other ways we can look at communication. Once many theorists thought that communication consisted of a one-way act, like shooting an arrow into a target. You hit the bull's-eye. You got close. You missed. But the whole activity of communication was centered around the one-way action of doing something to someone in that theory. How "good" the communication was depended on how well you shot the arrow or on how well you made your point. That also meant the emphasis was on constructing the message, organizing it, and delivering it—much like you would sharpen the point of your arrow, test its feathers, flex your bow, and then shoot straight to the target. Mission accomplished. This oversimplified view was also based on an idea that meanings are in words. If the sender had the correct meaning to the words, no misunderstanding could arise. If communication was not perfect, it was because you did not perform adequately—you did not shoot straight. There is a great temptation to the believer in this kind of communication to blurt out a great stream of important-sounding words and believe that they will therefore convince the listeners if these words are loud enough and plentiful enough. (This is like shooting a whole bunch of arrows into the side of the house and then going up and drawing the bull's-eyes and target circles around where they hit.)

Another favorite way of looking at communication is to compare it with taking turns in a Ping-Pong match. You say something. I answer. You say something more. I answer. Or if I start the serve, I make the statement and then you have to reply. We take turns being a sender or a receiver. Although this theory accounts for more of the complexities of human communication than the bull's-eye theory, it still tends to oversimplify the process by treating it as a simple cause and effect. You talk; I answer. Each exchange may be treated as an event by itself; one message causes only the next one.

A weakness in that theory is that our communication is not divided into Ping and Pong, stimulus and response, shot and return, action and reaction. Rather it is a flowing, spiraling process of interweaving: each *sender* is also *receiver* at the same time (catching the flow of the message sent and its impact) and each receiver is also sender (maintaining a stance of interest, attention, boredom, dismissal—both nonverbally and possibly verbally). The communication has also, very importantly, come from somewhere and is going somewhere. As we pointed out earlier, any communicative act which we try to stop and look at has a history and a future. It has been born in the mind of the speaker and relates to the mind of the listener, and these minds are not just appearing in front of each other as the words are said. They've lived in many places; they have said many things before, possibly to each other.

That is how we arrive at the "transactional" view of communication. Along with many other current theorists, we hold that communication is a transactional process. Your view of yourself and the world is essentially affected by your communication with yourself and with others. How you see yourself is closely tied to how you see other people around you respond to you. Your perception of other people's responses to you is itself affected by prior perceptions and prior responses—the history of your communicating we mentioned above.

If that is not sufficiently complicated, consider that the view you have of yourself (your self-concept) will have a very great effect on how you communicate with others; this will then affect how others will respond to you, and then how you respond back.

This transactional process is like a spiraling process and makes the analysis of communication difficult since every facet of the process is likely to be both cause *and* effect, stimulus *and* response, source *and* receiver, message *and* medium.

In a transactional view of communication, who we are can be both cause and effect of the communication event in which we participate. We will develop this idea further in the chapter on self-concept and roles.

To summarize our argument in favor of a transactional approach to understanding communication, let us for now make these three points:

1 We are who we are in relation to the other person with whom we are communicating.
2 That other person is the product of our perception of that person in that communication situation, and we are also a product of his or her perception of us.
3 We make up, define, or construct the other person as well as the environment in which we all are by (*a*) choosing from the infinite number of cues given off by the other person and (*b*) organizing the selected cues into a pattern which is our picture of him or her and our picture of the situation—a picture, incidentally, which includes what we think that person's picture of us is.

Such a view of communication has far-reaching implications which we will develop in the next chapter.

Communication Is the Sharing of Meaning

In describing communication, it is important to emphasize that it has a purpose. Although most communication scholars agree that communica-

Communication is a transactional process. *(Andrew Sacks/Editorial Photocolor Archives.)*

tion is related to symbol manipulation, there is not always agreement on the aims of communication. Some may view communication as designed to transmit information and to transfer ideas, but we agree with those scholars who have developed the view that *creation of meaning*, rather than the transmission of information, is central to the study of communication.

Ours is a world of booming and buzzing confusion in which we are assailed from all directions with messages and stimuli. Yet this world becomes understandable to us, full of beauty or ugliness, because we assign significance to what we perceive. It is like walking into a vast supermarket of noise and sights without any organization. From our experience we begin to sort things out—the vegetables are there, the canned goods over there, meats are back there, and so on—and we can find with the help of signs the order in the otherwise chaotic world or disorganized store.

In the supermarket we get help from a classification system known to us from our past experience and from the arrangement of signs and aisles. You don't expect to find the canned string beans next to the fresh string beans, just because they are beans. Would you expect to find milk with the other beverages such as colas, coffee, or tea? In fact, the classifications used by most supermarkets are not the only way things could be arranged, but they reflect some needs for displaying and preserving the goods, which is why fresh vegetables are not found with the canned ones of the same name and milk will be located in a cooler with dairy products rather than with other beverages.

As we communicate with our environment, we try to find meanings in the variety of stimuli or cues that originate from within ourselves and from outside. Because it would be impossible to attend to all the cues that impinge on us at any given time, we develop ways of responding to them *selectively* and we use a classification system to organize them. It is a classification system we have carefully developed over the years so that we can understand our environment. When we receive a message—that is, when we select a cue to pay attention to—it may call up a memory of a previous experience, just as when we see an object, we attempt to identify it in terms of what we already know. As our experience increases, the relationships with things around us expand what goes on in our world, so that it takes on more and more meaning.

As Dean Barnlund writes, "Communication, then, is an 'effort at meaning,' a creative act initiated by man in which he seeks to discriminate and organize cues so as to orient himself in his environment and satisfy his changing needs."[2] To communicate, thus, is to process stimuli from raw data into meaningful information. This creative act of generating meaning performs the function of *reducing uncertainty*. The cues we select out of our internal, physical, and social environment all serve the purpose of clarifying what any encountered situation is all about so we can adapt to it.

Meaning may not be the same in two individuals because they may select different areas and may have different classification systems; and thus they may have different experiences. If intrapersonal communication is an attempt to call up inside ourselves a meaning which has a close relationship with what is going on around us, interpersonal communication and a-personal communication involve our attempt to share meanings with others by providing them with stimuli or cues to which they will assign meaning; we hope their meaning will be similar to ours.

We strongly believe that the earlier theories of communication based on premises of information transmission and transfer of meaning are less useful for understanding human communication. It is much more fruitful to look at communication as the process of perceiving stimuli, assigning meaning to them, and behaving on the basis of that information to interact effectively with our environment. Our communication effectiveness thus rests largely on the number and kind of stimuli we perceive and how we develop meanings.

Consider that out of the buzzing confusion of our surroundings we choose some things to pay attention to. We place those things in some groupings, some categories, or lump them together with other things we know about ourselves or our world. The system we use for grouping, or classifying, or organizing, is one of our very own making. Surely we developed it with some help from significant other people in our world, but it is singularly our own to put into use. We use the system to put things in their proper place; new things get placed where we can understand them, old things are put in their usual or "proper" places. In

---

[2]Dean C. Barnlund, *Interpersonal Communication: Survey and Studies,* Houghton Mifflin, Boston, 1968, p. 6.

that way we construct meaning—deliberately and personally. We hope as we do this that we construct meanings somewhat along the same lines others will understand if we intend to share meanings with others, that is, if we intend to communicate.

COMMUNICATION IS A SHARING OF MEANING: APPLICATION

TALKING TO STRANGERS/TALKING TO FRIENDS

1 Imagine you are with a friend you have known for a long time. You meet each other in line at the cafeteria. Describe how you act—do you just begin talking as if you had not stopped since the last time you saw each other? Do you engage in some preliminaries to discussion? What do you need to know about each other to start a conversation?

2 Imagine you are sitting next to a person whom you've never met before. You will have to sit together for a long time (on a long bus ride, for example, or in the waiting room of an office). Describe how you act—do you just begin talking as if you knew each other? What do you need to know about each other to start a conversation? How do you find these things out? How do you feel about talking to a person you've never seen before? Is it as easy as talking to an old friend?

List the reasons you think it is easier or harder for you to talk with an old friend or a stranger:

Easier to Talk to a Friend   Easier to Talk to a Stranger

_____   _____

_____   _____

_____   _____

☐ COMMUNICATION COMPONENTS

Many communication theorists[3] have attempted to freeze the process of communication to describe it. They have developed "models," which give us a stop-action picture of this ever-dynamic process. A model is a replica of something and, as in model cars or model airplanes, it may

[3]Dean C. Barnlund, Ibid., p. 26. David K. Berlo, *The Process of Communication*, Holt, Rinehart and Winston, New York, 1960. Frank E. X. Dance, "Toward a Theory of Human Communication," in Frank E. X. Dance (ed.), *Human Communication Theory: Original Essays*, Holt, Rinehart and Winston, New York, 1967. Kathleen M. Galvin and Cassandra L. Bock, *Speech Communication: An Interpersonal Approach for Teachers*, National Textbook Company, Skokie, Ill., 1972, pp. 9–10. Harold D. Laswell, "The Structure and Function of Communication in Society," in Lyman Bryson (ed.), *The Communication of Ideas*, Harper & Row, New York, 1948, p. 37. Gerald R. Miller, *Speech Communication: A Behavioral Approach*, Bobbs-Merrill, Indianapolis, 1966. Raymond S. Ross, *Speech Communication: Fundamentals and Practice*, Prentice-Hall, Englewood Cliffs, N.J., 1965, p. 8. Claude Shannon and Warren Weaver, *The Mathematical Theory of Communication*, University of Illinois Press, Urbana, 1949, p. 98.

oversimplify the something it represents. Models are useful, however, since they allow us to see the relationships between the disconnected parts of an event and at least give us a rough idea of what that event looks like in the whole.

Most communication models include reference to a variety of terms which are used to describe components of the communication process. Although these terms may appear technical, they are needed to understand communication models. A glossary of these terms is included here.

Glossary

Source   A person, thing, or event which provides verbal or nonverbal cues to which someone can respond.

Sender   When the source is a person, it is also called a sender.

Message   A set of verbal or nonverbal cues sent by a source. Messages can be spoken or written words, gestures, movements, etc. They cannot have meaning apart from the persons involved in the sending/receiving process.

Symbol   Something which stands for something else. The something else is usually called a referent.

Encoding   The process by which a sender chooses symbols (a code) to describe the cues selected out of the environment and intends to share with someone else.

Decoding   The process by which a receiver translates or interprets the symbolic code and assigns meaning by associating the symbols with what they stand for. What must be noted here is that in interpersonal communication, what gets transmitted is neither the original cues selected by the sender nor his meanings. The code—the symbols—is what is transmitted. There is no guarantee that the symbols chosen by the sender stand for the same things to the receiver.

Receiver   A person who interprets a message sent by a source. A special note is in order here. We must emphasize that because of the transactional nature of communication processes, we are simultaneously "sending" and "receiving" messages. When we communicate with each other, we are both the *source* of communication messages—what we say to others, what we do, what we look like, what we wear, etc., are all verbal and nonverbal cues that others may "decode"—and the *receiver* of communication messages—our physical environment and the people in it are constant sources of cues for us to "decode."

Medium   The sensory means by which cues from an environment are sent and received. In human communication, the media will involve hearing, seeing, touching, smelling, tasting. Medium also refers to the *vehicles* of communication, such as speech, when verbal communication is involved, gestures or other nonverbal means, newspapers, radio, and TV.

Channel   The way information moves in a system from one individual to another; sometimes refers to the access one person has to another. For example, an employee may say, "I have a direct channel to my boss," meaning, "I can talk directly to my boss without having to go through someone else first." Sometimes, a communication channel may involve a series of people through which a message travels in a serial fashion. Serial communication is often typical of rumor transmission when one person tells a story to another person who then relates it to another, who tells it to another, and so on. Finally, channel is something used interchangeably with medium and refers to the means by which information is transmitted.

Feedback The response a receiver gives a sender as a result of the sender's message. The information the sender receives from the receiver may be used to adapt, adjust, or change subsequent messages. Feedback is thus a corrective mechanism which tells communicators "how they are going." Feedback is the key to understanding the transactional nature of communication. Two people communicating are constantly sending and receiving messages. As a result of the responses that they perceive they are getting from their past behavior, they correct and change their behavior. Thus, they elicit new responses, which in turn elicit new changes and new responses, etc. As we said earlier, communication is a dynamic process, an ongoing process, with no clear-cut beginning or end, no clear causes and effects.

Noise Any interference with the accurate transmission of a message. Noise, or the source of error in communication, can be external or internal. External noise can be anything from a purely physical noise—a jack hammer pounding in the street while you try to listen to a lecture—to an ambiguous or misused word. Internal noise can be a headache that prevents you from concentrating, anxieties or worries, strong prejudices or biases which contribute to narrow selectivity and message distortion.

☐ SWAPPING SYMBOLS

Our communication with others is called *interpersonal communication* or *a-personal communication*. The qualities of communication outlined in the preceding section affect us because we are people working with other people. The rules which guide our communicating are much the same for everyone.

Some Call It Common Sense

One of the criticisms leveled against the study of the systems of human communication has traditionally been that it is "just plain old common sense" and therefore does not really need to be studied. According to this argument, either a person has common sense or hasn't—it can't be taught. In reply to this, some communication scholars have pointed out (1) that there is really nothing very "common" about common sense and (2) that even common sense, as it is described by the critics, is a studied application of certain basic, logical cause-and-effect relationships, which actually can be identified and studied as part of human behavior.

Some Call It Obvious

Another point often made about studying communication is that "all that stuff about words and meanings" is simply obvious. Everybody knows that the *word* "snake" is not really the cold, crawly creature.

Everybody knows that the *word* "spider" is not that furry, frightening thing you see crawling on the floor. And everybody knows that the *words* "communist," "kike," "nigger," "redneck," "Spik," "Jap," "Chink," "fascist," "pig," and "yippie" are only noises. But in any of these cases, we may act as if the word were really a thing—as if the label were a physical blow. If we can argue that words and meanings are so "obvious," but then still make use of language to attack, hurt, revile, condemn, or stereotype other human beings, we are not behaving as if we know how we are using language. Also, if we can be taken in by phony sales pitches and by demagogues running for public office, or if we can be led by slogans and chants, we are not making use of the information we have about interpersonal communication.

This Is Your Life

Your communicating with others is what we are calling *interpersonal communication* or *a-personal communication*. It is your day-to-day speaking and listening. It is your attempt to influence others to your way of thinking about things or to your way of doing things. It is your way of explaining how something works or why you believe what you do. It is listening to a friend tell you about a date, her car, a course he is taking, or his job. It is listening to political speakers, comedians, or teachers; in small-group settings, it is listening to the ebb and flow of arguments and sharing ideas and feelings.

Your interpersonal communication and a-personal communication are as simple or as complicated as your language and your logic will permit. Your symbol system, joined with the settings and occasions, will impress an audience, whether a member of your own family or a great crowd of strangers.

Interpersonal Influences in Teaching Speech

In the past few years, the teaching of speech has become more and more concerned with the field of interpersonal communication. This has been due to many factors, including the acquisition of a great body of excellent research on human communication collected by some of the finest scholars in the country from many disciplines. Their research has provided us with more and more knowledge about how people interact in their communication settings. In addition, a number of techniques for teaching speech have been developed from this research. Teachers of speech have discovered that interpersonal communication is very closely related to the traditional areas of speech education. Rhetoric is related to research about persuasion and the influence of the public and of specific audiences. The artistic and competitive areas such as oral interpretation, reader's theater, debate, oratory, and the usual forensic activities are all related to the interaction of speaker and audience as clarified by scholarly research. Public speaking, as this book will demonstrate, is effectively linked to human communicative behaviors. By joining recent interpersonal findings with the more traditional approach to public speaking, we are convinced that you will (1) learn useful skills, (2) acquire greater understanding of yourself as a communicator, and (3) develop effective habits to use in the many encounters you will have with others.

■ LOOKING BACK

I. You have been communicating all your life in both formal and informal ways.

II. All your speech-communication activities are symbolic. However, they differ in their scope. You can distinguish between:
   A. Intrapersonal communication—communication within the self
   B. Interpersonal communication
      a. Dyadic—communication with one other person
      b. Small group—communication with up to about fifteen people
   C. A-personal communication
      a. Public communication—communication face-to-face with an audience
      b. Mass communication—communication generated through the print or electronic media

III. Your need to communicate is great; it's the only way to get things done in an interdependent world.

IV. Your communication serves several functions.
   A. A social function: You need to interact with others, to be wanted, to have intimacy.
   B. An information function: You need to exchange information to understand your world.
   C. An influence function: You need to communicate to change others' attitudes, beliefs, and behaviors.
   D. A decision function: You need to communicate, process, and share information to make decisions.

V. Your desire to communicate is great. Human beings require stimulation and self-expression.

VI. By recognizing basic communication postulates, you can better use all levels of your communicative abilities.
   A. Communication is not random.
   B. Communication occurs everywhere, intentionally or unintentionally.

C. Communication occurs on different levels.
D. Communication is continuous.
E. Communication is a transactional process.
F. Communication is the sharing of meaning.
VII. Communication activities have many components.
VIII. Rhetoric and rhetorical theory, forensic speech activities, and public-speaking situations and activities are all an integrated part of the human communicative act. Using the research of the behavioral scientists in speaking situations and in audience and listening occasions has brought to speech teaching the growing emphasis on what is now called interpersonal communication.

CHAPTER 2
YOU, THE SOURCE
OF COMMUNICATION

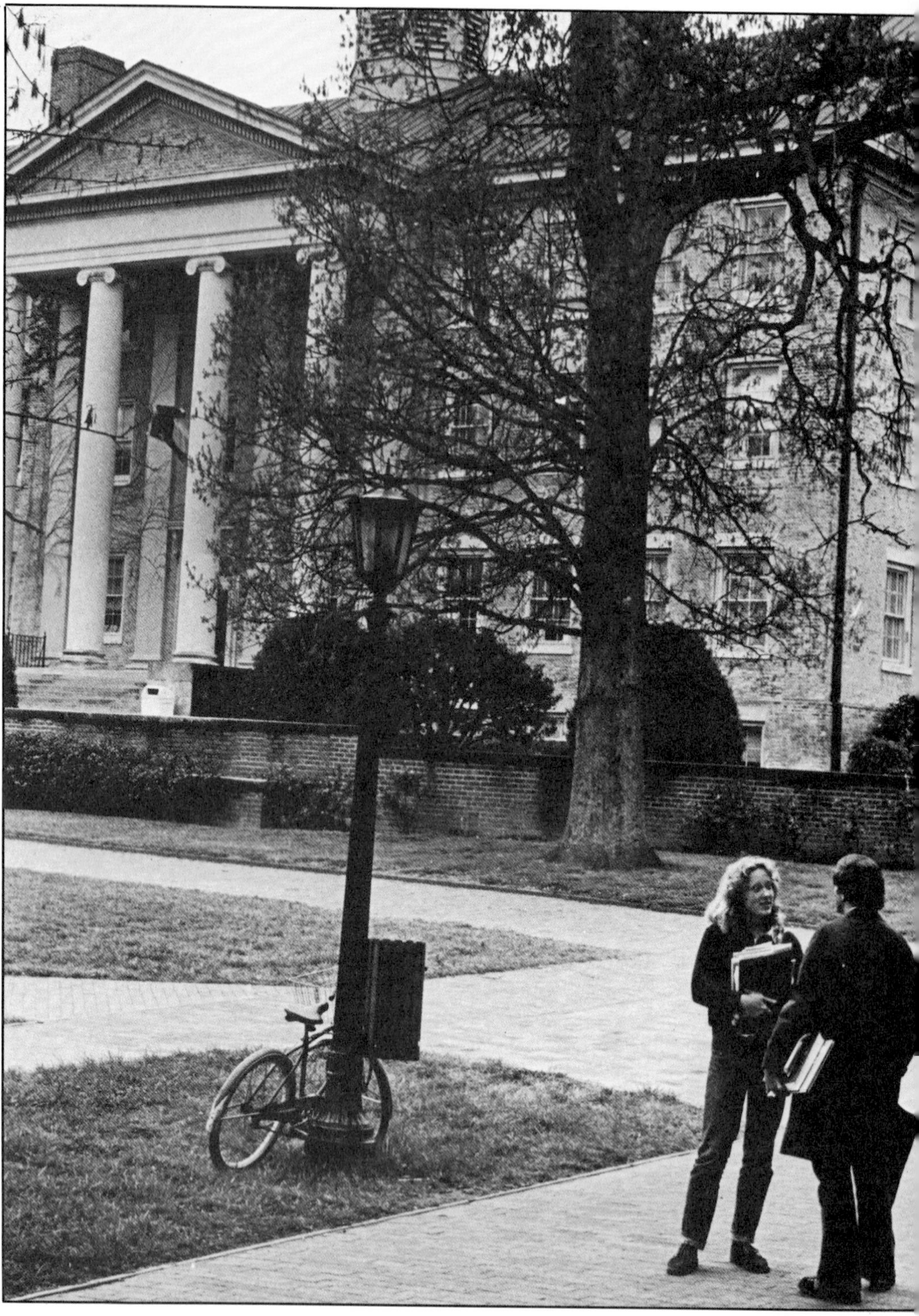

(Daniel S. Brody/Editorial Photocolor Archives)

CHAPTER 2
YOU: THE SOURCE
OF COMMUNICATION

People don't ask for facts in making up
their minds. They would rather have one
good, soul-satisfying emotion than a
dozen facts.

— Robert Leavitt

Another good thing about gossip is
that it is within everybody's reach,
And it is much more interesting than
any other form of speech.

— Ogden Nash

Once the realization is accepted that
even between the closest human beings infinite distances continue to exist, a
wonderful living side by side can grow
up, if they succeed in loving the distance between them which makes it
possible for each to see the other whole
against the sky.

— Rainer Maria Rilke

As the source or sender of countless daily communications, you constantly process information about your environment. Selecting, organizing, and interpreting the data about your world in order to produce a coherent and meaningful picture of that world is essentially a perceptual process. How you come to know "reality" through the process of perception, and hence, how you verbalize these perceptions, make up the basic ingredients of the communication process, whether you interact with one other person, a small group, or a large audience in a more public setting.

It is crucial that you understand your perceptual processes, because, as a sender of communication, you constantly make communicative decisions which are largely affected by (1) how you perceive your world—what you choose to communicate about; (2) how you perceive yourself; and very importantly (3) how your audience perceives you.

☐ HOW YOU PERCEIVE YOUR WORLD

You rely on your senses to tell you what is happening around you. You are continually bombarded by sensations of all sorts: tastes, smells, sights, sounds, feelings. You are forever the center of noises, things, people, and events. Perhaps you tend to consider yourself a passive receiver of all this stimulation—someone who can't help but perceive what is happening around you. Yet you know from personal experience that not everyone perceives the same situation in exactly the same fashion. Perhaps for you a particular painting is a masterpiece and evokes a multitude of feelings often hard to verbalize. For a friend, the same painting evokes only disgust. Eyewitnesses to an accident, reporting in good faith, often make contradictory statements about the incident they viewed. Examples such as these should give you some clue that there is more to your perceptual processes than meets the eye!

Communication is essentially a process of structuring reality through perception and symbolization. How you do this structuring basically shapes the information you gain from all the cues impinging on you, hence your "image" of the world. Your image of the world in turn affects how you behave and adjust to that world, hence how you communicate.

Although a thorough discussion of perception is beyond the scope of this book and of this chapter, some basic factors in perception must be understood.

Perception is a complex mental process of selection, organization, and interpretation of sensory stimulations into a meaningful and coherent picture of the world.[1] For example, the visual patterns which impinge on your brain are no more than light radiations of varying wavelengths, not solid objects in space. What reaches your brain is a

[1]Bernard Berelson and Gary Steiner, *Human Behavior: An Inventory of Scientific Findings*, Harcourt, Brace & World, New York, 1964.

pattern of impulses corresponding more or less to the brightness of the light reaching the eye. It is a pattern of moving light, shade, and color. What you see is no more the real event than the picture on your television set is the real cowboy, Indian, or news commentator. Your personal picture is made up basically of imagined solid forms, which have a degree of immobility, constancy, and permanence. These impressions of constancy and permanence, however, are a product of *mental* processes which took place in *your brain.* Objects in reality are neither solid nor immobile. Permanence is in your mind. What you see is a private creation of your brain. Since we can never "know" what happens in someone else's brain, we *act on the assumption* that most of us "create" a world similar to the private worlds of others. And in a large measure the assumption proves true. But you must not forget that your perceptions are no more than *theories* or guesses about what the world is like. A good deal of the time your theories work and your perceptions of reality are reinforced. However, when someone challenges your view of the world, a great sense of uneasiness or dissonance is created; and you may experience an anxiety when you realize that not everyone perceives objects, events, and people exactly the same way you do. The experience may be more or less unsettling, depending on who challenges you and whether the perceptions being challenged are particularly important to you. Discovering there is no Santa Claus may be a traumatic experience for young children who must then realign their whole sense of what is real. Discovering you have been deceived by an intimate friend can also be a shattering experience and may result in a reevaluation of your perceptions. If the experience is very painful it may result in an even more general readjustment of your ways of perceiving not only the deceiving friend but other people as well. Once "burned" you may resolve never again to trust another person enough to risk emotional involvement.

In summary, what you communicate about is *your perception* of what the world is like. Your statements about anything are in part statements about yourself. Having created for yourself a perception of people and events, you then go on to re-create for others, through the medium of language—oral, written, nonverbal—what you perceive, hoping they will translate your language into an image similar to the one you had in mind. You determine the effectiveness of the translation process by observing the feedback you get from your receivers. Here are a few comments that should point out what our discussion of perception has to do with the way you communicate with and relate to others. There are many ways to experience "reality." No two people ever experience it in exactly the same way. Two observers may perceive the same scene in a similar way or may disagree about its nature or content.

To the extent that many perceptions are common to most people, their "reality" (their "theories" about reality) will be common and they will probably understand each other when they communicate about it. To the extent that our perceptions of reality are different (because each

No two people ever experience reality in exactly the same way. *(The New Yorker.)*

of us is unique), perceptions can never be identical—we have difficulty in sharing them with others, and communication may not be effective if differences are great.

Because validation methods ultimately involve more perceptions which also have to be validated (a vicious circle), you can never be 100 percent certain that what you perceive is identical to what is out there. You can have only probabilities of fit between perceptions and reality. Although absolute certainty and absolute objectivity are impossible, some people's predictions about the real world are more often correct than other people's. Although all of us are biased, some may not even be aware that they are biased at all. The first steps toward increasing the probability that our perceptions yield accurate information about reality is (1) to become aware of the part you play in perceiving, (2) to realize that you have biases, (3) to interpret your perceptions in light of your biases and correct for them when you can, and (4) to realize that simply perceiving something does not give you a corner on the truth of the matter.

☐ HOW YOU PERCEIVE YOURSELF

In your study of communication, it is important that you explore a very important agent in the process, namely, *you*—who you are, how you see yourself, how others see you, what roles you play for the various audiences of your life, what your needs and values are. These are fundamental questions because who you think you are determines much of what you do and which roles you choose to play. Who you think you are is to a large degree determined by the responses you get from others to your behaviors. Therefore, your way of relating to others plays an important part in how your image of yourself is developed.

When you were born, some theorists claim, you were essentially a blank slate. You had almost no ability to think originally and almost no experience to rely on. Yet the way you were treated began to generate in you some feelings about yourself. Some of the early messages you received about yourself included being hugged, kissed, cuddled, being fed when you were hungry, changed when you were wet, held when you cried. These messages from others communicated to you that you were loved and good enough to be cared for. Some children may not be so fortunate. Their primary experiences may include being ignored when they cry, not being fed when they are hungry, not being touched very much, not being talked to. In such cases, children often internalize that they are not good enough to be cared for and to love.

As you grew older, you heard many more messages about how good or how bad a little girl or a little boy you were, and these messages were quite influential in your developing a sense of being OK or not OK.

Self-Esteem

Self-esteem is that feeling which we get when *what we do* matches *our self-image* and when that particular image approximates an *idealized version* of what we wish we were like. For example, you might see yourself as an "outdoor type" (self-image). You may imagine yourself as a successful forestry engineer (idealized self-image). You may go and register in a forestry school (action). That action matches your self-image and your idealized self-image. If you are accepted in the school and subsequently earn high grades, you are confirmed by others (peers and professors), and this confirmation will validate your feelings of self-worth and your self-esteem.

Maintenance of self-esteem is complex. Many times our attempts at maintaining positive feelings about ourselves are successful. Yet some of our attempts are sometimes self-defeating.

We sometimes try to hide parts of ourselves from others, fearing that if they knew these parts of ourselves, they might reject us. In his excellent book *Why Am I Afraid to Tell You Who I Am?* John Powell relates a poignant and real answer to the question: "I am afraid to tell you who I am because if I tell you who I am, you may not like who I am, and it's all I have."[2]

We hide parts of ourselves, for example, when we cover up feelings. We store up anger or frustration and keep a cool façade. Half the time

[2]John Powell, *Why Am I Afraid to Tell You Who I Am?* Argus Communications, Chicago, 1969, p. 12.

we don't really deceive others because our nonverbal behavior gives us away. But when we succeed in hiding, we tend to ''gunnysack,'' that is, to collect angry feelings inside us (generally in the stomach—a sure way to get ulcers) until the time when a trivial incident will ''make us'' explode—the straw that breaks the camel's back.

Sometimes we try to put on certain masks to appear something we are not. We give off false cues to the people around us and erect walls of intended impressions. This little game, a full-time job for many people, consumes much energy and concentration; to pay off, it must be carried off well. Most of us, however, are not professional actors, and thus our masks, deceptive as they may be for a while, are usually seen through by others. The more we pretend to be what we are not, the more we tend to believe the phony verbal world we hope to create and the more we tend to lose touch with the real world and our own reality.

Effective maintenance of self-esteem is based on a dual process of *self-exposure* followed by *feedback*. We expose to others, through our behavior, some parts of us; others give us feedback about their reactions to our behaviors, thus confirming us in some way.

Our doubts about who we are can be discarded only by checking them out through honest and direct exposure and direct and honest feedback.

THE PROCESS OF PERCEPTION: APPLICATION

THE DELINQUENT INTERVIEW

Connie, a seventeen-year-old girl considered a juvenile delinquent under Colorado law, visited a college class in juvenile delinquency to answer questions about herself and her reasons for violating the law. She had dropped out of high school in her sophomore year. Connie had been in court several times for drinking, but her most recent offense had been an attack on several college girls whom she and several of her friends did not like. Connie was accompanied by her parole officer and a woman from the community who held informal sessions with girls like Connie where they could discuss their problems. Class members asked Connie such questions as the following:

Class member: From what socioeconomic class do you come?
Connie: I don't understand what you mean.
Class member: Did you commit delinquent acts because all the people in your gang were committing these acts?
Connie: I don't know—I just wanted to, that's all.

Connie made some other comments—for example, ''If you really want to learn about people like me, you should get to know us, because just reading about us in your textbooks won't help you understand. A lot of the things that I have done are things that you have done too, but just haven't gotten caught.''

After the class session Connie, her parole officer, and a group of the students discussed the value of the interview to each of them.

Class member: We're glad she came. She gave us some new insights into the problem. I hope we made her feel welcome.

Parole officer: The session helped Connie as much as the class members, if not more. She needs to feel that she is important and that she has something to give.

Connie: I think that I helped the class understand juvenile delinquents much better.

1   If you consider the audience here to be the class conducting the interview, do you think they perceived each other's worlds accurately? What are some of the difficulties they might have in creating a "world" like that of the other?

2   If the audience were the parole officer (in the sense that he was critically viewing the communication situation), what do you think was operating within him to help or hinder perceptions? Can one person be an audience? Can that person affect what happens in this interview? Can that person affect future interviews of this kind?

3   Did Connie become an audience herself? What about her comment on the final effects of her appearing for an interview? Did that indicate that she was interested in self-esteem? What are the chances that her statement about the class response was an accurate one?

4   Role-play a situation in which one member of the class takes the part of a convicted felon and is interviewed by a class of students in sociology or criminology. After role playing, discuss the audience's conduct and perceptual habits. (Did anyone prejudge, deal in stereotypes, ask loaded questions, adopt the language of the interviewee, etc.?)

☐ HOW YOUR AUDIENCE PERCEIVES YOU

Your attitudes toward another person will affect both the way you perceive messages from that person and the way you expect messages to be perceived by that person. For example, if you think a person is dishonest, you may disbelieve or discredit what he or she has to say. If you think your roommate is strongly prejudiced against a certain group of people, you will interpret what he or she says about these people in light of your perception of that bias. The messages you receive are thus always mediated by your attitude toward the source of these messages. Conversely, the messages you send also will be mediated by the attitudes and the perceptions your audience has of you.

When you face an audience for whatever purpose—to persuade, amuse, or inform—you would like to know what they think of you. You have a natural desire for approval, and you are also concerned that the audience's attitude toward you will affect your speaking. Indeed it can.

How the audience responds to you as an individual is as important as how they respond to your message. The two responses really can't be separated.

Much of the communication that surrounds you in your everyday life is persuasive. You try to persuade a friend to go with you for coffee or to go on a date; you try to persuade your father to let you have the family car; you try to convince your teacher that you really worked hard on your term paper and that you deserve an "A." At the same time, you are at the receiving end of much persuasive communication in similar informal situations, as well as in many others, as when you are being pressured by a department store salesperson or are subjected to advertising on radio and TV.

Some people seem to be better salespersons, or better persuaders, than others. This is because effectiveness as a communicator depends on a variety of factors. Some of these factors are related to the audience you are speaking to and the degree to which that audience is likely to be persuaded. Other factors are related to the actual message you are delivering. How well you prepared your speech, what kinds of evidence you can present, how effectively you use different kinds of arguments, how well your speech is organized, and what kinds of topics you select may have a great deal to do with how well you can persuade your audience. These factors will be discussed in later chapters.

In this section, we will examine those factors related to you, the source of communication. We will specifically look at characteristics which your audience perceives in you and how these characteristics affect your attempts to persuade and inform. These characteristics are usually described as making up or contributing to source credibility.

Source Credibility

How an audience responds to a speaker is very much based on factors grouped under the label *source credibility*. The term "credibility," however, includes a variety of dimensions, some of which we will look at in this section. These source factors are *ethos, prestige,* and *charisma.* Other factors, chiefly physical ones such as sex and height, are often studied in research on credibility. They will not be included in this discussion.

ETHOS

The idea that the source of a communication message is important in understanding how the message is received can be traced as far back as the ancient Greeks. More than 2,000 years ago, Aristotle wrote that a speaker's personal character is just as important in communication as the audience and the message. "Good men" are more believed than others, he said, particularly when controversial topics are being discussed.

When Margaret Mead addresses anthropologists, their recognition of her achievements enhances her ethos. *(Mimi Forsyth/Monkmeyer.)*

To tell you that an effective speaker must be a "good man" or a "person of character" is of little use, however, unless we can tell you the effects of specific characteristics of "goodness" or "character" on your audience. In other words, what must your audience see in you to be persuaded by you?

What Aristotle called "character" is often called *ethos*. To be a credible speaker, you must have ethos. But what is this quality?

We must first stress the point that ethos is not a quality intrinsic to the source or sender of communication. Your characteristics *interact* with the attitudes of your audience and hence determine your audience's perceptions of you as well as their attitudes toward you. For example, an artist may be a recognized figure in her field, but in a group where artists are held in low esteem, her achievements contribute very little to her ethos. Among a group of people who highly respect artistic talent, her achievements will help increase her ethos. Thus, the same person may have high or low ethos depending on his or her audience attitudes.

Ethos is also a dynamic and changeable phenomenon. Brooks and Scheidel,[3] for example, demonstrated that a speaker's ethos can change several times during a speech. They measured the ethos of Malcolm X, a famous black leader, several times during a speech to a predominantly white audience. Eight measurements taken by these researchers showed that Malcolm X's ethos fluctuated, and the last measurement, taken after

[3]R. D. Brooks and T. M. Scheidel, "Speech as a Process: A Case Study," *Speech Monographs*, 35:1–7, 1968.

the speech, was significantly lower than the first one made at the beginning of the speech. In this case the speaker actually ended with less ethos than he started.

Whenever you confront an audience you have an ethos of some kind. Most of the time, however, you are known for something and that produces an image in the mind of your listeners. Whatever the image may be, it is there, a part of that communication encounter. It may contribute to, enhance, or detract from your effectiveness as a communicator. Components of that image, or ethos, are varied. Ethos has many dimensions; four which emerge consistently in most research studies are competence, trustworthiness, similarity, and attraction.[4]

Competence, or qualification, refers to the speaker's training in relation to his message topic, as well as his education, skills, information, ability, intelligence, and authoritativeness. *Trustworthiness* includes such general personality traits as warmth, kindness, congeniality, gentleness, unselfishness, sociability, calmness, fairness, hospitableness, and patience. *Similarity*, or *homophily*, refers to the degree of similarity your audience perceives between them and you. *Attraction* refers to the orientation your audience has toward you.

Competence   Competence refers to the degree to which you are perceived as knowledgeable or as an expert about the subject matter being discussed, and thus a source of valid information. If your audience thinks you know very little about what you are talking about, they are likely to dismiss or discount what you say. On the other hand if they think you have special information by virtue of your training, interests, experiences, education, etc., they are more likely to regard what you say in a favorable light.

However, competence is a relative concept. As McCroskey and Wheeless point out,[5] a person's perception of another's competence is mediated by the first person's perception of his or her own competence. For example, visualize a scale of 0 to 10 to measure competence, where 0 represents very incompetent and 10 very competent. If I perceive myself to be a 6 and perceive you to be an 8 on a specific topic, I will regard you as highly competent. However, if I perceive you to be an 8 while I perceive myself as a 10, then I will probably not judge you as extremely competent.

[4]C. I. Hovland, I. L. Janis, and H. H. Kelley, *Communication and Persuasion*, Yale University Press, New Haven, 1953; D. K. Berlo, J. B. Lemert, and R. J. Mertz, "Dimensions for Evaluating the Acceptability of Message Sources," *Public Opinion Quarterly*, 33:563–576, 1970; J. C. McCroskey, "Scales for the Measurement of Ethos," *Speech Monographs*, 33:65–72, 1966; J. L. Whitehead, Jr., "Factors of Source Credibility," *Quarterly Journal of Speech*, 54:59–63, 1968; D. Schweitzer and G. P. Ginsburg, "Factors of Communicator Credibility," in C. W. Backman and P. F. Secord (eds.) *Problems of Social Psychology*, McGraw-Hill, New York, 1966; W. J. McGuire, "The Nature of Attitudes and Attitude Change," in G. Lindzey and E. Aronson (eds.), *The Handbook of Social Psychology*, Addison-Wesley, Reading, Mass., 1969, pp. 3–179.
[5]James C. McCroskey and Lawrence Wheeless, *Introduction to Human Communication*, Boston, Allyn and Bacon, 1976, p. 102.

Perceived competence is an important factor in communication. An audience who feel you are competent are more likely to accept your opinions and follow your advice. By the same token, if you feel less competent than your audience on a specific topic, you are not likely to attempt influencing them, either for fear of exposing your own short-comings or because you realize the probable futility of your influence attempt. Because competence is such an important source of ethos, particularly in more formal situations, you should select topics on which you are competent and skillfully make your audience aware of your competence.

Many experienced public speakers will call attention to their competence as they discuss points for which they wish to be perceived as particularly knowledgeable. You must be careful, however, not to appear to be boasting, as this may adversely affect your audience. It is useful to provide pertinent information to the person who will introduce you to your audience; allow that introducer to build up your competence in the eyes of your audience.

SCALE OF COMPETENCE: APPLICATION

This scale, together with the scales of trustworthiness, similarity, and attrac-tion, cover the four main dimensions of ethos. They can be filled out by you individually or in a class or group assignment. Comparisons between your perceptions and those of others in the class can be useful in expanding your understanding of the principles of perception from the early part of this chapter. Why do you see these scales as you do? Are they the same for all class members? Why not? Do your perceptions change from one setting to another? From one topic to another? How do these placements you make on the scale relate to your self-concept? It is helpful to compare notes with others on how they see you and how you see the class and selected individuals.

If you are perceived as a valuable source of information or an expert on a subject, then the competence level is high for you on that issue or item. "The world's leading authority" on one subject may be a complete dullard on another. Also, you may be more knowledgeable about math than a six-year-old, but less knowledgeable than the world's leading astronomer. *Compe-tence Is Relative.* On any following scale mark yourself with an "S" (for "Self") where you think you belong in relation to most of the class which you will mark as a "C" (for "Class"). An alternate exercise would be to mark an "S" for "Self" and an "O" for "Other" by picking some other person to compare yourself with on any of the scales. See the example below on how to mark your scale or continuum.

Example: Suppose you are going to college in Georgia with classmates who have spent their holidays in that region, and you are the only one who knows how to ski in snow because you grew up in Vermont. On a scale of "Ability to

Snow Ski" you might make marks like these: "S" is for "Self"; "C" for the "Class" generally.

ZERO_____C_____S_____Expert

But if you were to rank yourself on this scale with the Olympic gold medal winner in downhill and slalom, your competency might change into something like this:

ZERO_____S_____O_____Expert

where the "O" stands for "Other" (in this case the champion mentioned).

ZERO_____Vocabulary; word meanings and their uses_____Expert

ZERO_____Baseball as a sport; playing and talking about_____Expert

ZERO_____Classical music and musicians_____Expert

ZERO_____Country-western music and musicians_____Expert

ZERO_____Computers; data processing_____Expert

ZERO_____Cooking; in general; not wok or some special_____Expert

ZERO_____Automobiles; auto repair and maintenance_____Expert

ZERO_____Taking pictures with a still camera_____Expert

ZERO_____Fishing in deep water_____Expert

ZERO_____Making jewelry; metal work_____Expert

ZERO_____Training a dog_____Expert

Make up items of your own on which you estimate a great difference between your own expertness and the rest of the class. If your expertise is very high and the class is very low, does that mean the topic would be a good one for a speech to them? Can you get to be so much of an expert that nobody wants to listen to you talk about your subject?

ZERO_____Subject:_____Expert

ZERO_____Subject:_____Expert

ZERO_____Subject:_____Expert

Trustworthiness   Trustworthiness refers to the appearance you give of being honest, just, and objective. Even though you may be perceived as highly competent on a given subject, if your audience does not think they can trust your truthfulness, you will not be believed. In the early 1970s, the Watergate affair eroded the already damaged credibility of the American government in the eyes of the public. Although many of the officials involved in Watergate were highly competent professionals, they fell ultimately because of the credibility gap they helped widen between the Presidency and the American people. When President Richard Nixon was perceived as untrustworthy, his effectiveness as Chief Executive was permanently damaged and he had to resign.

An important dimension of trustworthiness is *sociability*. Sociability refers to the degree to which we perceive someone to be friendly, likable, and pleasant. Sociability is an important factor in both interpersonal and a-personal communication. If you perceive some people as competent but highly unpleasant, you may avoid turning to them for advice because of the negative aspects of the communication encounter you anticipate. In television advertising, for example, great care is taken to select highly sociable people to advertise products simply because a sociable actor is more likely to catch and hold our attention than an unsociable one.

SCALE OF TRUSTWORTHINESS: APPLICATION

Using the same principle as in the Scale of Competence, make some comparisons between yourself (marked "S" on the scale) and some other group you want to compare yourself with—for example, you might want to put the letters "MP" on the scale representing "Most People." That means you see yourself as more or less trustworthy than most people you know. If you want to determine how the class might respond to a speech from you, place *yourself* on the scale (marked "S") and the *class* as you see them (marked "C").

NEVER	Telling the truth without embellishments	ALWAYS
NEVER	Taking exams honestly without any cheating	ALWAYS
NEVER	Paying income taxes without any hanky panky	ALWAYS
NEVER	Giving both sides to a story if they are known	ALWAYS
NEVER	Subject:	ALWAYS
NEVER	Subject:	ALWAYS
NEVER	Subject:	ALWAYS

Similarity   Homophily or similarity refers to the degree of commonality held between communicators. The more similar two communicators are, the more likely they are to engage in communication and the more likely it is that their communication will be successful. Simply, we tend to be more attracted to people similar to us than to people dissimilar from us. We tend to learn more from people whom we perceive as being like us, and they tend to influence us more than people who are unlike us.

The more similar you are to your audience, the more likely they are to accept you and your ideas. Extreme dissimilarity between you and your audience, even on factors unrelated to the subject of your communication, will vastly complicate your persuasive efforts. For example, you dress for a job interview the way you think people in the position you are seeking are likely to dress. If you apply for a job as a construction worker, jeans or overalls are appropriate because it is the way most construction workers dress on the job. If you apply for a job as a salesperson, a more formal mode of dress is indicated if you wish to be perceived as similar to those who work as salespersons.

The stressing of similarities between audience and speaker is often used in persuasive efforts. Kenneth Burke emphasized that "you persuade a man only in so far as you talk his language by speech, gestures, tonality, order, image, attitude, idea, *identifying* your way with his."[6] More recent experimental findings confirm the effectiveness of identifying with one's listeners.[7]

Similarity refers to the degree to which people are similar on objectively verifiable variables such as sex, size, age, race, religion, or education. It can also refer to less tangible variables which are deduced from those objective variables. If someone else looks like you, you believe that person must be like you not only in looks but also in the way the other thinks, feels, or may behave. For example, short people see other short people as more similar to themselves than tall people not only in height but also in other characteristics, such as sense of humor, likability, or tolerance. Perceived similarity in *background* is also important. If you are from New York City, you are likely to perceive other New Yorkers as more similar to you—in many ways—than, say, people from the South. If you are Catholic, you tend to perceive other Catholics as more similar to you than Jews or Protestants, not only in terms of religious observances, but also in politics, social norms and needs, and other factors not directly related to commonality of religion. In general, our feelings of similarity or the perceived similarity go beyond those actual objective similarities and have an effect on our communication behaviors.

If you perceive your attitudes or values to be similar to those of others, you will generally seek out communication with them. However, it is difficult to really know another person completely; thus much of the perceived similarity in attitudes and values is based on superficial judgments after relatively superficial disclosures. You probably have had the experience of meeting a person with whom you seemed at first to have a great deal in common. However, as the relationship developed, as communication increased and as intimacy and self-disclosure expanded, you may have discovered that the similarities were rather superficial and

[6]Kenneth Burke, *A Rhetoric of Motives*, New York, Prentice-Hall, 1950, p. 55.
[7]E. Burnstein, E. Stotland, and A. Zander, "Similarity to a Model and Self Evaluation," *Journal of Abnormal and Social Psychology*, 62:257–264, 1961.

that fundamental differences existed which made the relationship less desirable.

Similarity is very important. To the extent that you perceive another person to be similar to you or to the extent that another person perceives you as similar to him or her, attempts at communication will increase. If perceived similarity and objective similarity are fairly close, you will have a greater chance of communicating effectively with that other person. Most of us simply prefer to communicate with people we perceive to be like us, and we generally tend to avoid communication with people we perceive to be different.

SCALE OF SIMILARITY: APPLICATION

Using the principle again of a continuum or scale, mark yourself ("S") first against the class ("C") to get an idea of to what extent that class might perceive you as similar to them, which will affect how they would listen to you as a speaker. It might be interesting also to use this scale to mark yourself ("S") and some person you dislike ("D") or do not like to talk with to see what distances you can measure. Then mark the same scales with yourself ("S") and someone you very much like to listen to or communicate with. What differences do you see in these comparisons? What does that tell you about communicating with persons similar or different? Make some subjects of your own and then mark comparisons this same way. Are some items of more importance than others in feeling close to another person? Is height and weight as much a factor to you as some other values or characteristics? What are some of the most important characteristics to look for in another person for improving communication?

VERY DIFFERENT	Height	VERY SIMILAR
VERY DIFFERENT	Weight	VERY SIMILAR
DIFFERENT	Sex	SAME
VERY DIFFERENT	Religion	VERY SIMILAR
VERY DIFFERENT	Native geographical area	VERY SIMILAR
VERY DIFFERENT	Language ability	VERY SIMILAR
VERY DIFFERENT	Knowledge of sports	VERY SIMILAR
VERY DIFFERENT	Attitude about promptness, punctuality	VERY SIMILAR
VERY DIFFERENT	Interest in science and mathematics	VERY SIMILAR
VERY DIFFERENT	Political affiliation or leanings	VERY SIMILAR
VERY DIFFERENT	Age	VERY SIMILAR
VERY DIFFERENT	Financial status; income level	VERY SIMILAR
VERY DIFFERENT	Subject:	VERY SIMILAR

VERY DIFFERENT ———Subject:————————————————VERY SIMILAR

VERY DIFFERENT ———Subject:————————————————VERY SIMILAR

Attraction   Attraction refers to the moving toward rather than away from another person. Naturally, *physical attraction* has an impact on our communication. Physical attraction relates to your perception of people on the basis of their physical appearance. There is evidence that physical attraction is the most important factor in initial communication encounters. When you first meet someone, his or her physical appearance is what you will first notice and pay attention to. This dimension loses some of its importance as communicators get to know each other better. Physical attraction not only is affected by physical characteristics but also by the clothes people wear and their grooming.

Another dimension of attraction is related to the establishment of work relationships. You may be attracted to some of your classmates, for example, because of their intelligence and competence, and you may seek them out to work on a class project. *Social attraction* refers to the degree to which you perceive someone as a potential social companion. This particular dimension is important in interpersonal communication but plays only a small role in a-personal communication.

SCALE OF ATTRACTION: APPLICATION

As defined in the text, this is the degree to which your audience (or another person in the case of a dyadic situation) will move toward you or away from you on the subject. Communicating with an audience can be more effective if you can accurately guess how they are responding to you on this dimension. If they consider you attractive, you will more easily convince them, inform them, or amuse them.

On the three scales below, estimate how some person you know would be perceived by this class. For the person you pick, place a "P" on the scales. Is this person at the same place on all three scales? Would the position change if you imagined another audience besides this class?

It might be interesting to estimate how you would be located on these three scales by placing an "S" (for Self) where you think this class would place you. How about another audience you can imagine? Would your position change?

NOT AT ALL ——————Physical (see text for definition)——HIGHLY ATTRACTED

NOT AT ALL ——————Work———————————————————HIGHLY ATTRACTED

NOT AT ALL ——————Social——————————————————HIGHLY ATTRACTED

A dimension of attraction is related to the establishment of relationships at work, where we seek others out because of their intelligence and competence. *(Burk Uzzle/Magnum.)*

In summary, ethos is composed of the elements of competence, trustworthiness, similarity, and attraction.

If you have all these qualities, will you be a highly credible speaker? Not necessarily. Some audiences may perceive these characteristics in you, and some may not. Your topic and your audience influence your credibility. It is not a matter of a single characteristic like sex, age, or socioeconomic status. *Speaker credibility is determined by a set of perceptions on the part of an audience in relation to a situation.*

To some people, the President of the United States may be trustworthy, competent, and dynamic. Others may not agree. Still others may perceive him as trustworthy and competent in terms of foreign affairs, but not trustworthy in the area of domestic problems.

PRESTIGE

Prestige or status is another factor associated with your success as a speaker. Generally speaking, the more prestige you have, the more successful you will be in persuading your audience. But here again we

Speaker credibility is determined by a set of perceptions on the part of an audience in relation to a situation. *(David Krasner/Photo Researchers, Inc.)*

must caution you that the relationship between prestige and your credibility as a speaker is not simple. For example, a doctor might be more prestigious than a construction worker, but the construction worker may have more credibility if the topic under discussion is the technical feasibility of repairing city buildings or if the audience consists of members of the local builders union.

CHARISMA

Political figures and other leaders have been said to have "charisma" when they can enlist a large following of devoted adherents because of some kind of personal attraction or magnetism. This quality has been studied extensively in communication research. Like leadership, charisma has been difficult to define as a personality trait, as a set of behaviors, or as a physical manifestation. It appears to be a quality that an audience is willing to bestow upon some persons very consistently, and it may be a combination of the factors mentioned above. The late President John F. Kennedy, for example, was considered highly charismatic. His appeal to audiences in Europe as well as in the United States has been the subject of much speculation about charisma. Until there are better data on this elusive quality, we must assume that charisma is part of the interaction between an audience and a speaker and that it is based on what they know about each other and how they are expected to respond to each other.

Using Your Credibility

You can help improve or reinforce your credibility by the way you are introduced to your audience. Anything you have done that will make you appear more qualified in relation to your message topic and in relation to your audience should be mentioned. The suggestion that you have appeared in front of many groups may add to your dynamism in the eyes of the audience. Naturally, a good introduction will not compensate for a poor speech, but it can help enhance a good performance.

You may also try to boost your own ethos in the course of your speech, but you should be careful to do so only if you have been introduced favorably. In trying to bolster their personal impressions with boasting, some speakers have actually lowered their credibility.

Although your effectiveness as a communicator does not depend solely on how credible you are as a speaker, it is important to understand how credible your audience may perceive you to be as a source of communication messages.

■ LOOKING BACK

I. Your communication activities are largely affected by:
   A. How you perceive your world
   B. How you perceive yourself
   C. How your audience perceives you
II. What you communicate about is *your perception* of what the world is like.
   A. Your perceptions are the product of sensory stimulations *and* mental processes going on in your brain.
   B. Your perceptions are highly personal and in a large measure are your own creations or theories about what the world is like.
   C. You usually act on the assumption that you ''create'' a world similar to the private world of others.
   D. You determine the similarity of your perceptions to those of others by observing the feedback you get from the receivers of your communications.
III. How you see yourself largely determines the roles you choose to play and hence your communicative behavior.
   A. Who you think you are is influenced by the responses you get from others to your behaviors.
   B. Self-esteem is the feeling you get when what you do matches your self-image and when that image is close to an idealized image of what you wish you were like.
IV. How your audience perceives you affects communication.

A. The messages you send are mediated by the attitudes and perceptions your audience has of you.

B. Source credibility is the label given a variety of factors which affect your audience's responses to you and to your messages.

C. Ethos is the major dimension of source credibility and comprises various components:

1. Competence: the degree to which you are perceived as knowledgeable or as an expert, or as the source of valid information on a particular subject.

2. Trustworthiness: the degree to which you are perceived as honest, just, and objective.

3. Similarity: the degree to which your audience perceives you as similar to them.

4. Attraction: the degree to which your audience is inclined to move toward you or away from you.

D. Ethos is not a quality intrinsic to you. It is the product of an interaction between *your* qualities and *your audience's attitudes.*

E. Ethos is also a dynamic process. Your ethos may change with different audiences and with time.

F. Prestige and charisma are other dimensions of source credibility.

V. You can help establish and reinforce your credibility.

A. You can highlight specific points which will demonstrate your competence, trustworthiness, similarity, etc., to your audience.

B. You can give pertinent information to the person who will introduce you, to create a favorable image in the eyes of your audience.

CHAPTER 3
SYMBOLS AND MESSAGES

CHAPTER 3
SYMBOLS AND MESSAGES

When A annoys or injures B on the pre-
tense of improving B, A is a scoundrel.
— H. L. Mencken

Those who corrupt the public mind
are just as evil as those who steal
from the public purse.
— Adlai Stevenson

The one means that wins the easiest victory over reason: terror and force.
— Adolf Hitler

Basically, meaning is what communication is about. You have some meaning you want others to understand, agree with, appreciate, or simply share. So you try to communicate your meaning to them. Communication is your attempt to translate a meaning you have in your head into a symbolic system—language—so that other people will react to that symbolic system by translating it back into a meaning in their heads similar to yours. Symbolic systems, or symbolic codes, do not refer only to the spoken or written word. A very complex system of nonverbal symbols is also a part of your communication.

The function of symbolic systems—verbal or nonverbal—is to make meaning appear in people's minds. If symbolic systems elicit similar meanings in different people, then these people understand each other.

However, three basic factors are at work which often prevent the effective communication of your meanings:

1   Your internal meaning may not reflect accurately the realities of the situation.
2   The symbols you use may not evoke a similar meaning in the minds of your listeners.
3   The symbols you use may not clearly represent your internal meaning.

In the following section on verbal systems, we will discuss these factors in detail.

☐ VERBAL SYSTEMS

In this section you will take a look at language, how it works, how you use it, and what it does to and for you. You also will analyze the responsibilities that communication puts on you when you attempt to share meanings with others. A short discussion of *dialects*—or languages within languages—is included here, too, because much controversy is heard on the subject, and it seems difficult to reconcile opposing views.

Spoken language is only a part of communication, a handy extension of man's thinking abilities. Wisely used, language is helpful, effective, and successful as a means of getting information from one person to another. There are, however, some limitations to our language, one of the most important being our own mistaken beliefs about how language operates. Language, or symbolization, is more than a mere naming of the things you bump into in your environment. Language helps you dream of things that never were and perhaps never will be. Language is the major factor in producing your perceptions, your judgments, your knowledge. Language is the medium through which you organize, talk about, and make sense out of reality. Unless you understand the relationship between language (the symbolic system) and your environment (the observable world), you will be blind to the relativity and uncertainty which govern our universe.

Symbols and Reality

Study of language is really a study of our way of living, a study of our way of perceiving reality. Although our perceptions are unique to each of us, we need to know if one person's statement about the world is better than someone else's. We need to distinguish between, on one side, lunatics, careless observers, sloppy thinkers, charlatans, and on the other side, those whose relations with the observable world are more orderly, more accurately observed and reported, and more honestly evaluated. We need to have a way to know these differences.

More specifically, you need to know whether you are deluding yourself and others in what you perceive and report. You must find out how to tell delusions from accurate representations of what is out there in your environment. As was mentioned at the beginning of this chapter, one of the factors which prevents effective communication of your meaning is that your meaning may not accurately reflect the reality of the environment. This is why you must take a close look at the relationship between language and your perception of reality, and between language and your communicative behavior. In this section, we will specifically describe how language stands in relation to reality and how important it is for the structure of language to fit the structure of your experience if you are to (1) gain useful information from your perceptions, and (2) communicate honestly and accurately with yourself and with others.

Symbols allow us to translate experiences in the empirical world into a version that we can communicate to others. *(Raimondo Borea/Editorial Photocolor Archives.)*

SYMBOLS

Names of all things, events, people, and feelings you experience are symbols. A symbol stands for something else. Names are symbols: John, Mary, Pedro, and Hank stand for the real people who answer to those names. People can also be symbols. A minister stands for a church or for morality; an ambassador stands for his or her country. Even a physical gesture can be a symbol—a clenched fist, a hand waving goodbye, a hitchhiker's thumb. Words are symbols, too. They merely stand for the actual, real, empirical, honest-to-goodness objects that you can observe with your senses.

Symbols are shortcuts for two reasons. First, they can simplify the amount of information you need to communicate. Using a word like "chair," for example, is much simpler than describing the actual object, which consists of three or four legs, a back, and a seat; is made of wood, metal, or plastic; and has a color, a texture, a size, a style, and weight. The word "chair" does not convey all these details, but as a general term it helps you determine in one word the category of things you are communicating about. Second, symbols enable you to communicate about what is not always present to your senses.

Imagine yourself back in the days of the earliest human beings. Groans, grunts, and gestures were about their only means of communicating with one another. Pointing at something was about the only way they could say they wanted it. Without words, conversations are necessarily limited. Actually, the earliest humans were not much different from animals. An animal's survival depends mostly on being able to move around for food, and animal communication is generally limited to cries and grunts. Little by little, humans developed a *symbolic code*; that is, they agreed on a system in which certain sounds refer to certain objects, persons, events, and feelings.

Spoken language, a symbolic code, made possible communication beyond the boundaries of the immediate present. It became possible, by using words, to talk about the things these words named without having to point at the things themselves. Human beings could talk not only about the food they were eating at the moment but also about the food they ate yesterday and the food they were going to eat tomorrow. Words or symbols became links between the past and the future. They made it possible to store up experiences as memories in our minds and *later* recall them to ourselves or to others. The ability to communicate one's experiences to others made human civilization possible. When human beings became able to transmit their knowledge—the sum of their stored-up experiences and memories—to their children, and their children to their children, human civilization began.

You are the product of all the people who have preceded you. You do not need to start your education completely from scratch when you are born—the alphabet, the number system, the wheel, the steam engine, and the airplane are part of your education through the symbol system. Language is your human inheritance.

Symbols allow you to translate your experiences in the empirical world into a version that you can communicate to others. You can offer a symbolic version, a symbolic picture, a symbolic translation of these experiences.

What symbols accomplish, then, is to enable us to translate our firsthand experiences from the empirical world into a communicable version of these experiences. What we communicate to one another is not the experience itself, but a symbolic representation, a symbolic picture, of the experience. The symbolic picture of an experience is not the experience itself: the words we use to refer to the objects, persons, events, situations, and feelings from our empirical world are not the actual objects, persons, events, situations, sensations, and feelings. It is one thing to experience a toothache and quite another to say, ''I have a toothache.'' The words merely describe or refer to the pain and are a symbolic picture of the personal sensation you are experiencing.

This distinction is not as obvious as it sounds. Let's pursue it a little further.

We said that we communicate to ourselves (we call this thinking) and with others by using symbolic pictures of the experiences we seek to convey. When we communicate to ourselves, the process is extremely fast, of course. We feel something that is hot or cold, and as we feel it we label our feeling, we name it, and almost simultaneously we tell ourselves, ''I am hot'' or, ''I am cold.'' It is quite difficult to feel something and not immediately name it. Much of the time this labeling process is unconscious. When we communicate to others, the process of using symbolic pictures—using symbols to refer to a felt experience—is necessary and conscious because there seems to be no other known way to communicate a felt experience to someone else. *To be communicated at all, the experience must be translated into a symbolic picture of some kind, oral, written, or nonverbal.* Communication is oral when we speak words with one another; written when we write words to one another; nonverbal when we use gestures, facial expressions, and other symbols instead of words. The three kinds of communication are symbolic pictures, for all three refer to and are not the experience felt. Communication involves using symbols to represent, describe, or refer to whatever it is we experience, perceive, and remember.

WORDS AND THEIR MEANINGS: APPLICATIONS

WHAT'S IN A NAME?

When Humble Oil changed its name to Exxon, the company had to consider not only the 26,000 service stations with about 50 printed items each but also files, forms, tankers, oil-well signs, and billing forms. More than 300 million kinds of printed materials had to be changed. The company felt that the expense was justified by the impact the new name would have on the competitive market.

A small college in Columbia, Missouri, changed its name from Christian College to Columbia College because it felt that the very restrictive connotation of the name "Christian" was a deterrent to some students and donors and that the new name indicated a more academic tone. A few years prior to that change, the college advertised in national newspapers that it would be renamed after anyone who donated $5 million to it. There were no takers, however.

In Denver, an institution that had been known as Colorado Women's College was given the legal title to an estimated $25-million shopping center by a man named Temple Buell. The trustees renamed the college Temple Buell College as a condition of the gift. Not many years later, the name was changed back again, and the title to the gift was returned so that the college would be free to make other major fund-raising efforts.

1   What makes names so important that companies will spend millions of dollars to change them? Are they recognizable to an intended audience? Are they a "property" that the company needs to own? What things make names important?

2   Would you change your name? For what reasons? Every year, a large number of people (besides women who get married) change their names legally. How does a change of name change the person? What does your name tell others about you? Should women change their names when they marry?

3   Have all the members of the class say their names at once and then have each person say his or her name individually. Then ask whether the class members formed a different impression of others because of the way they said their own names.

WILL YOUR MOTHER UNDERSTAND?

The University of Iowa chapter of the Society of Sigma Xi adopted a program to encourage graduate students doing research to make their reporting of their work more understandable. They offered cash awards and established a series of public research lectures that would enable students to present their findings. The following criterion for basic clarity was suggested: "If you can't explain your research to your mother, you may not understand it yourself." The advantage of being able to explain research at that level was, according to the chapter, that it would help bridge the understanding gap between the scientific world and the general public on matters which really have some relationship to the public.

1   Have you ever tried to explain to your parents (or some other person with the same interests and background) just what it is you are studying in one of your courses? Have you ever tried to explain something to someone who had difficulty understanding you because the other did not have the background for it, such as the principles of snow skiing to a lifelong resident of Florida, the functioning of a carburetor to someone who knows nothing about cars, how to tell time to a child?

2 Form a group and select a subject to present to another group which you are sure does not have much information about it. (Someone in your group should be familiar with the subject.) Work out how you would go about telling the other group about your subject. What will you have to know about them? About your subject? About the words to use?

3 Imagine that you do not know how to put on a coat. Have a group start to instruct you in this, beginning with your standing beside a chair on which a coat has been thrown. Assume that you know nothing about the words that will be used—"sleeve," "collar," etc.—and that they will all have to be explained or pointed out to you. What is the simplest way to get a coat on someone? Is that method best for learning about putting on coats?

MAP AND TERRITORY

Language has the same relationship to experience as a map does to an area of land. When you plan to take a car trip to a part of the country you are not familiar with, you usually get hold of a recent road map—a symbolic picture of the actual territory. A map is a picture of a piece of land drawn by expert cartographers, not a free hand picture, as an artist might draw it. It is very carefully drawn to scale and maintains the spatial relationships between different points in the territory. Such a map is manageable in size, yet relatively accurate. It is a picture that shows you what the actual territory is like—a picture that helps you anticipate and predict what you will find in the actual territory when you take your trip.[1]

Accuracy   A map should not lie. If it lies, it misleads, and if you are misled, you get lost and confused. If maps are to be of any use in making valid predictions about unknown territory, they must present as accurately as possible the territory they describe.

Words or symbols are like maps because they describe a territory (your personal experiences or the experiences of others). If you say "I have a headache," you are describing a territory that exists inside your head. If you tell your little brother that "Indian people lived in America long before Columbus discovered it," you are describing an empirical territory of hundreds of years ago. If you tell a friend that you are "going to go on a diet tomorrow," you are making a symbolic map of a future territory. In all cases, your map should be as accurate as possible.

Advertisers flood us with symbolic maps about their products—"washes whiter," "makes teeth brighter," "no cavities," etc., etc. Are these maps accurate? Just as some road maps are better than others (they represent the territory more accurately), some verbal maps are better than others (they represent reality more accurately). For example, the Food and Drug Administration sees to it that the verbal maps that appear

[1]The extended analogy of the map and territory is based on formulations of Count Alfred Korzybski's General Semantics as developed principally in *Science and Sanity*, 4th ed., The International Non-Aristotelian Library Publishing Company, Lakeville, Conn., 1958.

on canned goods indicating the weight of the goods are fairly accurate. The labels describing the goods within the cans are also fairly accurate. If it says "corn," you do not expect to find peas or beans. You can predict from the label that eventually you will indeed eat corn from this can.

Appropriateness   Maps should also be closely related to your purpose in looking at a territory. If you are driving from Chicago to Los Angeles, you ought to have a road map of the states you intend to pass through. A geologic map of the Mississippi Basin would not do you much good in driving, although it would be appropriate if you were prospecting for oil or looking for gravel deposits. Thus one question you ought to ask about symbolic or verbal maps is: "How appropriate is the kind of map I am using?" Judging your academic success in higher mathematics by your performance in English grammar or literature may be like using a topographic map to drive across country. Similarly, the length of a man's hair wouldn't tell you much about his competency in computer programming. Responding to a casual "Hi, how are you?" with a lengthy description of all your ailments would be inappropriate. In a physician's office, however, such a response may be just what is needed.

Reliability   A second set of questions you need to ask about symbolic or verbal maps is: "Where does the map come from? Who drew it? What did the map maker know about map making?" In other words, "How good or reliable is the map?"

If you knew only what you had personally experienced, you would know very little indeed, and your world would be quite limited. But because your ability to use symbols allows you to make use of other people's experiences, you can enlarge your world considerably and "know"—if not at first hand, at least at second or third hand—an enormous amount. Since you cannot experience enough yourself, you depend on language to fill in for the real experiences. You listen (sometimes) to your elders, your friends, and your enemies; you read newspapers and books, watch television, and listen to the radio. In this way you make the maps of the world in which you live. You may learn that "all Republicans are rich," "all Catholics hate Protestants," "toads cause warts," "Mexicans are lazy," "mixed marriages never work," or "woman's place is in the home." You may never have met a Republican, a Catholic, a Mexican, or a career woman or never have known personally anyone involved in a mixed marriage. But someone has made the maps for you, in many cases. The map maker may not say it directly, but the message gets through: "Here, this is your map for dealing with the territory of politics, or religion, or ethnic questions, or toads, and if you follow this map you will not get lost." Perhaps because you have never been through these territories by yourself, you are pretty anxious to get some kind of map to guide you. You may buy your parents' or friends' maps without closely checking their reliability.

Who draws your maps for you? What do you know about their

expertise? If you need a reliable map about the state of your health, you go to a reputable physician. If you need to figure out what is wrong with your car, you go to a good mechanic. But ultimately how do you know that someone is reliable; for instance, how do physicians build their reputation? Someone watches what they do in the empirical world—how many people do they cure? This is the ultimate test of their performance. The final place for checking the reliability of a map is indeed the territory the map is supposed to describe.

Currency   Another question you ought to ask about maps is: "Are they redrawn when the territory changes?" We know, of course, that road maps are updated every so often because of our complex and changing highway systems. You would not take a trip in 1980 with a map made in 1910. But do you revise your symbolic or verbal maps periodically? Alvin Toffler's *Future Shock* describes vividly how fast our world is changing and how the rate of change can actually shock us physically. More than ever, perhaps, you must make it a point to revise your old verbal maps, or at least to check them against the reality of your changing world to see if they still fit. Many of the old maps must be changed, modernized, and updated. Reactions to beards or to long hair are changing each year as our experiences change. How long does it take a parent-child relationship to catch up with the changed ages and behaviors?

Sentimental Value   Perhaps one of the most interesting things about verbal maps is the way you cling to them. You defend the accuracy of your own map of a territory—your belief, your feeling about what your world is like—whether you have checked it or not. Because your map may fit some of the territory, you endow it with infallibility—and you try to get others to use it for all occasions. As Wendell Johnson said in *People in Quandaries*: "We do not like to have our attitudes criticized, even when they are attitudes that make us miserable and inefficient. We become sentimental about our maps, as it were, even when they lead us over and over again into blind alleys."[2]

You become attached to the symbolic maps that your friends, parents, teachers, ministers, and heroes give you. Although young people often question the values and traditions of their parents, a great majority of them will eventually have pretty much the same beliefs, attitudes, and values as their elders, according to recent political and social surveys.

BASIC POINTS ON LANGUAGE AND REALITY

Several important points here are directly related to the earlier discussion of perception.

---

[2]Wendell Johnson, *People in Quandaries*, Harper & Row, New York, 1946, p. 133.

Language is a symbol system we agree upon; like a map, it must be accurate, appropriate, reliable, current, and valuable. *(David Strickler/Monkmeyer.)*

First, *there is no absolute way of knowing what reality is really like.* There is no way to know whether you have a "correct" picture of the empirical world, since the word "correct" implies that you would know what the empirical world is like and thus could judge whether perceptions match it. Since your perceptions are only theories, predictions, about the empirical world, the best you can do is test the theories by acting, behaving, and communicating as if they were "correct" and then observe the results you get.

Second, *to describe our perceptions of reality (empirical world), we rely on language (symbolic world).*

Third, *language is to reality what a map is to a territory.* The map is useful only to the extent that its structure accurately reflects the structure of the territory.

Fourth—and this is the crucial point—because the structure of our language as we habitually use it is relatively static, and the structure of reality constantly changing and in process, *there can be no exact correspondence between language and reality, between symbolic maps and empirical reality.*

So here we are, imperfect human beings, forever encapsulated within our limited sensory equipment and within our even more limited symbolic tool—language—both of which we need to understand and describe an everchanging, ever-unknowable reality.

The fact that language and reality, maps and territories, can never completely correspond should not blind you to the fact that a good deal of the time you manage to predict your environment quite adequately. In spite of your perceptual limitations, you seldom bump into walls, furniture, people; in spite of symbolic limitations, you don't usually get the pepper when you ask for the salt.

However, there are times when you delude yourself into seeing what you want to see and into distorting what you see to fit preconceived ideas. There are also times when you do not get the salt when you ask for it. You may buy the right kind of toothpaste or mouthwash only to find out that you still don't achieve the popularity implied by the commercials. The symbolic world—that is, how we talk about what we perceive—must be treated with caution. Maps are not territories. Words are not the things they represent. One person's verbal map about something may be useful for you, but not useful for someone else. Verbal maps need to be examined carefully. Short of firsthand experience, they are all you've got to adapt to your environment. That's why you must evaluate carefully the verbal maps you make for others and the ones others make for you. That is why it is so important to develop criteria for evaluating the relative accuracy and usefulness of verbal maps.

Let us describe the relationship between language and reality another way and look more fully at the implications for our communication of the noncorrespondence between the structure of language and the structure of reality.

MATCHING LANGUAGE AND REALITY

The previous discussion on the relationship between symbols and reality points out that for language to be an effective tool in communicating your experience of reality to others, it must be structurally similar to the reality it describes.

Here are some pointers to help you remember to adjust the structure of your language to the structure of the reality you experience.[3]

Dating   Use dates mentally to indicate to yourself, and possibly to others, that you are aware that people and things change with time. If people and events are in process, then it is important to indicate your understanding of the changing nature of these supposedly static objects or occurrences. You today are not the same as you were in 1960, and a recognition of that difference is important to understanding one another. We tend to react to someone we have not seen for a while as if that person had not changed, and as if we had not changed. An ex-convict knows well what it feels like to be haunted by people who react as if lives were not in process, constantly changing. You recognize the process nature of our world when you get an up-to-date road map. You would

---

[3]The following discussion is based on Alfred Korzybski's "extensional devices." Op. cit.

not think of planning a car trip with a twenty-five-year-old map. Your verbal maps must likewise be kept current, so you will not be misled into thinking that things are just the way they used to be, that you never need revise the way you deal with your environment. Being aware of the "dating" device may help you adjust to a changing world and make your language reflect this adjustment.

Indexing   Look for differences within some supposed similarities. You can avoid stereotypes, help distinguish between things which may seem alike, soften attitudes, and reduce dogmatisms by a conscious effort not to lump together what look alike on the surface. This practice is called "indexing." Remember that differences are closer to the empirical world in which no two things are ever identical—similarities appear to us as a result of the abstraction process. We see similarities by disregarding differences. Our language should be similar in structure to our world of difference and uniqueness and represent the similarities we abstract. An index subscript attached to a generic noun can help maintain a healthy balance between the two aspects of our world. If the generic noun emphasizes similarities, the index shows the difference. $Professor_1$ ("professor" is the generic noun; "1" is the index) is not the same as $professor_2$, and $student_1$, $student_2$, and $student_3$ may all have different qualities you need to recognize so as not to treat all professors and students alike when you think and act about them.

Etcetera   This mental device helps avoid the idea that we can say all. Although the use of "etc." in an English composition may be frowned on, Korzybski suggested that we recognize our own limitations of observations and reporting by using this device to indicate there are things left out. "Education makes success" probably should have an "etc." after the word "education" and after the word "success" as well. Education, with some other factors, will produce success and some other things. Be wary of words like "always," "never," "everybody," etc.

Hyphens   The hyphen device indicates that our words often divide the world into two competing opposites, and that often this is not appropriate. This device helps avoid the either-or orientation of language and the polarizing thinking of dividing things into opposites. Good-bad, mind-body, and space-time are ways of indicating a relationship between the terms which may not make a dichotomy of them. Language is burdened with outlooks from common dichotomies of competing and mutually exclusive categories. Our thinking tags along with our language, and we often fall into the linguistic trap of dividing the world into either-or, into impossible blacks and whites without grays in between. If you want to indicate status or qualities about a person or group, it is not uncommon to use such terms as "socioeconomic" or "psychosocial." These alert a reader to recognize that the "social" qualities interact with the "economic'' or ''psychological'' ones and are not considered competing opposites.

Beware of the "Is" of Identity One of our less useful language patterns is to talk as if things, people, or events had inherent qualities. The structure of our language often compels us to identify, that is, to ascribe qualities to things and then react to those things on the basis of the labels. The verb ''to be'' in its various forms represents an easy temptation in that respect. When you say, ''John is lazy,'' you imply that ''John possesses a laziness quality'' and cover the fact that the statement represents only your perception of John, one among the many other things about him you could select to talk about.

If you could not use the word ''is'' in that sentence, what would you substitute which would make it correspond more to the reality of the situation? Well, the statement represents your attempt to express your perception of someone. ''John appears lazy to me'' would be better because the statement would move from one of absolute certainty to one reflecting some tentativeness. It would also show that you, the observer, are aware that you are talking about *your perception* of John, not about him as he ''really is.'' A more descriptive statement of what John did would provide more information, since it would give another person data about the behaviors you observed which led you to the evaluation you made. In other words, saying, ''John did not take the trash out for two days and it bothers me,'' gives more data about John and about how his behavior affected you. It also implies that the not-taking-the-trash-out behavior is only one specific behavior which he may not exhibit again, and does not represent all of John's repertoire of behavior. The ''lazy'' label, on the other hand, implies that that's the way John is, that's all he is, and that's all he'll ever be.

Granted, ''John is lazy'' is a lot quicker to say than ''John did not take the trash out for two days and it bothers me.'' But considering the complexity of any human being and the complexity of most human transactions, identification statements, convenient shortcuts as they may be, appear to oversimplify what they represent and ultimately to mislead.

Meaning and Communication

A great deal of the misery you often experience in your daily communication comes from very common, yet irritating mix-ups with language. You say something that you think sounds quite simple, but the other person does not understand it. Have you ever been invited to a ''casual'' party, only to find that all the men are wearing jackets and ties and the women are wearing long dresses? And there you were in your jeans and T-shirt. Or perhaps you were told by a friend to take Professor Smith's course because it was a ''cinch.'' In the class, much to your dismay, you learn that Smith requires an awful lot of hard work. The words "casual" and "cinch" did not give you any difficulty when you heard them. You thought you understood exactly what they meant.

Most communication breakdowns occur when different meanings are attributed to the same words by different people. It happens often, and yet you still find yourself arguing about the "real" meaning. But there is more to this business of meaning than meets the ear or the eye.

Two faulty assumptions about meaning that lead you astray are: (1) Meaning is assumed to be a characteristic of words—something that is contained in the words in a more or less permanent, natural, logical, and obvious way, and (2) words are assumed not only to have meaning but also to have *only one* meaning.

THE FIRST FAULTY ASSUMPTION: WORDS HAVE INHERENT MEANING

"Meaning" is the relationship you make between a symbol and what that symbol stands for. Meaning is not *in* words. Words are *not* containers. They are merely ink marks on a piece of paper or vibrations through the air. Meaning is in people's heads. People use words to *elicit* meaning in other people, that is, to evoke a particular relationship between a symbol and what the symbol represents. *There is no necessary, logical, or correct relationship between any symbol and what the symbol represents.* The relationship is man-made. It is arbitrary. It changes. Only to the extent that it is agreed upon by more than one person can it have communication value. For example, there is no necessary connection between the word "chair" and the object on which you sit. To call this object by that particular name—that particular set of letters arranged in that particular order—reflects only the fact that some people at some time have agreed to do so. It is not the word that means the object. You mean the object when you use the word.

You may be thinking by now, "So what, I knew that. What difference does it make?" As long as you talk about observable objects, it makes little difference. You can always point to the object to make the other person understand what you are referring to if he or she does not understand your words. This is basically what you do when you go to a foreign country and do not know its language.

However, when you begin talking about ideas and concepts which do not have a readily observable referent, what can you point to if the other person does not understand your words? For example, if you talk about "freedom," "democracy," "justice," "truth," there is no easy referent to point to. When you make an evaluative statement such as, "This is a good movie" or "Mary is an intelligent girl," the referent exists only in your mind. Symbols which communicate about value judgments and abstract ideas are telling us more about the person making the statement than the objects or persons to which they are applied. "This is a good movie" tells more about your reaction to the movie than about the movie. Yet you probably find yourself frequently arguing with other people over whether a movie is good, a professor is fair, a friend intelligent, etc. If you can remember that there is no relationship between the object and the word you use—except the relationship you make in your mind—you will be able to avoid such arguments.

Dictionaries   If people give words their meaning, then what is the use of dictionaries? Dictionaries do not set up authoritative statements about the "true" meaning of words, but rather record what words have meant to certain people, in certain contexts, and at certain times. They also report the *usages* of words at different times in different parts of the country. They do not provide us with one "true" or "correct" meaning for everyone. They simply give us the various definitions assigned to the words by people.

DEFINITIONS AND MEANING: APPLICATIONS

THE HORSE'S TALE
As a trial lawyer, Abraham Lincoln once asked a witness how he knew certain things. After the witness explained that he knew things because of what people told him and because of the names of various things, Lincoln posed this question:

"Suppose I have a horse here with four legs and one tail, which is usual for a horse. Now suppose I call this tail a leg. How many legs does the horse have?"

"Why, five, of course," answered the witness.

"Wrong," announced Lincoln. "Just calling a horse's tail a leg doesn't make it one."

1   Was Lincoln right in directing the question the way he did to make the point that naming things is not a way of making them real? How would you feel if you were a witness subjected to such a trick?
2   Have a group discussion in which you try to think of situations in which we treat things according to the names we give them. In other words, do we sometimes act as if a horse's tail were a leg because we call it that—and do we put too much confidence in something we have named just because of the name we have given it?

NOBODY SHOOTS SONGBIRDS
Hunters of game birds in the United States annually harvest thousands of pheasants, quail, partridge, ducks, wild turkeys, mourning doves, snipes (yes, there really are snipes), coots, geese, etc. They argue, among other

things, that most of these birds would die anyway and that hunting is a way of controlling the population of game birds, which has become unbalanced as a result of destruction of their natural predators. Those who are opposed to hunting argue just as strongly that killing these birds is needless, that the fact that they are good to eat doesn't justify shooting or wounding them, that the hunters actually upset nature's balance, etc.

South Dakota has been known for years as a center of pheasant hunting. Hunting is, in fact, in many ways the state's biggest industry, since a large hatch of pheasants will bring hunters from all over the world, who leave millions of dollars in that sparsely settled area in exchange for the privilege of shooting the pheasants.

Contrast the size of the big pheasant with that of the small mourning dove, which is considered by federal agencies to be a migratory game bird. (Hunters shooting mourning doves, as well as ducks, geese, and other migratory game birds, must by law have their guns plugged so that they cannot hold more than three shots.) A few years ago, when South Dakota had an open season on mourning doves, some citizens of this state objected to shooting the doves. They said that they should be considered songbirds rather than game birds, as they are in most states where they are in abundance, and called for a state referendum to determine which name should apply. A statewide election was held, and the songbird definition won. There will be no more hunting of doves in South Dakota.

1   Definitions are arrived at in many ways. Sometimes government agencies will set definitions, as in the case of pheasants, which are not considered migratory, and therefore may be hunted with automatic shotguns containing as many shells as they will hold. Sometimes categorization of various things will determine definitions, and sometimes people vote to determine what a thing is. In a group discussion, work out some kinds of definitions that result from (a) orders handed down by some kind of authority, like a government, management, or parents; (b) natural, observable physical characteristics; and (c) common consent, as when people vote.
2   Have a group develop arguments on both sides of the issue of shooting game birds. Would these arguments have been useful in South Dakota, which has a wide reputation as a great pheasant-hunting state? What special arguments have to be included or avoided if the commitment to hunting is already evident?
3   Did the election in South Dakota actually determine what mourning doves are? Did it simply define them for that state? Do you think they are songbirds? Is there some other category they would fit into? Did that election affect what a mourning dove is when it flies from South Dakota to the neighboring state of Nebraska or to Kansas?

Denotative and Connotative Meaning   To understand meaning, you must understand its two dimensions. The first dimension of meaning, *denotation,* refers to the relationship that people agree to make between a symbol and what the symbol stands for. It is agreed, for example, that the word "chair" refers to a three- or four-legged object that has a back and a seat on which we sit. The denotative meaning of a word is that arbitrary, but agreed-upon, relationship.

If the things we talk about were always present to us and to the people we speak to, we might not need names for these things because we could physically point to them. When what we are talking about is not present, however, we need pointers. Symbols perform this function. Words and other symbols vary in the number of details which they include in their pointing function. The word "cafeteria," for example, points to more details than the word "cup." The more general a word is—that is, the more details it points to, the more territory it covers—the higher its level of abstraction, and the more chance of misinterpretation. The details that you have in mind when you use the word and the details that will be thought about by your listener hearing the word may not be the same at all. The more details involved, the more chances there are that each of you will choose your own special ones. Specific, concrete words stay closer to the territory and point to fewer details, thus decreasing the chances for misinterpretation.

When children learn language, they proceed through trial and error to figure out which details are pointed to when a word is being used. If you give a one-and-a-half-year-old an ice cube and say "cold," that sound could conceivably point to many sensations the child experiences, such as the shape of the ice cube, its color, the melting ice dripping on an elbow, the cold feeling, etc. Later, the child might hear the word "cold" in relation to a drink of cold water. This time the child must remember which sensations from that first experience are similar to this second experience. The process of elimination is still not conclusive, however, because several characteristics of the two experiences are common, and the child does not have yet enough data to decide which one to pick. More experiences will be necessary to isolate slowly the cold sensation as the one to which the word "cold" refers. In a sense, children play detective with language and through a process of elimination determine the common denominators among their experiences and thus the probability that certain words point to certain characteristics of these experiences.

This is how the denotation of a word is learned. Denotation refers to the pointing process and reflects the agreed-upon relationship between a word and the critical details of its referent. Denotation classifies things and events and places them into categories on the basis of the critical characteristics we have agreed to emphasize. In very specific words which point to few details and which have observable referents, agreement on the denotative meaning of words is relatively widespread, and there is generally little confusion when we communicate. "Pass me the salt" will usually be understood without difficulty.

The connotative dimension of meaning refers to the individual experiences you have had with the things words stand for. *Connotation* refers to the feelings you have developed from all your contacts over the years with these objects. The word "mother," for example, is associated with the experiences you have had with your own mother and the mothers of the people around you. As a baby, "mother" possibly meant to you primarily food, warmth, and security. These were the things you experienced whenever your mother was around. Your experiences with your mother, of course, became more diversified as you grew older, and other "meanings" developed as your experiences developed. If the sum total of your experiences with your mother in particular and other mothers in general is positive, warm, and reinforcing, your connotations for the word "mother" will be positive and pleasant. But think of a child beaten by its mother, for example. That child's experiences with a mother are cold, hateful, fearful, and insecure. For such a child, it is unlikely that the connotation of the word "mother" will ever be warm, loving, and pleasant; the word will instead evoke unpleasant reactions. Finally, the word "mother" in some cultures has a significantly different use, and hence a different connotation.

DENOTATIVE/CONNOTATIVE MEANINGS: APPLICATION

Make a list of words for things that you can point to in the environment to communicate. (Example: "chair")

_____

_____

_____

_____

Make a list of words for things that cannot be pointed to when we want to communicate. (Example: "liberty")

_____

_____

_____

Which of these two lists will other people understand better? Which kinds of words make our communication more accurate? Try talking with someone using primarily words of the type in the first list—denotative words of things you can point to. Then try talking with someone using primarily words from the second list—highly connotative or abstract words. What differences do you notice?

IMPLICATIONS FOR COMMUNICATION

The concept of connotative meanings has some extremely important implications for communication.

1. *Words Can Have Similar Connotative Meanings for People Only to the*

People can have similar connotative meanings only to the extent that they have similar experiences. *(Gail Myers.)*

Extent that People Have Similar Experiences. If your experiences with something are different from someone else's, your connotative meanings will be different. For example, suppose you are talking about dogs to a friend. The dogs you have known have always been nice, friendly, and fun, but perhaps your friend was once bitten and had to undergo painful rabies shots. Your friend's meaning for the word "dog" is going to include those unpleasant memories and perhaps some fear. You may never convince such a person that dogs are all right to have around children.

Unless you and other people have had similar experiences with what words stand for, you are not likely to understand one another, for you will never be talking about quite the same thing.

For instance, the word "money" means one thing to a middle-class child who is accustomed to having most needs satisfied, but it means something quite different to a ghetto child or a person brought up during the Depression. Many misunderstandings between generations come from attitudes about money and can be traced to the different connotative meanings that people have attached to the word.

The term "LSD" means something quite different to a scientist studying the effects of certain dosages of this drug on the chromosome structure in rats, to parents afraid their child is experimenting with it, to the college student who has used LSD without apparent bad effects, and to the student who had a really "bad trip" and ended up in a hospital after a suicide attempt. It's not true that any one of these people knows more or less about LSD. But their experiences with it are different, and therefore their meaning for the word will be different. If they talk to each other, they may never quite understand what the other person "means."

Consider the word "car." To people who have never had any difficulties with cars, it may be a fairly neutral word referring generally to some means of transportation. To those living in crowded cities, it may mean awful traffic jams and the pollution associated with car exhaust systems. To the person who has had a very serious accident and perhaps killed someone or who has had a relative or close friend die as a result of a car accident, the word may never be neutral. It will bring up a whole series of painful associations.

Because people never have identical experiences, they can never have identical connotative meanings. One hundred percent successful communication is thus impossible. Heraclitus, the Greek philosopher, once wrote that a man cannot step in the same river twice. This is because the person changes and the river flows. You are not the same from day to day. Your experiences with your environment change constantly, even if slightly. As long as you live, you grow and change. If you do not remain the same, how can any one else be like you? No two people are ever identical or have identical experiences—not even brothers and sisters raised in the same family. Parents act differently with each child, with boys and with girls, with the firstborn, and with the baby of the family. What you experience is the product of who you are and how you filter things from your environment.

Although you never can meet your identical twin, it is still possible to arrive at similar meanings through similar kinds of experiences. So, on some matters that are nearly universal, you might reach a fairly good level of understanding. You know, for example, that if you have been through a very painful and traumatic experience along with another person, you have little difficulty communicating with each other about the experience. It is considerably more difficult to explain what you went through to someone who was not there. You understand your close friends better than strangers. That is because you have had common experiences.

Again, we must stress that misunderstandings occur primarily at the connotative rather than at the denotative level. Agreement on many basic words like "chair," "table," "house," and "car" can be achieved. Misunderstandings occur primarily in two ways:

> When we use abstract words that have many connotations, such as "parent," "freedom," "love," "hate," "education," and "teaching."

> When we treat a word as if the other person automatically uses it the way we do. Our misunderstandings happen when we are not aware of the possible differences in meaning each of us may attribute to a word.

2. *Meanings Are Not Fixed.* Your experiences with things, people, and events are never static. They change constantly as your environment changes. You change too—even similar experiences are perceived differently at different times in your life. Your reactions to and feelings about what is around you differ as you change, and thus your meanings change, too. Your meanings of the word "parent" are quite different

when you are ten years old, fifteen years old, eighteen years old, and twenty-five years old, and when you become a parent yourself.

3. **You Respond in Terms of Your Experience.** You tend to think that everybody reacts to things the same way you do. It is difficult to think otherwise because you feel your experiences have a quality of universality and somehow must be shared by everyone. Yet they are not. No two people ever have exactly the same experiences. Even when exposed to the same kind of experiences, each will perceive them in a personal and unique way. The abilities to recognize that your experiences are unique, to figure out what other people's experiences are like, and to try to see the environment as another person does are all keys to effective communication.

This combined ability has many names. Some call it "empathy," some "sensitivity" or "communication awareness." Whatever the name, it refers to a conscious awareness of human differences and a genuine attempt to see the world through another person's eyes. It is an effort to understand why another human being feels that way about something, and perhaps how that feeling came about. This ability is premised on a great deal of curiosity about human behavior and a genuine interest in people. It is a curiosity without judgment, an attitude that says "I am OK and you are OK, even if we may be different." Communication often breaks down because of a lack of such efforts— because of the feelings that *my* way of seeing the world is the *only way* that makes sense.

THE SECOND FAULTY ASSUMPTION:
THE FALLACY OF SINGLE USAGE

To complicate things further, we are often under the delusion that one word has only one usage. Take the word "run" as an example:

> You can *run* a 50-yard sprint
> *run* a business
> *run* your hose
> have a *runny* nose
> have a *run* of cards
> *run* out of something
> *run* out on somebody
> *run* over someone with your car

The 500 most common words in the English language have about 14,000 different meanings, an average of 28 different meanings per word. That does not even consider the infinite number of private connotations each of us will call up in our minds when we hear a word. We are talking about the public or denotative dimension of word meaning.

Clues for figuring out what is meant by a given word come generally from the context in which the word is used, that is, from the other words with which that particular word is used. A native of this country will undoubtedly understand quickly which meaning of the word "run" is intended by looking at the rest of the sentence in which the word appears. However, someone who is not a native speaker might get confused by an expression like "a runny nose" because the words are taken in their literal usage.

The importance of context for understanding a message cannot be overemphasized. When words or sentences are taken out of context, the meaning of a message can be drastically changed.

Private Usages Language is a code. When you know the key to the code, you can decipher the messages you receive. If you know the people who send the messages, you can decipher their messages even better because you are more in tune with their private meanings.

A code is a powerful tool. It includes you in the group which shares it, but it also excludes anyone who does not know it. Young people familiar with the latest slang, for example, can carry on a conversation which adults would probably not understand. Most trades or professions have developed their own "jargon." Scientific disciplines develop their own language to be more precise and to narrow down the number of usages for a given word. For example, we commonly refer to marijuana as "grass," "weed," or "pot," rather than *Cannabis sativae* or "tetrahydrocannabinol." The term "gastroenteritis" is more specific than "tummy ache" or "sore gut" to a physician, but it will draw a complete blank from a four-year-old child. Different groups use different codes to communicate similar messages.

Sometimes the highly esoteric jargon of specialists can be an obstacle to communication. A classic example is the story of the plumber who wrote the Bureau of Standards in Washington that he had found hydrochloric acid to be fine for cleaning drains and wanted to know whether it was harmless. Washington replied: "The efficacy of hydrochloric acid is indisputable, but the corrosive residue is incompatible with metallic permanence." The plumber wrote back that he was very glad the Bureau agreed with him. The Bureau replied with a note of alarm: "We cannot assume responsibility for the production of toxic and noxious residues with hydrochloric acid and suggest you use an alternative procedure." The plumber wrote again that he was happy to learn that the Bureau still agreed with him. Finally Washington exploded: "Don't use hydrochloric acid; it eats hell out of pipes."

Dialects In a given society, we have codes within the main code, languages within the language, that only certain groups are familiar with and really understand. English, as it is spoken in the United States, is really many different languages. The language of black ghettos, sometimes called "black English," has its own rules, structure, and vocabu-

"I can't put it into layman's language for you. I don't know any layman's language."

Sometimes the highly esoteric jargon of specialists can be an obstacle to communication. *(The New Yorker.)*

lary. There is "street language" as well as Southern, Mexican-American, and Northern dialects, to name just a few.

But in addition to geographic differences, there are socioeconomic as well as ethnic differences in the ways Americans speak. Even in the same geographic area, the black worker's speech is different from that of the white worker, and the lower-class person speaks differently from the way the upper-middle-class person does.

The spoken mass media, however, generally use a standard dialect known as *General American Speech.* Most radio and television announcers learn to use this dialect and thus bring that speech pattern into homes where it might never have been heard otherwise.

Is General American Speech the "correct" way to speak American English? Is it the only "standard" speech in this country, putting all other dialects in a "substandard" category? Experts generally agree that no one dialect should be considered better than any other as long as it communicates meaning effectively and is appropriate to the situations in which it is used. However, General American Speech is considered by many to be the most widely acceptable speech dialect. It is a fact that many people tend to look at language as an index of a person's level of education, social class, and intelligence. When people believe that one speech dialect is better than others, more prestigious, or the only way for educated people to speak, the consequences can be quite damaging to those speaking other dialects. This problem was particularly apparent in the case of children from the black ghettos in the late fifties and sixties. Because it was found that black children were not reading or writing at the same rate as white children, some scholars contended that the problem was caused by the "substandard" dialect spoken by the black children. This dialect, they said, caused them to be culturally "impoverished" and inadequately prepared for schooling. The key to solving the problem, they argued, was simply to make all black children learn standard American English. Controversy immediately arose when other scholars took the position that black English was in no way inferior to General American English. The language of the black ghetto not only was valid, they maintained, but also contained subtleties that were missing in standard English. One example cited was the distinction black children make between "He sick" and "He be sick." A ghetto child, asked why his father wasn't at a PTA meeting, might say "He sick"— meaning that he had a cold, for example—or he might say "He be sick," describing a continuing or permanent condition. The scholars pointed out that in standard English, the child would have only one, less descriptive answer—"He is sick." They concluded that the ghetto dialect should have equal acceptance with standard English in schools attended by black children. These scholars emphasized a growing sense of black pride in black culture. Teaching black children that their language was inferior and was holding them back in school, they felt, would severely damage their newly won pride.

The controversy continued when other scholars maintained that usage of certain language forms did not make them generally acceptable. They said that the "everything goes" approach to language was unacceptable because it really implies the racist view that black children are not capable of learning the language that other Americans use. They further argued that continued use of the black dialect would hold back these children from success in our culture, where many people who speak predominantly the standard American dialect are intolerant of those whose speech is different.

What needs to be underscored here is the fact that "better" or "correct" language is not better or correct because of any inherent qualities in the language itself or because of any qualities inherent in the people who speak it. Language is essentially arbitrary, and common usage or common agreement is what makes it go. Those who speak black English consider it a correct language, not less acceptable than any other.

Those who speak General American English think it is the correct language. Someone who never intends to leave the black community has little reason to learn to speak General American English, except perhaps out of curiosity, as some people learn Latin or Greek. However, in our complex, changing, and mobile world, the chances are that isolation in any one group, to the total exclusion of other groups, is unlikely. If you increase your repertoire of "languages," you increase your choices. The more languages you are able to master (and we do not mean only foreign languages), the better able you will be to fit your language to the varied situations you are likely to encounter in a complex society.

DIALECTS: APPLICATIONS

LEGISLATING LANGUAGE LAWS

For nearly 150 years the Belgian government has disagreed over the problem of which language is to be spoken in which parts of the country. Belgium was founded in 1830 and has debated ever since that time whether its citizens should speak French, Flemish, or German dialects. Both French and Flemish are spoken in Brussels, the capital. In mid-1972 the government was forced to resign over an issue involving some 6,000 farmers in eastern Belgium living in six villages where residents speak a mixture of French, Flemish, and Walloon, but seem to prefer French. The Flemish-speaking parliament members, however, say that these villagers have been assigned the Flemish language. This debate has been going on for ten years, as one government after another has tried to make an acceptable linguistic decision.

1   How would you feel if a government said you had to stop speaking the language you grew up with and adopt another one? Has that happened with American Indians in reservation schools? With Chicano children in the Southwest? With ghetto black children?
2   What are the arguments, do you think, for imposing a language on one section of a country? Is there an "official" language in the United States? Is it possible for a nation (or a state or a district) to have one written language and several spoken ones?
3   Why do people feel strongly about their language? Is it more than just sounds or squiggles on paper? Does it represent a culture? A way of looking at the world? A familiar force binding people together?

OVERHEARD ON A BUS

On a bus in Hawaii, a woman of Oriental extraction made this remark when she was pushed aside by another woman for a seat.

"You high fo lookin Potagee hoa, you no fit be on bus. You push folk roun an you git trouble. Think you big cuz hapa haole."

The other woman replied in a nasty tone: "You pau now Pakay bag, or do I send you head up puka in roof?"

1   Although Hawaii is supposed to be a melting pot and a symbol of the ability of diverse groups to mingle with ease and lack of prejudice, there are times when cultural and racial differences seem to cause friction. A common language is spoken, which a Mainlander would find difficult to follow. Can you interpret the exchange above, which contains some Hawaiian words and some words that are spelled as they might sound to a listener?

2   Would you expect either speaker to use another language with her own family or friends that would be different from this pidgin English?

3   Is this a substandard language? Is it a dialect? Do you think both women managed to convey their emotions to each other and exchange a message? Would you be likely to use this language (or dialect) at the university when analyzing literature or chemical compounds? Would students use it in the coffee shop? Would roommates use it?

The Humpty Dumpty Attitude   Lewis Carroll's *Alice in Wonderland* illustrates what language is really about:

> "I don't know what you mean by 'glory,'" Alice said.
>
> Humpty Dumpty smiled contemptuously. "Of course you don't—till I tell you. I mean 'there is a nice knockdown argument for you.'"
>
> "But 'glory' does not mean 'a nice knockdown argument,'" Alice objected.
>
> "When *I* use a word," Humpty Dumpty said in rather a scornful tone, "it means just what I choose it to mean—neither more nor less."
>
> "The question is," said Alice, "whether you *can* make words mean different things."
>
> "The question is," said Humpty Dumpty, "which is to be master, that's all."

Can you make words mean whatever you want them to mean? After all, if the relationship between a word and what the word stands for is arbitrary, and if "correct" spelling, pronunciation, and language structure are only conventions, then what prevents you from changing all this—from calling objects by names you would coin, spelling any way you please, and speaking words in whatever order you wanted to? Nothing prevents you from doing it, really. Actually, you do this a good deal of the time with your friends and those who live closely with you. You have your own names for various things and your "in-jokes," for example. The rather esoteric slang used by some young people is an attempt to form their own language, understood only by the in-group.

However, the value of language, or of any symbolic system, rests in the fact that it is a *shared* system, that is, a system known to more than one or even a few individuals. You *can* make words mean whatever you want them to mean, but for that freedom you pay the price of not being understood by the rest of the world. Language with shared symbols is what binds us all together. If you choose to speak your own language, then you forgo human contact and the chance of being understood by others. You can invent your own private language or use a language understood by only a few, but unless you can make other people learn it, accept it, and use it, you will not be able to communicate with anyone else. Human communication, however imperfect it may be, is still the central thread of our sanity and humaneness.

WORDS OUT OF CONTEXT: APPLICATION

IS IT HONEST?

This statement was made by a member of a committee studying innovation. The context is given in the statement itself.

> In our quest for innovation and fresh approaches to the concept of interdisciplinary studies, it is important to have a healthy attitude. Some of our educators are simply faddists, ready to leap on whatever academic bandwagon appears to offer a new way of doing things without any necessary testing of results. On the other hand, there are those whose own selfish interests appear to be best served by having a wait-and-see attitude—to hold off until the wave has passed and the innovation has been so widely adopted that little case can be made for its freshness. What we are asking for in this commission is that we adopt an attitude somewhere between these two extremes and that we be ready to innovate and support fresh programs with funds, but cautious about scattering our efforts by swaying with every breeze.

Following is a statement made by one person who is attempting to interpret this summary in a particular way. Notice how the speaker distorts the original statement by taking parts of it out of context.

> The committee has rightly accused educators of being—and I am quoting—'simply faddists, ready to leap on whatever academic bandwagon appears to offer a new way of doing things. . . . ' In support of that view, I am proposing that we go on record as opposing any new schemes of teaching which have not been adopted by a majority of the schools in the state and that any experimental teaching methods or programs be withdrawn from the budget. The committee was quite right in challenging us to be 'cautious about scattering our efforts by swaying with every breeze.' The proposed program for reading innovation is just such a 'blowing breeze' and must be dropped immediately.

1   What qualifications should the speaker have made in quoting the committee report? Was the report misquoted? Did the speaker use the same
words the committee used in its original report? What did the speaker do
then which made the reporting of those words slanted?

2   If you were a member of the original committee and heard this statement
made in reference to your report, what would you say to the speaker? How
would you attempt to bring the statements into better balance with the
original report? Assume that this is a meeting of a school board in a public
setting to discuss the report of a study committee of outside experts, in
which case this speaker against the innovative program has been heard
by many people who probably have not read the original committee
report. Would you, as a member of the committee, stand up and correct the
new statements? Would you simply ask the audience to read the report
carefully to determine whether the speaker's interpretation is correct since
it is given out of the context of the report?

3   Assume you oppose this "selective" quoted report. Make a statement to be
read to the public meeting using the same words that appear in the
committee report but taking the other side. How would you support
innovation by using the words of the original report?

4   Find a public statement made by a politician, by an official of the city or
the university, or by some other public figure. Divide the class into two
groups and have one group develop an argument in favor of an issue and
one group develop an argument against that same issue—using only
quoted arguments from the public statement. Role-play a meeting in
which the two sides have assembled to "prove" their respective cases by
use of the original public statement.

Offensive Language   Use of words that some people consider obscene,
dirty, or simply distasteful often becomes a problem in informal and
sometimes formal-speaking situations. Some say, "Why all the fuss?
Words are only combinations of letters," and yet many people are
offended by off-color jokes and language. Other groups use such
language extensively and punctuate almost every sentence with words
that others would find objectionable. Some people may use offensive
language because of the feeling of freedom from social restraints it gives
them. In some groups or regions, such words are so widely used that
they have lost much of their strength and have become a common part of
everyday vocabulary.

However, as a speaker, you must often decide whether to use
potentially off-color language and to what extent. Your decision has to
take into account the setting and the occasion of your speech. Will you
be in a locker room, at a funeral, at a formal dinner, at a beer party with
your friends, or at a large family gathering? If using off-color language
will give the impression that you are "one of those good-for-nothing
youngsters" (unless this is precisely the impression you want to create),
it may be advisable to tone your language down a bit.

It is true that the public is generally more tolerant of offensive language than it used to be. Although the issue of obscenity is still raised in many letters to television-station managers and newspaper editors, fewer words are "bleeped" from television programs or appear as dashes in print.

When you are dealing with an audience that you are sure tolerates and even enjoys off-color language, you may be tempted to adopt their norms and try to speak "their language." For example, some teachers attempt to ingratiate themselves with their students by using swearwords or adopting the latest slang terms. Such attempts should be handled with care because you may sound phony or "put on."

This discussion points out the dilemma of language use. On the one hand, you want to be sensitive to your audience's level of tolerance for language in order to avoid shocking them needlessly. On the other hand, if you try too hard to speak on their level, particularly when you are not like them (the teacher who uses an overabundance of slang, for example), you may be unconvincing. The way out of the dilemma is to be sensitive to the audience, the setting, and the occasion and to be yourself as much as possible. If "being yourself" means that you use profanity with an audience that would offended by it, perhaps you have to reconsider your priorities. You can't blame the audience and expect them to tolerate language they consider unacceptable. Your choice depends on the effect you want. If you want to shock them, you may succeed. If you want to win the audience over to your cause or gain their confidence, you may not succeed. This is just as much of a problem for a speaker who never uses swearwords and who faces an audience that normally does. Such a speaker too must adjust to the audience sufficiently to be listened to, without sounding as though a foreign language is spoken. Mark Twain's wife once scolded him for swearing so much, and to make her point she repeated back to him the words he had used. He laughed and told her: "The words are right, but the tune is all wrong."

OFFENSIVE LANGUAGE: APPLICATION

MEANINGS ON THE BBC

Recently a new code of conduct for the British Broadcasting Corporation (BBC) was instituted to control what the BBC officials thought was an increasing use of offensive language and nudity. The BBC maintained that it may not be necessary to offend viewers in order to make a point about language or situations.

The BBC criticized a scene from the television series "Elizabeth" in which a naked girl was shown leaving the bed of the French king. Commented the BBC: "The scene added nothing to the plot and very little to an understanding of the character of the King of France."

In addition, the BBC objected to the use of such words as "bloody," "bleeding," and "God" to give force to lines or situations, saying: "The BBC regards the use of these in such circumstances as indefensible."

1 Are you offended by these words? Are they typically British words and not ones that Americans find offensive? Are there words used in television programs in the United States that offend you? Would those same words offend a person in Britain?
2 The decision to ban certain nude scenes was made by a group of people in responsible leadership positions in the BBC. How did they determine which kinds of scenes would be offensive? Form a group to role-play the meeting of this board at which the decision to ban some kinds of nudity was discussed. Do you deal with public morality or with your own private attitudes and values about what would be offensive to "the viewers" as you see them? How do you know what the viewers like or do not like and what they will tolerate or will not tolerate? Do you get mail from viewers, have many viewers actually talked to you, or do you guess at what will offend them?

The Effective Use of Symbols

Although you may be confident that your internal meanings are structurally related to the reality you wish to describe, and sensitive to the fact that your listeners' meanings for certain words may be different from yours, your task as an effective communicator has not ended. The symbols you use may or may not clearly represent what you wish to communicate. Your *style* of expression may do much to enhance or detract from the communication of your intended meaning. How you choose words and arrange them so as to best express your meaning to your listeners is the subject of this section.

ACCURACY AND PRECISION

Precise meanings are difficult to express unless words are chosen carefully. To tell your garage mechanic that there is a "rattling sound in the *whatchamacallit*" and that you need "*a gadget* to fix it" is at best vague. It is not that much more vague than the politician exhorting a crowd to vote for "true Americanism." Abstract words, that is, words which do not have a readily observable referent to point to, are more subject to private connotations—hence are more likely understood only in terms of personal, idiosyncratic meanings. "Democracy" does not mean the same to a citizen of Poland and to a citizen of the United States. What is "expensive" to you may be "cheap" to a very wealthy person. However, if you know that your audience is in many ways like you and has a background similar to yours, then you can assume that its personal connotations will be essentially similar to yours. This is why conversations between intimate friends often seem so obscure to the eavesdropping stranger.

Precise and accurate and technical language enhances communication only if both communicators share an understanding of the nuances expressed. Abstract and general words are often ambiguous and do not express clearly enough the precise nuances you may wish to convey. Unfortunately, some people sometimes deliberately use language ambiguously and vaguely in order to cover up rather than explain reality. When this is done, language becomes an unreliable instrument for communicating. Euphemisms sometimes are harmless: saying "powder room" instead of "toilet" does not create any particular problem. In other cases, reality becomes so verbally distorted that listeners lose their ability to assess and evaluate what might be actually happening. For example, a statement is labeled "inoperative" and later turns out to have been an outright lie. The term "police action" replaces war. The expression "liberating a town" is a substitute for capturing it.

SIMPLICITY

No matter how accurately words express your intended meaning, they are ineffective if your audience does not understand them.

Use simple words rather than complicated ones. Use short and concrete words rather than longer and more abstract ones. Be concise rather than wordy so that your meanings will not get lost in a sea of words. Administrative memoranda (and some students' papers) are often classic cases of needless wordiness. Meaning often can be communicated more effectively in a few words.

APPROPRIATENESS

Your language should fit you, your audience, the subject on which you are speaking, and the occasion of your communicating.

Obviously, you do not use a string of light jokes in the middle of a solemn eulogy. Formal and dignified oratory is not appropriate among a group of friends informally chatting at a party.

Your speaking style must represent *you* if you wish to develop trust and credibility with your audience. If you are an educated person, you must speak like one, even if you are speaking to an uneducated audience. However, you must carefully gear the level of your speaking to the level of your audience. A person with Ph.D. in physics speaks differently to a group of physicists than to a group of high school students. The level of the vocabulary will change. Educated speaking does not mean using long and complicated words; it simply means an adherence to basic rules of grammar and style used by that group of people.

Most interpersonal situations and some public situations demand an informal style. As Bradley points out in his summary of the research on informality,[4] an informal style is characterized by shorter sentences, fewer different words, larger number of short words, more self-references (I, me, we, our, us), more pseudo-quantifying terms (much, many, a lot), more allness terms (none, all, always, never), more terms indicating an awareness of the subjectivity of perception (to me, apparently, seems), fewer quantifying terms (precise numerical terms), more informal language (contractions and colloquial words), more qualifying terms (if, however, but).

IMAGERY AND ORIGINALITY

Trite phrases and cliches are often colorless because of overuse. Some figures of speech have become so overworked that no originality of expression is left. "Cute as a bunny," "sleeping like a log," are examples of common figures of speech that have become predictable and uncreative. Overused words like "cool," "fabulous," "terrific," "far out," often become substitutes for more original expressions and are sometimes intended to cover up a lack of more precise vocabulary. After all, when a pair of shoes, a girl, a book, a pizza, and a philosophical idea can all be "far out," the word obviously loses precision.

On the other hand, metaphors and imagery can be used to produce sensations in your listeners which help them recreate and recall images of previous experiences. Visual, auditory, gustatory (taste), olfactory (smell), tactual (touch), kinesthetic (muscle strain), and organic (internal sensation) images are all powerful tools for recreating sensorial experiences and can be used quite effectively. Using figures of speech to add imagery to your communication is like putting seasoning on your food—it doesn't change the nutritional content, but it makes the whole effect more palatable. That preceding sentence is an example of a *simile*, a figure of speech which usually uses the word "like" to connect the parts of the statement.

The *metaphor* compares items or activities or events or persons which are alike in some characteristics. "I wandered lonely as a cloud . . ." is the kind of poetic metaphor which is familiar to us. A few years ago a group of reporters were given special information to disseminate to the public about governmental events in Washington, and that was called "news by leak." The "ship of state" metaphor for the United States government has given rise to many associated nautical references about "steering," "at the helm," "shoals of indecision," and so on. Former President Gerald Ford introduced sports metaphors into the jargon of government with "team play," "end runs," and other sports-language references applied to activities of running the nation.

---

[4]Bert Bradley, *Fundamentals of Speech Communication: The Credibility of Ideas*, W. C. Brown, Dubuque, Iowa, 1974, pp. 195–196.

☐ NONVERBAL SYSTEMS

So far, our discussion of the processes of communication has focused on verbal language and verbal systems because verbal symbols are essential tools for your communication with others.

However, you should not overlook another important facet of the communication process—the *nonverbal system*. In this section we will examine the elements of the nonverbal system and the way they work in informal and formal speaking situations.

All of us send and receive a very complex system of nonverbal signals when we speak. These signals include tone of voice, body movements, gestures, clothing and accessories, and a whole range of messages conveyed by touch. These nonverbal signals often determine whether we like someone or not. In our interpersonal communication we make many decisions on the basis of an intuitive interpretation of the nonverbal code. When to laugh, when to move, when to relax or tense up, and when to continue or end a conversation can all be decided by "reading" someone else's nonverbal signals.

Paralanguage

The spoken word is never neutral. It is always affected by your tone of voice, your emphasis and inflections, the breaks or pauses in your sentences, the speed of your delivery, how loudly or softly you speak, and the pitch of your voice. These nonverbal factors are called *paralanguage*.

As you know from your experiences in informal speaking situations, a simple "yes" can be said in many different ways—it can express anger, frustration, resignation, disinterest, agreement, or challenge.

In formal speaking situations, paralanguage certainly affects how your listeners will respond to you and what you have to say. Voice quality is important to the delivery of a prepared speech, although it should be less important than content in the evaluation of a speaker's performance. However, some unpleasant voice qualities may affect an audience negatively. Breathiness, for example, suggests weakness. A harsh or husky voice indicates tenseness. A rough tone often suggests bad temper and induces tension in the listeners. Flat voices may suggest boredom, and thin voices insecurity.

In everyday life we naturally rely on the words themselves plus paralanguage features to develop meanings. Sometimes, however, we become distracted and do not hear the words themselves. Rather than admitting that we have not been paying attention, we often rely on the paralanguage features alone to interpret what was said. This may happen, for example, at cocktail parties, where people often don't listen carefully to conversations and respond almost automatically. If you use the right tone of voice, you might get away with, "My parents just died; I am fine, thank you, and how are you?"

All societies have a system of meaningful gestures that either accompany oral language or stand alone in conveying a particular message. *(Charles Gatewood.)*

We often are upset not so much by *what* people say as by *how* they say it: "He sounds so sure of himself that I always want to contradict him." We tend to respond to people in relation to such paralanguage features without quite realizing what it is we are reacting to.

Some people, no matter how interesting what they have to say might be, will bore you. This is invariably a matter of voice quality— usually their pitch or intonation, and perhaps their rate of speech. Most of us have listened to a speaker who spoke so slowly and monotonously that we found it hard to stay awake and interested. This is definitely a liability in speech-related activities. More specific suggestions in relation to voice qualities will be given in another chapter.

GESTURES

Gestures were probably one of the first means of communication human beings developed, long before oral language. All societies have a system of meaningful gestures that either accompany oral language or stand alone in conveying a particular message. We nod to say "yes" and shake our heads to say "no." Extending our hand is a gesture of friendship, not of hostility.

You usually accompany your speech with a considerable number of hand gestures. Have you ever given directions to someone over the telephone and found yourself frantically waving your hand? Members of some cultures are more expressive with their hands than others. French,

Spanish, Italian, Mexican, and Arab people, for example, use many more hand gestures than Americans or the English. Sometimes certain individual gestures become automatic. Students are usually quick to recognize the familiar gestures of their professors. Impersonators of famous people rely on pose and gesture as well as on voice. Gestures are also used for emphasis, and if your timing is off, you may appear insincere.

FACIAL EXPRESSIONS AND BODY LANGUAGE

You are almost never expressionless or immobile. Your face moves and your body moves, and these movements communicate a great deal about your feelings, emotions, and reactions. Some of these movements are conscious and intentional—when you deliberately smile at a friend, frown to express dissatisfaction, or raise an eyebrow to show surprise, for example. Sometimes, however, you make such movements unintentionally. When you attempt to hide a feeling, you may give yourself away without realizing it: by the way you move toward or away from a person or by the way you sit—tense, relaxed, on the edge of the chair, or slouched. You tend to lean forward when you are interested and involved, and to lean back when you are not. Even the way you walk indicates to others how you feel—tired, good, happy, cheerful, or gloomy, for example.

In more formal speaking situations, an audience will often form an impression of the speaker from the way he or she stands or sits. Posture provides subtle clues about your personality. These clues may, of course, be misleading, but they are influential. Many people think they can size up speakers and judge their sincerity, their friendliness, their respect for their audience, and their enthusiasm by the way they stand, sit, or walk.

When you analyze another person's facial expressions or body posture, remember that one expression or one movement alone is not enough to base an opinion on, just as one word lifted out of context cannot give you the meaning of a whole paragraph. Movements, expressions, and gestures are not isolated from the whole context of postures and other behaviors. If another person stands with arms folded, for example, you should not infer immediately that the person is hostile. Try to notice other movements and see whether they form any pattern that is meaningful rather than relying on a single nonverbal "utterance." And be aware of your own movements and how they might be interpreted by others.

OBJECT LANGUAGE

The term "object language" refers to the meaning of the objects you surround yourself with. Clothes, jewelry, and decorative objects in a home, for example, are all part of object language. They say something about you because they represent to some extent deliberate choices you have made. Clothing and jewelry are particularly revealing. They communicate something about your sense of appropriateness, your upbringing, your values, and your attitudes. Clothing is symbolic. Some people are so concerned about clothes that they will buy them only in stores that guarantee them the particular image they want to present, whether these are army surplus stores, secondhand stores, or the most fashionable boutiques.

We react to others in terms of what they wear in a particular setting and for a particular occasion. You dress differently depending on the setting, the occasion, and of course the audience. You usually dress to fit the role you find yourself in. The police officer's uniform tells us a great deal, if not about the officer personally, at least about the kind of role he or she can be expected to play. The man wearing a jacket and tie and carrying a briefcase is probably not headed for a picnic. The woman in a white uniform or coat is more likely to be headed for a surgical visit than the opera. And unless you are going to talk to a crowd of your friends at the beach, you will not wear a swimming suit to give a prepared speech. Your physical appearance thus gives people clues to your personality, your attitudes, your values, and the roles you are likely to play.

People often make wrong assumptions from a quick look at someone's physical appearance. We often resent the speed with which others draw conclusions about us on the basis of things we may consider trivial or superficial, particularly when these inferences are incorrect. But outward signs such as clothes and hairstyles do communicate messages. You cannot ignore them and decide they do not count at all, just as you cannot decide that a person's words do not count. Of course, you must be cautious in interpreting the nonverbal messages communicated through dress and other material objects, just as you must be cautious in interpreting a person's words.

But the choice of what to wear, like the choice of what to say, is still ours, and we have to take the responsibility for the misunderstandings that might follow. If you wish to communicate effectively with others, you cannot assume that it is their responsibility to understand you. Just as you would not speak Chinese to an Italian and expect understanding, you should not be surprised that certain clothes or certain hairstyles may be misunderstood by certain audiences. You may not *like* to be judged by what you wear, but your choice is a part of your communication.

NONVERBAL SYSTEMS: APPLICATION

LANGUAGE OF FEATHERS

Certain groups of young men use two feathers in a hatband to indicate their dating status. If the feathers are together, the wearer is all tied up. If they are crossed, he has a date for tonight but not necessarily for tomorrow. If both feathers are sticking straight up, it means he is on the prowl. If the plumes are pointed outward, he is available.

1 Do members of a group develop such "codes" in order to communicate basic information to one another, or does a common code or language establish a deeper relationship between them?

2 In a group discussion in class, try to make a list of the kinds of special codes that members of certain groups may develop as a means of (a) imparting information to one another, (b) building up a feeling of belonging, and (c) excluding others whom they do not wish to let into their group.

3 Are all codes as formal as the one described above? Do we use our clothes and the way we walk, stand, or sit to develop understanding just as much as we use formal codes?

4 How did the Morse code (dots and dashes) come into being? Who used it? Why was it limited to just short and long noises? Is it typical of codes that are limited by the kind of medium they are used in? Is the Morse code a truly international language? Do people whose languages do not use our alphabet make any use of the Morse code?

5 Your nonverbal communication system includes all the messages you give to others around you—whether it is the feathers in your hat or your blue jeans. Have some members of the class work out an entire system by which a particular group could be identified, including, for example, clothing and how it is worn, symbols of different status, and things that outsiders cannot be let in on.

Our communication with others in formal as well as informal situations is very much influenced by spatial relationships. *(Shelly Katz/Black Star.)*

PROXEMICS, OR SPACE AND YOUR COMMUNICATION

Your communication with others in formal as well as informal situations is very much influenced by spatial relationships. People communicate by the way they use space in relation to others. You have your own "personal space," an invisible bubble which is yours and which you do not like to see intruded upon without some direct invitation. We all set our own boundaries, but there are some recognizable cultural patterns that regulate the handling of personal space and interpersonal distance.

Pioneering studies of physical distance by Somner (1959) indicated that distance implies remoteness and detachment, while proximity connotes feelings of attraction and pleasantness. These studies also showed that in face-to-face informal conversations, the average distance between people is about 5 feet. Anthropologist Edward T. Hall has identified three major interpersonal distances: intimate, social, and public. These three, in turn are divided by Hall into a total of eight categories depending on the kind of message and the voice-loudness relationship of the communicators. Hall's categories, then, can be stated as follows:

Intimate—very secret or intimate information in a soft whisper: 3 to 6 inches
—very confidential information in an audible whisper: 8 to 12 inches
—less confidential information in a soft voice: 12 to 20 inches

Social—personal information in a soft voice:20 to 36 inches
—nonpersonal or neutral information in a regular voice: 4 1/2 to 5 feet

Public—general information in a full voice: 5 1/2 to 8 feet
—addressing an audience in a full voice: 6 to 10 feet (or beyond)
—hailing and departing distance: up to 100 feet

When people violate the unspoken rules of interpersonal distance (get too close when they should be at a social distance or stand too far away when they are expected to be more intimate), we tend to feel uncomfortable. Somner calls this the "friction of space," referring to the tension you may feel when someone intrudes on your personal space. When someone you did not invite to approach you comes too close, you tend to move away. If someone sits too close to you at the library or the cafeteria, you will unconsciously move your books, your tray, or your chair away from the intruder. If the other does not get the message and for some reason moves even closer, you will try other avoidance behaviors, or you may even leave.

Appropriate interpersonal distances vary from culture to culture. As Hall points out, most North Americans feel comfortable at a distance of about 3 or 4 feet during social conversation. In France, Mexico, and Latin America, the distance is under 2 or 3 feet. Should a North American engage in conversation with a Latin American, for example, a subtle ballet is likely to follow. The North American may back up the entire length of a hall while the Latin American tries to catch up with him. To the North American, the Latin American comes on as pushy; to the Latin American, the North American seems unfriendly.

Other spatial elements besides interpersonal space also affect our communication. For example, physical space is important in determining how people try to orient themselves to their surroundings. In purely physical terms, proximity is simply the distance that people maintain in their face-to-face interactions. In psychological terms, proximity consists of the meanings attributed to the relationships between people and their surroundings. Strangers, for example, prefer to maintain greater physical distance and prefer to sit side by side rather than face-to-face. In crowded places or in public elevators when sufficient distances cannot be maintained, people keep their privacy by avoiding looking at one another and by staring at the ceiling, the floor, the elevator buttons, or the lights.

Orientation of the body also makes a difference in the feelings we have about a communication encounter. If you meet two other persons and one of them shifts his body and head slightly toward you, then you are likely to perceive that person as having a more positive attitude toward you than the one who did not.

Arrangements of a room will definitely contribute to the atmosphere. Although one can hold a solemn ceremony in a gymnasium, the atmosphere is certainly not the same as if the event were held in a massive cathedral. In atmospheres that are considered ugly, people tend to have reactions such as headaches, drowsiness, irritability, and hostility. In atmospheres considered pleasant, their reactions also tend to be pleasant. Effects on people of particular settings are certainly not trivial. A class held in a colorful seminar room furnished with comfortable chairs will not have the same atmosphere as the same class held in an old, green-walled, traditional classroom furnished with beat-up metal and plastic desk chairs.

How people locate themselves in a room in relation to one another is also a significant factor in their communication. If a boss asks an employee to come into the office, it will make a difference if the boss stays behind the desk and keeps the employee standing on the other side or if the employee is invited to sit down. It will make even more difference if the employer stands up and goes to meet the employee halfway through the room or comes out from behind the desk and sits with, or next to the employee, not using the desk to separate them. The employer might stay behind a desk but have a chair located almost next to it so that the two communicators will occupy two sides of the desk at right angles. These may seem like trivial differences, but they communicate the employer's desire to be formal and impersonal or to be informal and more friendly. They also tell a lot about the relationship between the two people.

You may want to watch for such factors in interview situations, for example. Check which of the interviewer positions or locations in the room in relation to your own position makes you comfortable, tense, or relaxed. Feelings you have after an interview are often connected to proxemics of the situation as well as the verbal exchange.

In group meetings a variety of factors related to proxemics affect how the group works and how communication flows between group members. The shape of the meeting or conference table, for example, affects patterns of communication of those sitting around it. At a *rectangular* table, the ends of the table are seen as the positions of power; group members sitting there are more likely to talk and be talked to than any other members of the group. They are likely to be regarded as group leaders and to be called upon to perform certain leadership functions in the group. At *round* tables, communication is usually more evenly distributed. If you watch the way people sit at a meeting, you can tell a great deal about the dynamics that are likely to occur in that group. You can discover something about the personal likes and dislikes of group members, about competition for leadership and influence in the group, and about the likely flow of communication in the group. Of course, other nonverbal signs such as body movements (for example, whether people lean forward or slouch in their chairs, in what direction they turn their bodies when they sit or talk, and whom they look at when they talk or listen) will also tell you a great deal about the interpersonal dynamics of a group.

In more formal speaking situations, how and where you stand in relation to your audience also has implications for your communication with that audience. Are you on a raised platform addressing a large audience in an auditorium? Are you located on a stage and speaking from a high podium and lectern? Will the audience see only your face when you speak? Will you be able to move from behind the lectern and come closer to the edge of the stage? Will they be able to see you move? Will you decide to use the PA system? Is that PA system a fixed microphone, or a lavaliere mike with a long cord that you can pull as you pace the stage? Are you able and willing to come down from the stage and continue your speech in the midst of your audience in an effort to lessen the public distance and make your speech sound less formal? Will you stand on the stage as you speak, or will you elect to sit down on the edge of the stage in an attempt to be informal? Answers to all these questions will say a great deal about the situation, the occasion, the setting, and the kind of audience you are speaking to. Your choices must certainly be made with a full awareness of these factors. An informal stance during a formal occasion is inappropriate, particularly when the audience expects a formal presentation.

There is some controversy about the size of an audience in relation to the size of the room in which it is gathered. Politicans and show-business people have long maintained that it is better to address a small, packed room (the "full house" feeling) than a larger room containing the same number of people sitting in scattered positions. There is no doubt that from the point of view of the speaker, addressing a full house, scary as it may be at first, is more exciting than speaking to a few isolated souls in a large auditorium.

However, speaking to a crowded audience is somewhat more difficult because people in crowded situations react with greater force to the speaker. Listeners in a crowded audience feel more anonymous and thus less inhibited and freer to do things they may normally not do. When you add to this the fact that behavior in crowds is highly contagious, you can see that a crowded audience may be harder to predict and control than a smaller one. If one person starts applauding with vigor, for example, you may benefit from the effects of the contagion and get a standing ovation. But if someone starts booing or dozing, you will feel the effects of audience infection and you may be in for great embarrassment.

PROXEMICS: APPLICATION

HOW CLOSE SHOULD YOU BE?

Have another person (your "assistant") help you demonstrate the factors involved in how close to get (interpersonal distance). You should be across the room from your assistant. For each of the situations described below, ask your assistant to tell you when you have come close enough. Take only a step or two at a time and then check your distance with your assistant.

"How far away should I be to give a lecture or make a speech?"
"How far away should I be just to say 'hello'?"
"How far away should I be to talk with you about the weather?"
"How far away should I be to talk with you about going to a movie together?"
"How far away should I be to tell you a secret?"

Ask your assistant to help you figure out how we know the "proper" distance for each kind of communication. Where do we learn this? Do we generally agree, within a short distance, on how close to get in these situations? If we disagree, what factors in our backgrounds or our relations make a difference in these "proxemics"?

I. Communication is your attempt to translate your meaning into a symbolic system so that other people will react to the symbolic system by translating it back into a meaning in their mind similar to yours. Three factors often prevent the effective communication of your meaning.
   A. Your internal meaning may not reflect accurately the realities of the situation.
      1. Symbols are used to name and represent what we sense.
      2. In the map-territory analogy, language has the relationship to reality that a map does to the territory it covers.
         a. Maps should be accurate, appropriate, reliable, current.
         b. We often cling to our verbal maps.
         c. Remember to date, index, use the etc. device, hyphen; beware of the "is" of identity.
   B. Meaning is the relationship you make between a symbol and what that symbol stands for. If symbols elicit similar meanings in people, these people understand each other.
      1. One faulty assumption about meaning is that it is inherent in words rather than in people.
      2. A second faulty assumption about meaning is that words have only one meaning.
   C. Dialects are different languages or codes within the main language.
      1. Many groups develop their own language.
      2. Language is considered by many people to be an indicator of ethnic, education, social, and economic background.
      3. No language or dialect is substandard if it communicates meaning effectively in the situation where it is used.
      4. In a complex and changing world, you will encounter people who speak a variety of dialects, including the one most used in this country today, General American Speech; for this reason, you will find it useful to master the dialects you will encounter in your life.
      5. You may invent your own private language, but if other people do not learn it, you will have no one to communicate with. The value of language rests on the fact that it is a shared system.
      6. The use of profanity in speaking may offend some audiences in some settings and may be well accepted by other audiences; therefore, you should adjust your speech to your audience's level of tolerance for profanity.
   D. Your style of expression may do much to enhance or detract from the communication of your intended meaning.
      1. It is important to be accurate and precise.

2. Use simple rather than complicated words.

3. Your language should be appropriate to you, your audience, your topic, and the occasion of your communicating.

4. Imagery can be used to produce sensations in your listeners which help them re-create images of previous experiences.

II. The nonverbal system is another important part of your communication process.

A. Paralanguage refers to your tone of voice, your inflections, speech delivery, speed, and the softness, loudness, and pitch of your voice; it affects your communication because it represents *how* you say things, rather than *what* you say.

B. Gestures accompany verbal language and are used for emphasis; they can also communicate meaning by themselves.

C. Facial expressions and body movements communicate your feelings and reactions.

D. Object language and physical appearance give others clues about you as a person.

E. Proxemics, or how you communicate by your use of space in relation to other people, is another part of the nonverbal code.

1. Four kinds of speaking distances can be distinguished:
   a. Intimate (a few inches to about 1 foot)
   b. Personal (1 to 1 1/2 feet)
   c. Social (1 1/2 to about 5 feet)
   d. Public (6 feet to the end of listening distance)

2. The arrangement of a room contributes to its atmosphere.

3. How people locate themselves in relation to others and to the furnishings in a room communicates something about their relationships.

4. The shape of a meeting table will influence the communication flow among the people sitting at the table.

5. In a large audience situation, where you stand and how you stand affect your communication with the audience.

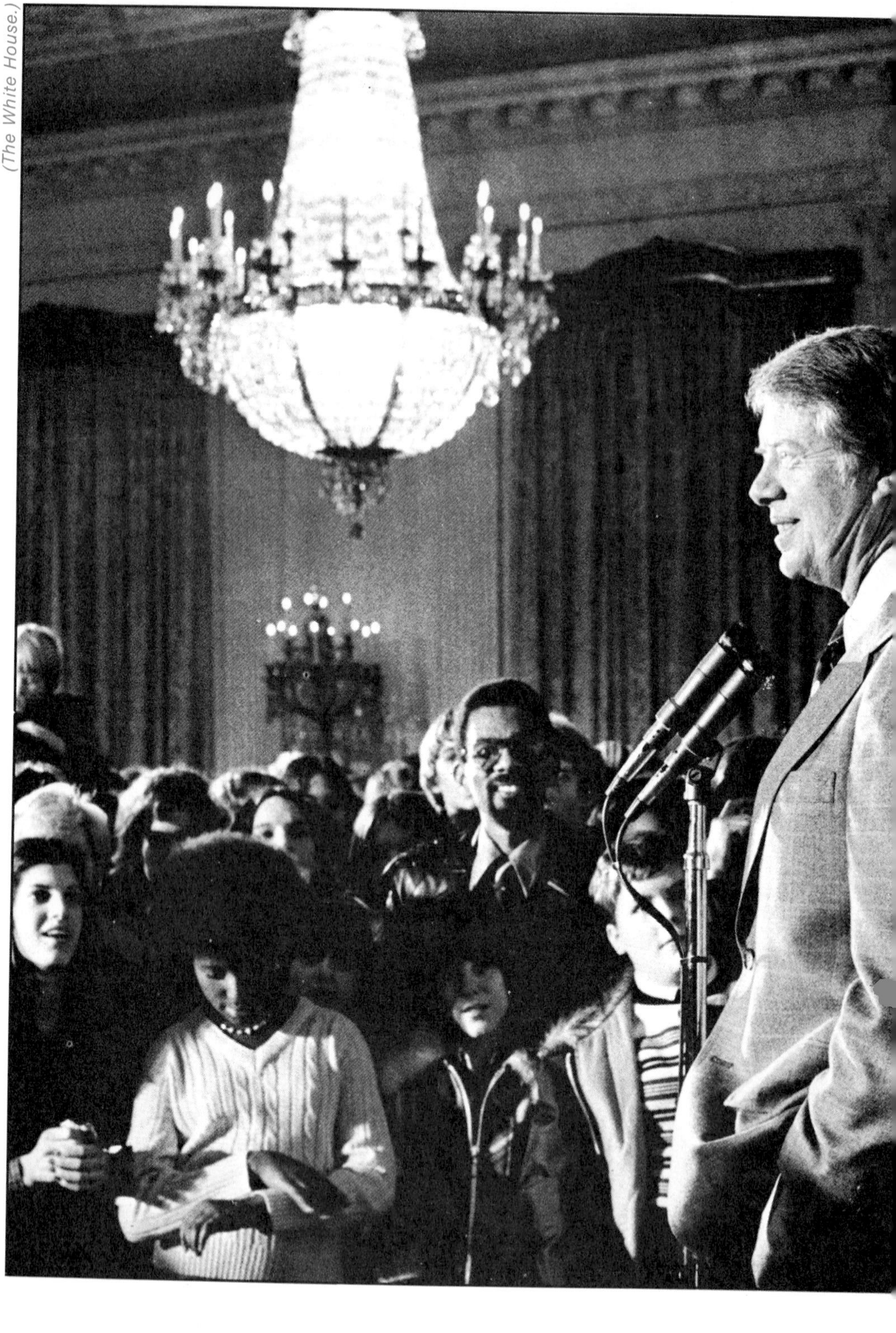

(The White House.)

CHAPTER 4
COMMUNICATING TO YOUR AUDIENCE

There are two kinds of people who blow
   through life like a breeze,
And one kind is gossipers, and the other
   kind is gossipees.
                — Ogden Nash

Herein lies the tragedy of the age:
not that men are poor — all men
know something of poverty; not that
men are wicked — who is good? Not
that men are ignorant — what is
truth? Nay, but that men know so little of men.
            — William E. B. DuBois

There is a holy mistaken zeal in politics
as well as in religion. By persuading
others, we convince ourselves.
                — Anonymous

Audiences are listeners, and listening is a behavior. Thus audiences have behaviors which include complex sets of moods, habits, values, beliefs, motives, attitudes, drives, needs, and opinions. You as an individual will take to a listening situation the same qualities of moods, habits, values, etc. Does this mean that you can treat an audience as one large person? Not unless the audience consists of only one person listening to you, in which case speech teachers call that person an *auditor* rather than an audience. If the audience is composed of many people, it contains all those individuals with their own moods, habits, values, etc.

As far as we know, no member of an audience was born there. Each came from somewhere and has had many experiences. Each has personal motives and needs, and each is affected by things over which you as a speaker have no control. Thus you ought to be aware of two possibilities relating to your success with an audience:

1 You might be able to guess or discover its needs and motives.
2 You ought to work as hard as possible on the things you *can* control.

In this chapter we shall develop some reasons for having an audience-centered emphasis within an integrated approach to communicative speaking. We shall discuss informal and formal audience situations and analyze the audience as listeners. In order to do that, we shall discuss the steps involved in listening and expand on the kinds of listening that audiences tend to do. Because the audience attitude will have an effect on your approach to the speaking situation, we shall also talk about friendly and unfriendly audiences and some that fall in between.

□ THE IMPORTANCE OF YOUR AUDIENCE

To be most effective, communication should be audience-centered. The other approaches are all somewhat limited.

The Speaker-centered Approach

Here the speaker carries the communication load; he or she has the most important role and should be studied for style, vocabulary, pronunciation, enunciation, movements, and total vocal skills. The speaker-centered approach may also focus on morally proper techniques. Another kind of speaker-focus analyzes the motives of the speakers—the hidden meanings behind oral utterances. A third type of focus might be on the eloquence of the speakers—we listen to their rolling phrases and multisyllabic words just as we would listen to a concert or a theatrical performance. All these approaches have one thing in common: They focus on the speakers' central importance in communication. This

To be effective, communication needs to be audience-centered. *(Gail Myers.)*

becomes a limitation because other aspects of the communication are studied only as they relate to the speakers; that is, the messages they give, the audience they speak to, and the occasion for the speech are all merely background to the speaker as a performer. Another limitation of this approach is that it is circular in its design; if the speakers perform only for the sake of their own speaking, they might as well talk to mirrors.

The Message-centered Approach

Focus on the speech itself is the primary object of concern. This approach may emphasize logic and make a perfect outline of the reasoning presented in the speech. Using this approach, you would be able to show that each argument is properly supported with validly logical systems of comparisons, examples, premises, and propositions. A message could also be analyzed for its content and the development of its ideas. The message could also be analyzed in terms of the style or mode of presentation. Analysis would look for a flowing development with an elaborate style, including analogies, metaphors, alliterations, etc. The limitation of the message-centered approach is that it tends to ignore the human actors in favor of a rather sterile focus on the message itself. It also takes the drama of speaking out of the context of human behaviors we call an ''audience.''

The Medium-centered Approach

How is the message sent from the speaker to the listeners? This approach makes it clear that messages do not flow intact from one person to another. They must go through some sort of medium or channel. This may be as simple as the wave of a hand or as complex as the electronic miracle of satellite television. In studying a speech situation using the medium-centered approach, you might look at phonemes (the smallest possible unit of spoken sounds) and the sound-wave patterns they produce. Or you might use the medium-centered approach that involves a mathematical system called *information theory*. This theory breaks information into "bits" that are transmitted through a medium at any time under any conditions in various forms. Another way of using the medium-centered approach would be to look at the differences between various media such as personal oral reports, newspapers, radio broadcasts, and telecasts. Marshall McLuhan, noted theorist of communication, describes messages in terms of the media used to transmit them. His now-famous assumption is that the medium itself is a vital part of the message because it has a tremendous influence on the speaker and the speaker's approach to the listener. Obviously, approaches that center on the medium itself do not exclude listeners; rather, they treat the audience as a terminal, without considering the moods, needs, settings, and occasions that affect reception.

An Integrated Approach

The communication process forces us to understand that each part of the process relates to the others. Without an audience there is no speaker. Without a speaker there is no message, audience, or medium. The process of communication and public speaking is spiraling or circular, enclosing within its circle the speaker, the message, the medium, and the audience. These are inseparable. Yet we might study some part of that involved process, as we might stop the action in a baseball game to see the close play at first base.

Taking a look at any single part of the communication process as a separate element is very much like looking at one play in an entire ball game. So many interactions are involved in the total time of play that you can rarely choose any one moment to show how the game turned out as it did. However, to study the form of the players, their particular strategy, or an action that had a significant part in the game, it is useful to have stop-action, slow-motion, or other devices to enable you to analyze crucial points in the game.

So it is in studying speech. We have to stop this complex, busy process in a way that is not natural in order to analyze and learn more about human communication. One way to integrate all these factors is to

An integrated approach: Who says what, to whom, how, when, and with what effect? *(Wide World Photos.)*

consider *who says what to whom, how and when, and with what effect or result?* Let's illustrate how this integrated approach leads to a serious consideration of, and a primary emphasis on, an audience. If the *who* is you and you want to communicate a *what* (a message), then the next elements are *how* and *where* the message is going.

Suppose you are a man who wants to ask a woman for a date. That establishes many of the features of the process integrating the speaking situation—the *who* is you; the *what* is asking for a date; the *to whom* is the woman; the *when* and *how* are to be established. Then you get the *effect*. If you concentrate on the speaker and delivery, on the message, or on the medium, you may not be as successful in your speaking attempt as if you had concentrated on the audience. You should know all you can about the audience (listener, or auditor) to make this appeal successful. You should know how the integrated parts of your speaking situation affect the auditor. This is why we have said that the audience is an important element—perhaps the most important.

Suppose you see a woman standing in the street and a car approaching her at a fast speed. You want to alert the woman (the audience) to the situation because you think she does not see the car coming. You yell, "Look out!" She jumps out of the way of the car. The message was received and acted on successfully. Suppose she had been deaf? Suppose she had not understood English? What did you have to know, or assume, about your audience before you could get the message across? You need to know very little about yourself. The relationship between the speaker and the medium and the message content is much less important in this situation than the abilities of the audience to hear, to understand, and to jump.

☐ THE AUDIENCE-CENTERED APPROACH

Very few textbooks on speaking or communication focus on the audience, or the listener, as the primary part of the communication act, partly because it is difficult to generalize about audiences and to study them adequately. Many different kinds of public-opinion polls give us audience information, but they are useful only in very special circumstances. We also have many kinds of data about people that we can use to estimate audience reactions to different kinds of messages, speakers, and media. But again, these must be tailored to specific instances, and they are difficult to generalize from or use in predicting audience reactions. You cannot always expect an audience to react the same way to the same messages because the contexts may change, and then the reactions will change. Even if you are sure how any one person in an audience feels about an issue, giving a speech on that issue in the presence of other people can produce a different effect from the one you anticipated. People are often influenced by the reactions of those around them.

We tend to measure audiences (1) statistically or (2) functionally. In the first instance we are interested in how old, how rich, how well educated, etc., an audience is—which means that we want statistical data about the audience so that we can judge which means, medians, modes, and variations will elicit unfavorable reactions. For example, if an audience is young, we might assume they are liberal in their views, unless it is a meeting of young conservatives. If they are all well educated, they will be interested in art, music, and culture, unless they like detective stories and X-rated movies. To measure audiences functionally, we find out what brought the group together—what common purpose they have for assembling. Obviously, it is safe to say that a gathering of the Tuesday Chamber Music Society will want to hear a Mozart quartet rather than a lecture on big-game hunting. Determining what the members of an audience have in common—either statistically or functionally—will help you plan your message and medium and your own presentation as a speaker.

One of the reasons we focus on the audience in this text is that you spend so much of your time as an audience yourself. In the give-and-take of a conversation with a friend, you spend a portion of your time as an audience. Listening to the radio, watching TV, hearing speakers around you, listening to lectures, or simply getting information, you are an auditor or part of a larger audience. The things that happen to you as a speaker also happen to someone else when you are part of an audience. Much of what happens to you when you are in an audience you can imagine happening to a member of any audience you may speak to. If you get bored when some speaker talks too long, remember that feeling when you are the speaker. If you have trouble hearing a lecturer, try to learn what you can do when you are hoping to be heard by a classroom of people. If you don't seem to follow the logic of the speaker or if points are presented poorly, remember that when you get up in front of a group to explain something.

COMMUNICATION AS AN AUDIENCE-CENTERED ACTIVITY: APPLICATION

GETTING ORIENTED

Every fall, college students or staff members spend some time during "orientation week" or "freshman week" welcoming incoming freshmen and acquainting them with the college.

Administrators (especially those in student services or student personnel) give speeches about social opportunities, dormitory life (if there are residence halls), and the various services offered. Often a dean or a faculty member will discuss the academic program. Then a student leader (usually the chairperson of the orientation week) will tell the freshmen how great it is to be in school here and how many things they have to look forward to; upperclass students may also conduct campus tours so that the freshmen will know where their classrooms and other facilities are.

1   Select a panel of three members of the class to role-play the following: (a) the dean of students, who offers advice on being a student while on campus; (b) the dean of faculty, who explains the educational and academic opportunities; and (c) the chairperson of orientation week, a student, who gives advice on where to go to get certain things and tells what your year will be like.

2   After a brief preparation period, these three will appear before the class as an advisory panel during orientation for freshmen.

3   Select three or four observers from the class whose job it is to check audience reactions to the speakers. Their assignment will be to watch for the nonverbal signals the listeners are sending the panel and for any attempts to adjust (make use of the feedback they get) on the part of the panel members. After the brief speeches are over, these observers should check their observations with the class members to see whether the signals they observed were the ones the audience members intended. They can also check with the speakers to see whether they caught the feedback signals.

4   The remainder of the class are the freshmen at the orientation meeting. .

You may respond in whatever way you think a freshman would react to the kinds of things being said to you. Try not to overact (there are no Academy Awards for this performance); instead, try to give real kinds of feedback to the speakers.

Informal Audiences

Much of your communication will be with informal, one-to-one audiences as well as with larger, more formal groups. You should be experienced in approaching many different kinds of audiences. Informal audiences may consist of individuals just like you, with the same habits of listening (good and bad) that you have. They are classed as informal because the situation just happens—no one got the group together so that you could give a speech. Much of what goes on can't be planned or predicted. Preparations made by either the speaker or the audience in an informal situation are likely to be minimal.

After those generalities, here is a specific example. Your friend asks how you are. You start to say that you have a bad headache and tell how you got it. Your friend couldn't care less and doesn't want to hear your whole response, being not really interested in your health.

As another example, you ask your father for the family car, and he starts his familiar lecture on what to do and what not to do with it. You tune out this message because you think you know it already. Similarly, if a friend has already heard you tell how you were stopped for speeding and the cop let you off with a warning, that friend will tune you out and think about something else if you start to tell the story again, even if you use different lines in hopes of making it more interesting.

Other informal audiences face us all the time. For instance, when you enter a store, sometimes the clerk performs for you, and sometimes you perform for the clerk.

Before class starts, for another example, a group sits around in the classroom and raps about some topic—usually the discussion is led by one person, who becomes the informal speaker for that informal audience. (After class gets under way, usually the instructor is the speaker, and you in the class are the audience.)

In another case, you are eating dinner with your family and start to tell about something funny that happened to you that day; the other family members then become an audience of some kind. What do you already know about your family that makes it easy or hard for you to address them as an audience? Who listens to you carefully? Who doubts things you say? Who pretends to listen and then chides you for talking with your mouth full? Who interrupts you with "Hey, pass the butter"?

You have already collected much information about the informal audiences you face in your daily life. You use that knowledge to make a

In the give and take of a conversation, you spend a portion of your time as an audience. *(Catherine Ursillo.)*

better approach to your audience, to watch for the audience's response, and to test its tone and attitude at the beginning and end of your "speech."

In summary, the audiences that you face every day in an informal way are subject to many of the same moods and limitations as the audiences you would face in a formal-speaking setting.

Formal Audiences

As you might imagine from your informal-speaking experiences, one duty of a public speaker is to find out as much as possible about an audience. In your day-to-day informal brushes with others in speaking settings, you may have little chance to discover a lot about your audience. When you are involved with a more formal audience, it is more likely that (1) you already have some useful information about the audience, (2) you have time to find out more about your audience, and (3) you have more potential outside sources of information about your audience. At some point in your investigation of your audience, make sure you are not simply generating the information about them inside your own head. It will be useful to check your perceptions of the audience with another person—preferably someone who has talked to that same group or a similar one before. If you find discrepancies between what you think and what the other person thinks, look again at your ideas of what the audience is really like. See whether the two of you can agree on some perceptions of the group. There is no way you can learn *too much* about an audience you are going to face.

Audience Characteristics

FRAMES OF REFERENCE AND REFERENCE GROUPS

Much of what happens between you and your audience is related to the audience's attitudes about the world in general, about your topic, and about you. Whenever you speak to a group of people, even total strangers, you are not starting from scratch. You are dealing with live human beings who believe in certain things, like some things, dislike other things, and generally have patterns of values and attitudes that make up their views about the world. This whole complex of attitudes and values is called a *frame of reference.*

People generally do not receive messages in a vacuum, but filter them through their frame of reference that relates to the particular message. They test and evaluate these messages, see where they fit, and ultimately figure out how to make sense out of them. When people's frames of reference are well developed, they tend to reject information that does not fit in.

Your frames of references have been built up as a result of your experiences, your education, the groups of people you have associated with, and the understanding you have developed about people and

We build frames of reference by contact with, or membership in, particular groups called *reference groups. (Laima Turnley/Editorial Photocolor Archives.)*

groups. Of course, your frames of reference depend on situations you find yourself in. For example, imagine a man shopping for some hunting gear. The salesperson might develop a pitch to tap his frame of reference regarding outdoor fun, spending the day with the guys, etc. But if his girl friend or wife is in the store with him, the same sales pitch might fail because he would hear it with a different frame of reference. This time his frame of reference could include spending money for nonessential things, the pleasure of spending time with family or girl friend rather than with the guys, or the attitudes of wife or girl friend toward hunting.

Although it is almost impossible to predict with complete accuracy which frame of reference will be used to evaluate a given message, we can make some predictions about how another person may react to a message.

Frames of references are built up by contact with, or membership in, particular groups, or *reference groups,* as they are called.

Reference groups can be the groups you belong to without making any choices—involuntary groups. Examples of these are sex groups, age groups, and ethnic groups. Your reference groups can also be groups you joined voluntarily or groups that you like or admire. For example, your church, your school, and your friends are voluntary membership groups. Athletes, physicians, and artists may represent groups you do not belong to but identify with and admire.

What help will it be to you, as a speaker, to know the sex, age, ethnic, and other involuntary groups your audience belongs to? It should help you predict the kind of reactions they will have to your message.

For example, there are differences in the way men and women react to persuasive messages. As is discussed later in this chapter, there is some evidence that women are more easily persuaded than men. Older people are less easily persuaded than younger people because their frames of reference are more complete and more stabilized. New information creates relatively little impression and thus results in few behavior changes. Young people's frames of reference are still being established, and new information may serve to complete them or start new ones.

However, many factors besides age or sex ultimately influence someone's reactions to your message. And quite often different factors will pull a person in different directions. Will a younger man be more persuadable than an older woman? If you considered only sex, you would say "no." If you considered only age, you might say "yes." Obviously, without any more information about the two people you can't tell which one might be more persuadable.

In practical terms, what can you do with your knowledge of frames of reference and reference groups when you are speaking to a particular audience?

1 If you know that your audience has a connection with a voluntary reference group, you can try to develop a relationship between your message and that reference group. For example, if you are speaking to people who have strong ties with the Boy Scouts, and you want to convince them that parks and forests ought to be protected, mentioning the Boy Scouts and their attitudes toward the outdoors and nature could give your audience a frame of reference that will support your ideas (called "audience identification" in an earlier chapter).

2 Although it is hard to predict which reference group a person might use in evaluating a message, some reference groups are commonly used by a large number of people. Family is one, church is another, and neighbors and close friends are still another. Well-known public figures such as athletes, movie stars, or television personalities are often used as reference groups. If you can make a relationship between any of these reference groups and your message, you may be able to strengthen your appeal. Advertisers make good use of this principle when they have public figures endorse products on television.

3 Nonverbal cues may be helpful in creating an environment that will suggest a favorable reference group to your audience. For example, the President delivers most of his televised speeches from the Oval Office in the White House, with the flag of the United States and the presidential seal clearly in evidence. This environment evokes reference groups with patriotic connotations and respect for the office of the Presidency.

PERSONAL CHARACTERISTICS OF AUDIENCES

When you analyze an audience, whether formal or informal, you might ask yourself whether the individuals in that audience have certain personality traits that make them more or less receptive to what you have to say.

Several factors can be isolated which seem to have an effect on a person's response to attempts at influence or persuasion.

Intelligence People differ in their ability to respond to a particular message. Not everyone understands nuclear physics, complex arguments, and generally difficult material. Intelligence is a factor in learning and applying knowledge to new situations. Although there is evidence linking intelligence and persuasibility, there is reason to believe that a more intelligent and informed audience expects sound reasoning, supportive evidence for the points made, and a more thorough treatment of the issues raised.

Age It is commonly accepted that as people grow older, they become more resistant to change and to persuasive appeals. Children tend to be more flexible since their frames of reference are being formed.

Sex Generally, women are found to be more persuasible than men. However, the research findings are not conclusive. It is quite possible that the nature of the topic under discussion produces the conflicting results. Culturally, women may be conditioned to be more persuasible than men on certain topics, and may be more resistant to influence on others. However, we need to emphasize that generalizations based on sex differences must be treated with much caution.

Self-Esteem Students of the relationship between personality and communication have found that people with high self-esteem, that is, people who feel confident, worthwhile, competent, and generally in control of their lives, are less susceptible to persuasion than people with low self-esteem. The reason is fairly simple. People with high self-esteem tend to perceive themselves as equal or superior to most people with whom they interact and who may attempt to influence them. People with low self-esteem, on the other hand, perceive other people as more credible and better informed than they are. Hence, they are more likely to be influenced by those sources they believe superior.

Dogmatism People with authoritarian personalities (those who are highly dogmatic) tend to rely heavily on the moral authorities of their reference groups, to be preoccupied with power and status, and to adhere rigidly to their values and express them in absolute terms. Such people tend to react to factors other than the ideas presented in a communicative message. They will react more to who sends the message than to what the message says. People with authoritarian personalities are not necessarily more persuadable than less authoritarian or less dogmatic people, but messages that emphasize the source of trusted authorities are likely to be more successful with them.

Highly dogmatic people are not easily persuaded or influenced by rational arguments. They need the influence of a person in authority or strong group pressure to conform in order to be swayed. Highly dogmatic people tend to have a strong need to conform to their reference groups. If a highly dogmatic person becomes aware that his or her views conflict with the views of his or her reference group, considerable influence can be exerted toward a change of position.

Machiavellism Highly Machiavellian people want to influence others and are usually quite good at it. Low Machiavellians act in the opposite way: They are not very interested in trying to influence others and when they do try they are not particularly effective. While highly Machiavellian individuals, however, are not very susceptible to influence, low Machiavellians tend to be more easily persuaded and influenced.

Principles of Audience Analysis

Some basic principles of human differences should be considered whenever you analyze your audience.

MOTIVATION AND NEEDS

People differ in their motivation, and a common situation may trigger different needs in different people. We know that people's behavior is motivated; *motivation* is usually defined as the process of directing behavior in such ways that basic needs will be met.

One of the most widely accepted descriptions of people's basic needs was formulated by the late Abraham Maslow.[1] According to Maslow, humans are motivated by five basic needs:

[1]Abraham Maslow, *Motivation and Personality*, Harper & Brothers, New York, 1954.

1 Physiological—The need for food, water, sleep, sex
2 Safety—The need for shelter, clothing, and protection from the environment
3 Social—The need to belong, to be accepted, to be loved, and to have friends
4 Self-esteem—The need to respect oneself and to be respected by others
5 Self-actualization—The need to be what one can be, to develop oneself to one's highest potential, the need to give love and respect

Maslow further contends that these needs are arranged in a hierarchy. This means that people must fulfill their basic needs to a large degree before they can concentrate on the fulfillment of their higher or less basic needs. For example, unless physiological needs are satisfied—those needs vital for survival—people will not spend much energy attempting to fulfill safety or social needs. Once the physiological needs are satisfied, energy can be spent to fulfill the next level of needs—safety needs. Once safety needs are reasonably met, an individual will attempt to satisfy social needs. Self-respect, respect from others, and self-actualization come next.

Another of Maslow's contentions, and a direct corollary of the hierarchy idea, is that once a need is satisfied it no longer acts as a motivator. If you have eaten a full dinner and feel satiated, it is unlikely that you will respond to a message about food. Appeals to people's needs when these needs are satisfied are not effective. Appeals to needs not entirely satisfied are much more effective, provided the needs appealed to are not too far up in the hierarchy in relation to the lowest satisfied need. For example, appealing to the self-respect and self-actualization needs of a group of workers may be of little value when they are striking for pay hikes in a recession. Appealing to their security needs (the threat of losing their jobs in a time of high unemployment) is likely to be much more effective.

AUDIENCE MOTIVATION AND NEEDS: APPLICATIONS

THE CASE OF THE BENSON JOB CORPS

When the Job Corps was first being established across the country, some difficulties arose in communities where camps were to be located. One such situation is described below, based on an actual event and a real town. Even the quotations are real.

A camp of about 100 boys between the ages of sixteen and twenty-one was to be established at the old U.S. Reclamation Bureau project headquarters near the town of Benson (not the real name). The boys, all of them school dropouts, would get job training. The old headquarters had been vacant and would not be activated for other government purposes, although its closing had left an impact on the economy of the small town of Benson. The citizens were divided in their response to the plan, about half being *for* the project for reasons which included:

The project would bring some tax dollars back to Benson.

The project would really help some kids become better citizens when they got jobs.

Caretaking costs of the bureau project headquarters would no longer be a drain on the taxpayers of Benson, who tried to keep the camp from falling apart.

It is the obligation of any community to help the national effort to give our youth a break.

Renovations of the camp would be carried out by the Job Corps boys, and after the program was finished (in the future years), the town of Benson would have an excellent recreation facility for its own youth and adults to enjoy.

About half the citizens were *opposed* to locating the camp near Benson for some of these reasons:

The boys in the camp were already beyond help as useful citizens, and Benson should not have to put up with some 100 young criminals living near town.

The local police had enough to do already without trying to control these juvenile delinquents.

The influence on the local youth would be bad—morally depraved, dishonest boys should not be brought into contact with the more innocent young people (especially the girls) of Benson.

The town had begun to make good use of the camp as an occasional meeting place for civic celebrations (like the Fourth of July picnic sponsored by the local veterans organization) and had spent some money for improvements, including putting up a baseball backstop and making horseshoe-pitching pits.

The Job Corps was a government boondoggle designed to keep more bureaucrats in office and money flowing into Washington.

The citizens of Benson did not actually know how the governor of the state stood on the issue, but the fact that he had sent a representative to talk to the citizens for two days made them sure he was interested—either pro or con—and they didn't want his interference.

The governor of the state was supporting this venture only because he wanted a federal appointment for himself, said some townspeople who were against the bill.

The governor of the state was against this venture because he wanted to impress the voters of this county and give the camp to the town of Benson.

There is to be a meeting of the citizens of Benson, and appearing as speakers will be (1) the regional director of the Reclamation Bureau from the county seat, which is about 50 miles away and has had control over the camp; (2) his assistant, who is a resident of Benson and grew up there; (3) an aide to the governor, who is present to hear testimony, not to speak for or against the issue; and (4) the leader of the town council, who will be moderator of the meeting. This leader has already told the citizens that they should write to the governor and has been quoted in the press as saying that sentiment was "divided about fifty-fifty for and against the Job Corps project." In addition, the town council chairman said, remarkably, "Even those who are dead set against it are pretty open-minded."

1 Working in groups in class, construct the major speech to be given by the person you select. Will it be the town councilman? The regional director from out of town? The local assistant director? The governor's aide? Someone else? Your group will select the speaker, prepare a speech to persuade the citizens to accept the Job Corps, and then be ready for questions.
2 Another group should prepare a speech to be made on behalf of those opposing the Job Corps camp. Who should deliver the speech? What should be said? What balance of emotions and logic should you strive for? Which part of the audience do you appeal to? Those who are with you? Against you? Neutrals? The governor's aide? The Reclamation Bureau representative?
3 A group should be designated the town council and assign its spokesperson to give a speech to the group assembled for a hearing. What tone will this speech take? Is the speaker free to express personal and private views? Those of the town council? Those of the majority of the townspeople, if there is a majority, who seem to be divided fifty-fifty? Outline the speech and estimate when during the meeting it should be given (remember that the head of the town council will be serving as moderator) and how it should be presented.

SUPPORTING YOUR COMMUNITY

One of the most familiar types of speeches given to service clubs and civic organizations is about community affairs. These speeches have been analyzed and the following themes have been found to recur in them:

1   Boost your hometown
2   Cooperate with other groups
3   Provide for our young people
4   Trade at home
5   Encourage new industry
6   Become a part of the community
7   Help solve our community problems
8   Support the church of your choice
9   Support the local community fund drive(s)
10 Explanations of taxes or taxation

Such speeches are more inspirational than analytical. Speakers need to inspire themselves as well as others to believe everyone is part of a good community. One of the basic rules of these speeches is that you don't need to knock something down to build something better, so the tone of such speeches is upbeat and positive, reassuring and optimistic. People are generally sensitive about a hometown or a community area. Whatever organization you belong to must become a part of a community before being able to interact to improve the community.

1   How would you find material for a speech on any of the subjects listed above? Are you convinced that the "home community" (maybe a campus) is worth supporting? Are there things you must overlook in the community (campus) in order to be enthusiastic about parts of it?
2   What does your audience have in common when you speak on this topic? Do you see them as old, young, affluent, poor, male, female? Where do you get your own attitudes about your audience for this kind of speech?

VALUES

Values are fairly enduring conceptions of the nature of "good" and "bad," of the relative worth we attribute to things, people, and events in our lives. They usually form the basis of the moral and religious systems found in all societies. Values serve as guides for our actions and are designed to enable us to make choices or select alternatives when several courses of actions are possible. Values grow out of a complex interaction between basic needs and the specificity of a given environment. For example, all humans need to eat in order to survive, but they do not all value the same foods. In America, beef is our basic meat, while in India the sacred cow must not be touched. What is valued in a particular area, region, or country is often determined by the availability of certain foods.

Values are fairly enduring and resistant to change because they are tied to fundamental human needs and because they are learned very early in life in an absolutist way. Yet many of our values conflict with one another. In order to act, then, we must decide which of the conflicting values is more important, more basic, takes precedence over the others, and thereby establish priorities.

BELIEFS

Beliefs represent the way you view your environment. Beliefs are concerned with specifics about the nature and the probability of things. They usually represent what you agree with and what you think is true. Some things you believe to be absolutely true; others you believe to be probably true; and others you are not sure about. Some beliefs are more easily verifiable than others. Some are more central than others. The more central or important a belief is, the more likely it will resist change.

It is not always easy to determine which of the beliefs a person holds is central and which ones are less important. According to Milton Rokeach,[2] the importance or centrality of a belief is determined by its *connection* to other beliefs and by its *consequences* for those other beliefs. Central beliefs are connected to a larger number of other beliefs and have deeper consequences for these other beliefs.

Rokeach distinguishes between five types of beliefs:

Primitive Beliefs—100 Percent Consensus   These are the most central beliefs of all. You learned them from direct experience and they are reinforced by unanimous consensus among the people with whom you associate. They are fundamental, taken for granted, seldom questioned axioms which rarely provoke controversy. For example, you believe in the constancy of things. If you see a rectangular table from several angles, you continue to believe that the table is rectangular and that its shape does not change. The belief that things remain constant in the physical and social world is a primitive belief which is very important. If such a belief is disrupted, you begin to question the validity of your own senses, your competence to deal with reality, and sometimes your sanity. These beliefs are the most resistant to change.

Primitive Beliefs—Zero Consensus   Some primitive beliefs are not shared by others and do not depend on social consensus but arise from deep personal experiences. Because they need not be shared by others to be maintained, they are usually quite resistant to change. Many of these unshakable beliefs are about yourself. Some are positive (what you are capable of); some are negative (what you fear). If you are convinced that the world is a hostile place, no matter what others tell you, you will probably hold on to that belief. These beliefs can be changed with the help of a therapist, a counselor, or by deep personal experiences, but will seldom be affected by superficial influence attempts.

[2]Milton Rokeach, *Beliefs, Attitudes and Values*, Jossey-Bass, San Francisco, 1968.

Authority Beliefs   At some point in your childhood you discovered that not everyone believed the same things. If you believed in Santa Claus and your best friend at school told you Santa did not exist, you probably turned to an authority to figure out the dilemma, perhaps your parents or an older sibling. As you matured, you wrestled with the question of which authorities to trust and which not to trust, which reference group to identify with. When you deal with authority beliefs, you learn to expect controversy and differences of opinion. Hence, these beliefs can be modified more easily than primitive beliefs.

Derived Beliefs   Once you put stock in an authority for a particular belief, you tend to buy some other beliefs from that same authority, even in areas in which the authority has no expertise. This is the principle behind endorsement practices in advertising. If your favorite athlete shaves with a particular brand of shaving cream, you may believe his testimonial and buy the product on faith. Would Joe Namath lie to you?

Inconsequential Beliefs   Matters of taste are usually considered inconsequential because they seldom have any connections with other beliefs. If they change, there are few consequences for other beliefs you may hold. To say they are inconsequential does not mean you may not hold them strongly. Nor does it mean you don't think they are important. You may be absolutely convinced that skiing is more fun than swimming. The belief is inconsequential, however, because if you change your mind, it will not necessitate a massive reorganization of your entire belief system.

ATTITUDES

Attitudes are relatively lasting organizations of beliefs which make you tend to respond to things in certain ways. Attitudes are not directly observable. We infer their existence from what people do. If people act consistently in certain situations, we infer the existence of an attitude which predisposes them to act that way. Attitudes can be examined along three dimensions: their direction (how favorable, unfavorable, or neutral you tend to be in relation to something or someone), their intensity (how strongly you like or dislike something), and their salience (how important the attitude is to you).

Attitudes, beliefs, and values, we must emphasize, are *learned.* You are not born a liberal, a conservative, an atheist, a football fan, or an anti-Semite. All attitudes, beliefs, and values are learned from the people you associate with and with whom you live. Because they are learned, they can be unlearned, that is, changed, although change often may be resisted.

Attitudes, beliefs, and values are learned from the people with whom we associate. *(Sybil Shelton/Monkmeyer.)*

COGNITIVE CONSISTENCY AND BALANCE

As we pointed out earlier, you can hold many different attitudes, beliefs, and values, and it is quite common for some of them to come into conflict with others. A group of psychological theories called the *consistency theories*[3] deal with this phenomenon. These theories say basically (1) that we need consistency among our values, beliefs, and attitudes; (2) that the awareness of inconsistencies will produce tensions; and (3) that we will usually do something to reduce the tensions.

Our desire for cognitive consistency causes many attitudes, beliefs, and values to be formed and changed. If an imbalance occurs in your belief, attitude, or value systems, it means generally that some new state of balance will come about. The change will usually follow the principles of balance. For example, if a person you admire praises something you dislike very much, you are faced with cognitive inconsistency or cognitive dissonance. To restore the balance you have a number of alternatives. You may:

1 Decide you were in error about the person you admired. Hence you may develop a negative attitude toward him or her.

[3]F. Heider, *The Psychology of Interpersonal Relations*, John Wiley and Sons, Inc., New York, 1958. T. M. Newcomb, "An Approach to the Study of Communicative Acts," *Psychological Review*, vol. 60, 1953, pp. 393–404. P. Lecky, *Self-Consistency: A Theory of Personality*, The Shoe String Press, Inc., New York, 1961. C. Osgood and P. H. Tannenbaum, "The Principle of Congruity in the Prediction of Attitude Change," *Psychological Review*, vol. 62, 1955, pp. 42–55. L. Festinger, *A Theory of Cognitive Dissonance*, Row, Peterson & Co., Evanston, Ill., 1957.

2 Decide you were in error about the object you dislike. Hence you may develop a more positive attitude toward it.
3 Decide you were in error both about the person you admired and the object, and develop a less positive attitude toward the person and a more positive attitude toward the object.
4 Deny the reality of the situation, in this case that the person you admired made the statement at all. This alternative is not always available and depends on the degree of ambiguity of the situation. Some realities are not easily wished away. Some lend themselves to a multitude of interpretations, and fudging becomes easier.
5 Acknowledge the inconsistency but maintain that your relationship to the object is insignificant and unrelated to your relationship to the person. You simply deny the importance of the inconsistency.
6 Accept the inconsistency and do nothing at all. This is possible but unlikely, since most people find inconsistency uncomfortable.

In summary, you need to be aware of the following principles of human differences:

1 People differ in their ability to respond to a particular message. Not everyone understands nuclear physics or football.
2 People also differ in the way they approach a communicative situation. Some bring to it a wealth of information regarding the topic to be discussed, while others have relatively little knowledge of the subject. The responses of these people may be quite different.
3 People differ in their motivation, and a communication situation may trigger different needs in different people. Advertisers are well aware that they can manipulate your behavior by appealing to your needs. Biological needs are probably the strongest, in spite of the fact that those of most Americans are reasonably well satisfied. You still respond to messages about food, even if you are not hungry. For another example, a great deal of television advertising is based on appeals to sex. A certain brand of toothpaste not only will get your teeth clean but also will guarantee popularity with members of the opposite sex, or so the commercials tell you.
4 People respond better to communication situations in which they can be actively engaged rather than passively detached. If the purpose of your speech is to persuade your audience, try to have them *do* something besides just listen to you. Try to get them actively involved by participating in the discussion, asking questions, or getting up and moving around; whenever possible, you should take them to see whatever it is you are talking about.
5 Once people make a choice (buying a car, enrolling in a college, voting for a candidate), they want to convince themselves that they have made the right decision by selecting the messages that reinforce their choice. As a communicator, you can make people feel better

about the decisions they have made by giving them additional reassurance that these decisions were good and justified.

6 When people are placed in unbalanced situations—situations that produce conflicting ideas or attitudes—they will attempt to restore the balance. For example, you may believe that abortion is a moral crime and then find out that your best friend favors it. This situation calls for some effort on your part to restore the balance. Little children tend to try to restore balance by fighting it out physically. So do some adults and, unfortunately, some groups, such as nations that go to war to fight for a "principle." However, in most interpersonal situations people rely on communicative efforts to convince one another of the rightness of their position.

One way for you to restore the balance in the above example would be to become negative toward your friend. You might take this approach if your feelings about abortion are stronger than your feelings of friendship. If you feel more strongly about your friendship than you do about abortion, however, you might reconsider your point of view on the subject.

Some other strategies are available to you which might restore balance temporarily but which really do not solve the conflict. For example, you might distort your friend's position by convincing yourself that your friend really does not mean what was said. Or you may disassociate yourself from the topic on which you and your friend have opposing views and tacitly refuse to talk about it again. Abortion becomes a taboo issue and is no longer brought up.

AUDIENCE ATTITUDES AND BELIEFS: APPLICATIONS

LET US ENTERTAIN YOU

You have been assigned to make a speech to entertain this class. This means that you are more interested in amusing the class than you are in convincing them about something or informing them on some subject. You have to make them at least relax or smile (if not actually laugh) or simply give them a few minutes of enjoyment. The speech will be about three minutes long, and you have several weeks to prepare for it.

1 What do you have to know about the class in order to prepare this speech? What kinds of questions do you have to ask to get the information you need? Do you know the class so well that you don't have to ask questions? Will previous experiences with speakers in this class help you guess what will amuse or interest them?

2 Make a list of the kinds of things you might do to entertain the class and a

list of things you know about the class. Match these up to see whether you can arrive at a satisfactory approach to preparing an entertaining speech.
3   Compare notes with another class member (or a small group of several students) to see (*a*) what factors each of you selected as important about the class and its tendencies as an audience, (*b*) what kinds of approaches to an entertaining speech you each came up with, and (*c*) how well these fit together as an "audience analysis" for the preparation of your speech.

CURE-ALLS AND OTHER FRAUDS

Old-time medicine men used to sell "elixir of swamp root" to cure all human ailments; now methods have been updated, new diseases discovered, and "cures" developed for our worst illnesses.

Some of the cure-alls discovered by field investigators for the American Medical Association (AMA), who make many speaking engagements each year and work closely with federal agencies to expose frauds, included:

A bottle of Atlantic Ocean water which was claimed to be an antidote for cataracts, gray hair, Parkinson's disease, and schizophrenia

A "miracle tonic" for diabetes and stiff joints, which AMA representatives said had been responsible for one known fatality

A cancer-cure solution which was 95 percent tap water and cost $100 a pint

An electric appliance designed to cure baldness, toothache, varicose veins, and other minor ailments

1   Is the power of suggestion responsible for the success of these "cures"? Why would the AMA be interested in these alleged cures? What effect does a traveling representative of the AMA have in convincing people that these cures are ineffective? Who comes to such meetings? What audiences should hear these speeches?
2   Who needs protection against these frauds? What is the government's role in giving that protection? What do private agencies do?
3   Plan a speaking engagement for the purpose of exposing health frauds in your city. Whom would you ask to speak? Whom would you invite to be the audience? How would you promote the speech? What things would be included in the presentations?

Some Reminders

Here are some things you might want to ask yourself about an audience in order to plan your speech better:

1   Does the audience consist of a group organized for some purpose, or

is it a collection of people gathered accidentally? (Formal or informal setting?)

2 Does the audience have strong common interests (such as partisan political views), or does it represent a wide spectrum of interests?

3 Is the audience well informed on the subject you will be speaking about, or do you need to provide a great deal of information? (How elementary or complicated should you be?)

4 Has the audience heard others speak on the same subject? Recently? A long time ago? Ever? (Is this old stuff?)

5 Will the audience be free to react to your message, or is there anything beyond your control that will inhibit their responses? (Will they be under constraint not to act for personal, professional, religious, or other reasons?)

6 What do you hope to achieve, and is it possible? (If you ask them to vote, are they old enough? Are they registered?)

7 What physical circumstances might affect the audience's listening that you may be able to do something about? (Can you use a public-address system, open doors or windows for ventilation, or move the audience closer to the front of the room, for example?)

8 What are the basic audience attitudes about you and your topic? (Do they love you, hate you, or have no opinion?)

☐ THE AUDIENCE AS LISTENERS

An audience is a collection of potential listeners. You should know something about audience listening possibilities and about different types of listening audiences may do.

Steps to Listening

HEARING

This must occur first; some sound from the speaker must reach the audience. Thus you must make sure that the audience can hear you before you worry about whether or not they are listening. You must speak clearly as well as loudly enough; you may need the aid of a microphone or other means of projecting your voice.

FOCUS, OR CONCENTRATION

If your message is just random noise to the audience, there is little chance it will make sense to them. They will have to work at understanding you. Audience responsibility is involved as they focus their attention on the sounds they hear.

COMPREHENSION

Having sorted out the noises, the next step is to make some sense out of them. The speaker's language, gestures, inflections, and the rate and volume of his speech are all perceived by the audience, who must give meaning to these factors.

INTERPRETATION

After comprehension comes the stage of analysis, or putting things together. It is closely related to the next step.

EVALUATION

When the listeners put together a series of interpretations to make a judgment about how the message relates to their needs, they have evaluated the speaker and the message.

REACTION

This is the response that the auditor makes to this whole sequence. Reaction can be almost instantaneous within an audience or part of an audience. The kind of feedback the speaker receives identifies this reaction: nods or shakes of heads, smiles, laughs, groans, clapping, frowning, etc.—the obvious and also the subtle messages the audience sends out. The speaker also learns from reactions after the speech how the audience responded to advice, information, argument, or pleas.

Types of Audience Listening

To understand better what might be going on in an audience, the speaker should know more about the different kinds of listening that may take place. It is not likely that all the following kinds of listening will occur together.

INFORMATIVE LISTENING

This is the kind of listening an audience does when it wants to hear some general information, some answers to questions, some opinions, some directions, or some instructions about how to get somewhere or do something. Classroom lectures tend to fall into this category, as do "speeches to inform" in the traditional classification of speech types. In order to get your audience to engage in informative listening, you must start at their level—if you are too elementary, you will bore them, and if you are too deep or technical, they will become confused. Clear, step-by-step instructions; well-organized material; and carefully developed explanations from the simple to the complex are important if you are going to reach your audience.

APPRECIATIVE LISTENING

This is listening done mostly for pleasure—audiences that want to relax, enjoy themselves, or increase their cultural or emotional understanding engage in appreciative listening. Much of this kind of listening is done without a conscious effort. To be successful in getting an appreciative-listening response from an audience, you need to be particularly aware of their mood and comfort when you begin. Your own relaxed approach will elicit a relaxed mood in this kind of audience, and overseriousness will not be effective. Speakers should also be aware that appreciative listening has an infectious quality; if a few people respond well, others will too. Here the audience is listening on an emotional level rather than on an intellectual level. In this category you would find the traditional class of "speeches to entertain" or "speeches for ceremonial occasions."

CRITICAL LISTENING

This is the most demanding kind of listening because it requires the audience to make judgments about what is being said and why. The audience must be alert to the devices of a propagandist, to the persuasive manipulations of a demagogue or advocate, or to the biases and prejudices of speakers who want to convert them, direct their interests, divert their attention from realities, or plead for justice or the righting of wrongs. Becoming a better judge of right and wrong is one of the outcomes of critical listening. Speakers who want to approach an audience on this level must be ethical, logical, and morally consistent to be successful. Critical-listening audiences put the greatest intellectual responsibility on the speaker because these audiences realize the value and the limitations of the spoken word. They can be very demanding in their assessment of speakers. The traditional category of "speeches to persuade" fits here.

THE AUDIENCE AS LISTENERS: APPLICATION

HOW DO THEY LISTEN?
Look at the list of informal and formal audiences you made earlier. For each informal and formal audience on that list, label the kind of listening described in this chapter: informative, appreciative, or critical listening.

Informal audiences: 1 _____

2 _____

Formal audiences:

3 _____

4 _____

1 _____

2 _____

3 _____

4 _____

☐ AUDIENCES YOU WILL MEET

In analyzing an audience, you will want to know whether they are for you or against you, and whether they don't care or don't want to care. Some audiences may have a favorable attitude toward your communicating. These would be groups of people who believe generally the same way you do—for example, members of your own political party or a group of friends you are addressing on the subject of longer spring vacations. There may be other occasions when you will face audiences who have a variety of reactions to you and your message because of the variety of people in the group. In all speaking situations you want to achieve an effect: If you are speaking to persuade, you want to convince people; if you are speaking to inform, you want your audience to learn something; if you are speaking to entertain, you would like to amuse them. Some audiences are with you, and some are against you; some don't care. That is true in any kind of speaking situation—some listeners will simply not be persuaded, informed, or entertained regardless of how hard you try. At least some audiences appear that way when you face them. Knowing some ways to deal with these various audience attitudes may make it easier for you to succeed in your speech purpose, whatever it is.

They Love You

This is the believing audience. They are easy to talk to because they are ready to accept what you have to say. There is a wide range of acceptance, however. The audience may be enthusiastically on your side, in which case you can receive applause for almost everything you say. If you cough at the right moment, you could get an ovation! At the other end of the spectrum is an indifferent acceptance or uncritical acquiescence—the "I'm not fighting it" attitude. Wildly enthusiastic supporters can be found at political rallies, pep meetings, and social gatherings of members of many kinds of clubs and organizations. The apathetic accepters are likely to be seen in large lecture halls, at a family dinner table, or at a picnic when the boss gives the annual report.

The point of your speaking to a believing audience is to solidify their support or make them believe even more strongly. You may want them to do something with their beliefs which has not been asked of them before. In order to make such a group continue to support you, you should not be patronizing of their support; you should indicate genuine pleasure that they follow you. Do not try to be too instructive. They need one of two things to bring them further along in their acceptance or to guarantee that they will continue to follow you: (1) They must have their existing beliefs and emotions reinforced by your message, or (2) they must be given new, stimulating ways of looking at those beliefs. This means giving them new reasons to believe as they do—a fresh set of logic or information to keep them going. If they think you have a good amount of information, try to find more data which they have not heard before and which they are not likely to hear soon from another source. If they are already laughing at your jokes, tell even better ones to reinforce their belief in your ability as a storyteller.

You need to inspire this group. Use their enthusiasm to support yours. Encourage their participation in your message by asking questions or responding to theirs. Use your common experiences to tell your story and to relate to them. Get new data or bring a fresh approach to old data. Make sure to let them know you are all together in whatever the situation is.

They Love You Not

A hostile or uninterested audience is not much fun. You do not have the same friendly faces out there. You also have a bad feeling that this audience has already made up its mind and is rigidly opinionated on the wrong side. If you let these feelings show through, you can expect only negative reactions. If you want to entertain them and they don't seem to appreciate your humor, you might try to make them laugh by talking about situations which you all have in common and which you are sure they'll appreciate. If you want to inform or persuade them, do not argue. Instead of launching a full-scale attack on their beliefs, try to get them to the point where they will at least listen to you. However, you don't do this by lashing out at their beliefs; they will be ready to protect them just as they would their own lives.

How do you go about getting them to listen, and perhaps even to modify their views or in some cases even change them? You should state the audience view as accurately and fairly as possible. If you are arguing, you should concede any points to the audience that you honestly can. You must show respect for the audience as an intelligent group. Insulting them or implying that they are dumb will not make them listen. In stating your own case, do not exaggerate or overdramatize your stand. Use as friendly and appealing a manner as possible. Do not become angry or show impatience with their attitudes or ideas. You will notice that when you have made these modest assaults on another person's (or an audience's) beliefs, you will be more successful in getting support for yourself. If you present fairly any common ground of two opposing views, your audience will characterize you as fair and believable; thus when you present your own case, they will also believe you if you do not exaggerate or make wild claims that will tax their credulity. If this sounds like a cop-out or a manipulation to make a reasonable, conciliatory approach to a hostile or opposing audience, just try it the other way and see whether you can get anybody (1) to listen openly to you or (2) to move from fortified position to join your side. Your purpose is to inform or persuade to your view—and if others hold opposing views, this is the most effective way to reach them.

If your objective is simply to lecture an opposing or hostile audience and tell them how wrong they are, that is also your choice. This may be a form of catharsis and make you feel better, but it won't gain any converts to your cause.

The audience that has not made up its mind is not easy to deal with. *(Daniel S. Brody/Editorial Photocolor Archives.)*

They Are Neutral

The audience that has not made up its mind is not easy to deal with either. Although they may be more inclined than a negative audience to listen to both sides of an argument and more receptive to your attempts to persuade, inform, or entertain them, they are still critical in their evaluation of you. The fact that they are neutral doesn't mean that they don't care, however. In fact, they may be very strongly committed to not doing anything either way in a situation. This makes their reactions very hard to predict. If they have already made up their minds not to be on either side, it takes a good deal of persuasion to move them from dead center.

This is an important group. In elections it is often the "undecideds" who make the difference. If you have difficulty pulling the opponents over to your side, there is still the hope that you can reach those who have not yet joined one side or the other. To do this, you must present very good, logical evidence. You should again approach the subject by using examples the audience is already familiar with—demonstrating your common experience and showing them that you are actually working together. Being too dramatic will turn off most neutrals, while being coolly logical may have a good effect. You should be able to relate to the audience with anecdotes about them and yourself. You should further relate to them by offering to answer questions. The give-and-take of questions and answers is most useful if you can reinforce things you have already said, rather than introducing new data at this time. When questions are asked, you should take them seriously. Acknowledge the implications of each question and give a brief answer. Then ask the questioner whether he or she is satisfied with your reply.

They Couldn't Care Less

Although the apathetic audience and the neutral audience are often discussed together, there are enough differences between them to justify separate consideration. The apathetic group will fight against even listening carefully to you. It has certainly made no commitment to remain neutral; it simply is not sufficiently interested. Perhaps it has been forced to attend (as in the case of an army training lecture, a required session of a lecture series, or some club meetings), or perhaps the members of the group wish they were somewhere else right now and have their minds on other things.

Dullness will drive this group into further apathy. Routine statements, stories, or jokes will turn this audience off even more. A monotonous delivery or boring examples will put them to sleep.

The approach here is to be dynamic in your delivery and creative in your examples and stories. Say things they have not heard before; that will surprise them because part of their apathy may be the feeling that they've been here before. Use humor as much as possible—live, fresh, even somtimes shocking anecdotes. Use things with an *emotional appeal* first to get the group's attention so that they will be more responsive to intellectual examples or arguments.

They Are Consistent, or They Are Mixed

When you have decided what your predominant approach to your audience should be, you can use some of the techniques mentioned above. Again we must emphasize that the audience may be very homogeneous in terms of attitudes as well as age level, sex, educational status, general intelligence or informational level, language facility, and common affiliations or loyalties. By using audience analysis, by making inquiries of members or others who have been associated with the audience, or even by employing very formal statistical analyses or taking polls of the group, you can arrive at the proper focus for your audience.

It is difficult to tailor a speech for a group whose attitudes toward you are very mixed or whose makeup is varied as to educational level, age, occupation, etc. You will very likely decide which part of the audience is most important to your purposes or which part is dominant in terms of size or your own interest. That is the group whose attitudes and other characteristics you will have to take into account when you get to the stage of preparing your presentation.

☐ FEEDBACK

Whenever we talk about a process like the communication process, we imply the notions of continuity and growth. Yet to be studied at all, a process must be stopped and fragmented so that its various parts can be looked at in instant-replay fashion. One of the central parts of the communication process is *feedback*.

The thermostat in a house provides a classic example of feedback in the physical world. We set it at a certain temperature, and it sends a signal to the furnace when more or less heat is needed. In this respect, the heating system is self-regulating because as more heat is needed in a room, the furnace responds accordingly.

Our goal in communication is to achieve some specific purpose such as giving information, socializing, or giving directions. In order to know whether or not the goal has been achieved, you need to watch for feedback. What reactions do you get? Did what you intended to happen in fact happen? The other persons involved may respond to what you do with a shake of the head, a smile, or a shrug; they may talk to you, frown, or otherwise indicate how your message is being received. This is feedback: *the reaction you get from your actions.* Just as you steer a car, a bicycle, or a boat or direct your own movements when you walk on a crowded street, you need to steer your communication. You will notice that when you are walking on a crowded street, you seldom bump into other people. This is because as you approach them and as they approach you, you are watching for the kind of moves they make in response to your moves. A little bit to the left or to the right, and the walking ballet continues without accidents.

Mathematician Norbert Wiener wrote about feedback as an essential part of the system he called *cybernetics*, which deals with control of machines and human beings. Implicit in the concept is that watching for feedback and receiving feedback will help us monitor our communication to adapt it better to the situation. When we touch a hot stove and feel extreme heat, we move our hand away. The feedback we got accomplished its purpose. Pain is essentially a feedback device that protects us against injury.

Examples of feedback in our communication would include tests by a professor who wants feedback on what students are learning and who in turn provides feedback to the students by giving grades to let them know how they are doing.

More specifically, feedback is an essential part of your contacts with others. You ask questions and expect answers. You speak to someone and expect a response in the form of words or nonverbal signs that will tell you that you have been heard. After receiving a response, you adjust your next communication in relation to how you interpreted the feedback you received. A cheery ''hello'' to your roommate met by a sour ''get lost'' is telling you that your next move ought to be at least cautious. The same ''hello'' met by a friendly ''hi there'' will encourage you to continue the communication you initiated. In both cases, feedback from the other person told you how to adjust your next move.

Being alert to the feedback you get from an audience is a most important part of your communicating with others because feedback tells you how you are doing and helps you adapt more adequately to the situation.

However, to be useful, the feedback you are getting must be (1) sent truthfully and (2) deciphered accurately. The parent who praises its child constantly and becomes ecstatic about every scribbling the child produces on a piece of paper may be giving positive feedback that is pretty unrealistic. By the same token, the child whose every attempt at painting or drawing is ridiculed will soon get the idea of total incompetence as an artist. In both cases the unrealistic feedback will give the child an inaccurate picture of what that child can do.

Of course, you have no control over how truthful your audience will be. But when you decode the feedback you get in your speaking situations, you can at least ask yourself how truthful, honest, or realistic that feedback is. Is your audience really free to be honest? Are they trying to be nice in order not to hurt your feelings? The parting remarks after a boring party are usually of the ''We had a wonderful time, thank you'' type. Students who praise a professor to the skies may be more grade-conscious than really honest.

On the other hand, we do not always accurately decipher the feedback we get from an audience. Some responses may be damaging to our ego. We often rationalize the negative feedback by blaming others or the situation rather than ourselves. Many students will rationalize a failing grade by blaming the instructor (the teacher was not fair; had it in for me; or played favorites) or the assignment (it was too hard or too confusing; we never covered that material).

In face-to-face situations, feedback is verbal as well as nonverbal. In the more formal setting in which one speaker addresses a large audience, feedback is ordinarily nonverbal. Individuals in a large audience are less likely to interrupt a formal speech with statements or questions. The way to get feedback in this situation is to watch closely the nonverbal reactions of your audience. Do they frown, look puzzled, or seem confused? Do they look interested? Do they seem to be enjoying themselves? Do they laugh at your jokes or the humorous parts of your speech? Do they squirm in their seats? Do they make noise with their chairs? Do they talk to those around them? Each of these reactions should give you an indication of the mood of your audience and thus tell you what your next move should be. A large class of students will often tell its lecturing professor that the time is up by closing their books and notebooks, putting things away, and squirming in their chairs. The message usually gets across, and the professor knows that students are no longer paying attention and that it is time to stop.

The purpose of feedback is to help you decide what your next move should be. If your audience nonverbally indicates to you that they are puzzled or confused, this is a clue to review the material you have already covered, trying to clarify what may not have come across. Perhaps you will even want to ask your audience whether they are confused and would like you to make your point in a clearer way. Do they look as though they are having difficulty hearing you? Ask them whether they can hear you and then adjust the loudness of your voice so that you can be heard by everyone. Do they seem impatient with what you are saying, perhaps because it is old stuff to them? You may want to shorten that part of your speech. You can acknowledge that you are covering familiar ground and assure them that you will soon get to something different. Do they look as though they have had enough and are anxious to go? Then you *must* cut your speech short—skip some less important points you were planning to make and get to your conclusion as rapidly as you can so as not to tax your audience's patience. If they are ready to leave, chances are they have stopped listening already.

Looking at your audience as much as possible rather than at your notes will maintain the necessary eye contact that makes you more real to your audience, and it will also help you watch for the visual feedback you need in order to judge audience reactions and adjust to them appropriately.

Several factors may make it very difficult for you to interpret an audience's reactions. First, the audience may give you little or no feedback. The poker-faced audience is the most difficult to talk to because you never know what their reactions are—whether they like what you are doing or are bored. You feel, and rightly so, that you are speaking almost in a vacuum. There is not much you can do to loosen up such an audience. If they don't even laugh at a few good jokes or funny remarks, then you must simply go on and hope that you are doing all right. They may love you, but they won't tell you until you are all done.

Second, the audience may give you weak feedback that you cannot make out. If you are not too sure of the kind of feedback you are getting near the end of your speech, and people appear anxious to leave, it is good to announce, in passing, that you are coming to the end of your presentation: "One more point and I'll be finished," "I want to summarize in just three minutes," or "I want to leave you with these final thoughts." It may set your audience at ease to know that you do not intend to go on speaking forever.

Third, sometimes several members of your audience will give you loud, distracting feedback. This heckling behavior may come from an individual who wishes to gain personal attention rather than give a reaction to the speaker. Such feedback is usually directed more toward impressing the audience than toward impressing you. It is difficult, at best, to cope with such distractions without embarrassing yourself or the individual who started it all. You may want to enlist the help, patience, and understanding of the audience if you see that they are also bothered by the antics of this overactive listener.

FEEDBACK: APPLICATION

THANKS TO ROTARY FROM JOE

Joe, a student, is selected to give a fifteen-minute speech to the local Rotary Club to thank the club for its annual gift of a scholarship to his college. Joe puts together a speech telling why people who have money should support those who do not. He tells the club members that adults are obligated to help young people who want to go to college or get started in business. He ends up speaking for nearly half an hour because he strays from his notes to talk about some personal experiences he has had on campus and in the community.

1 Do the Rotary Club members have a stereotype about college students? Does Joe have a stereotype about Rotary Club members? What did each expect of the other?

2 What preparations should Joe make for his talk? What should he know about his audience? (Have many attended college? Are they all in favor of scholarships? How old are they? What do they do for a living?)

3 What physical conditions will Joe face when he makes his speech?

Waiters may be clearing the tables after the big dinner, and the club members may be sitting at scattered tables, where they can talk to one another without difficulty but may have trouble hearing a speaker. Are they easily distracted by the passing of coffee pots, the lighting of cigarettes, noises from the kitchen, etc.? Do they have a very tight schedule for adjournment so that they will resent a long speech?

4   What are Joe's obligations to this audience? Should he try to please them? Should he try to educate them? Reform them? Entertain them?

■ LOOKING BACK

I.   Communication needs to be an audience-centered activity.
   A. You may select an integrated approach to putting all parts of the speaking system together, and that is very true to life where all parts are independent.
   B. An audience-centered approach helps you focus on the effects of communication rather than on smooth delivery, the message content, or the situation.

II.   Informal audiences are composed of people just like you.

III.   Members of formal audiences seem to have an influence on one another just as a result of being in the same setting on the same occasion.

IV.   Reference groups you belong to will have an effect on what you choose to believe and what you will listen to.

V.   Your audience characteristics will include such factors as intelligence, age, sex, self-esteem, dogmatism, and Machiavellism.

VI.   It is important for you to know the needs and motivation of your audience so that your appeals may be effective.

VII.   To be effective, your audience analysis must focus on your audience's values, attitudes, and beliefs. By understanding the principles of cognitive consistency, you will better understand your audience reactions.

VIII.   If you can treat the audience as listeners, you can better understand the kinds of things that will happen in them.
   A. Listening occurs in steps: focus, concentration, comprehension, interpretation, and then reaction.
   B. Listening can also be studied by audience types (or speech types).
      1. Informative listening occurs when the audience is being given instructions or data.
      2. Appreciative listening occurs on ceremonial occasions and during some kinds of entertainment.
      3. Critical listening occurs when audiences are being persuaded or are hearing special pleas to believe in something or to take action.

IX. Audiences may be for you, against you, neutral, or even apathetic, or they may have a mixture of any of these attitudes.

X. Feedback is the reaction you get from your actions or communication.
   A. The purpose of feedback in speech situations is to let you know how you are doing so that you can judge what your next move should be.
   B. Feedback from your audience in informal situations is both verbal and nonverbal.
   C. Feedback from your audience in formal speaking situations is more often nonverbal than verbal.

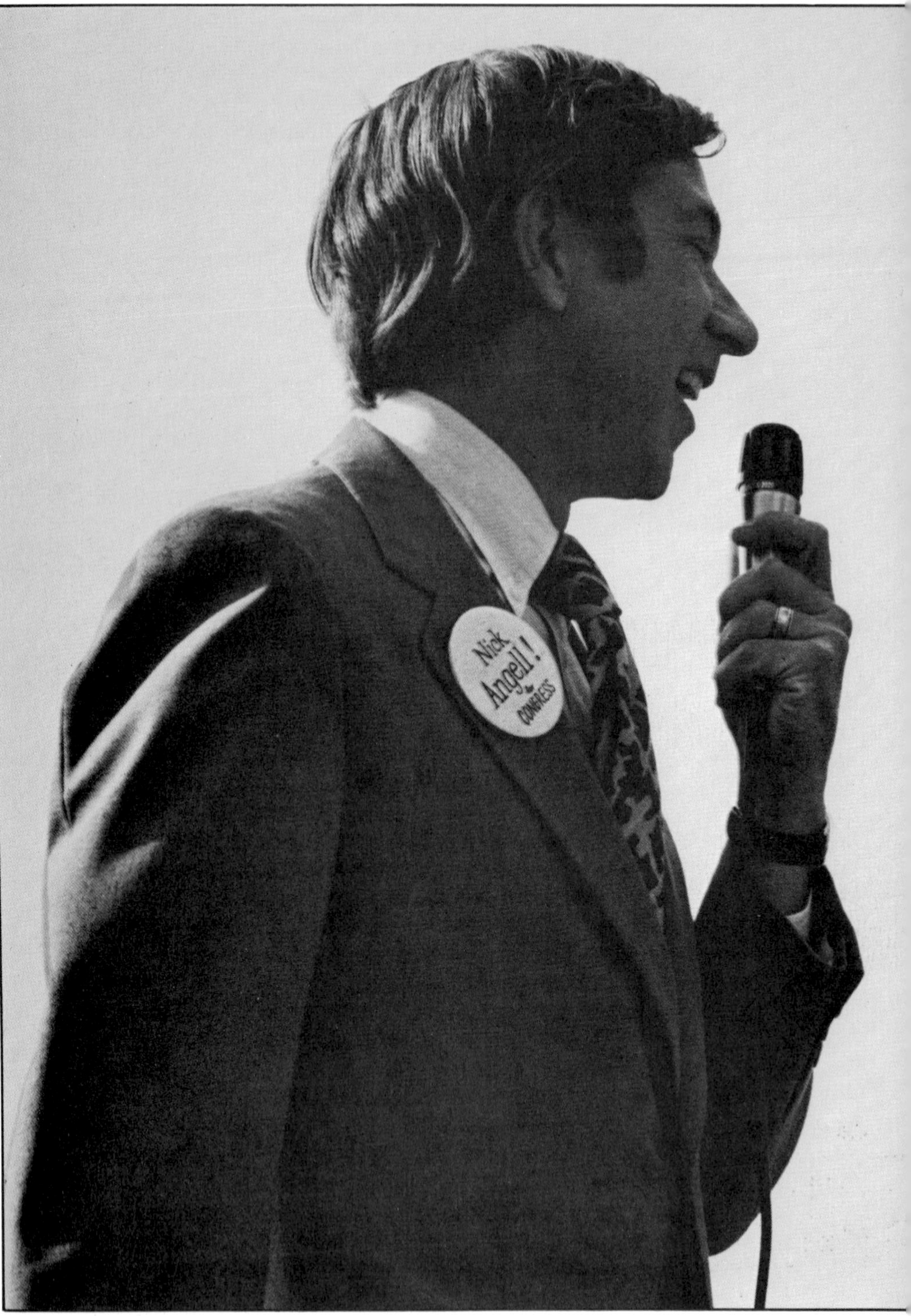

(Mimi Forsyth/Monkmeyer.)

CHAPTER 5
COMMUNICATING IN A SPEAKING SITUATION

Since wars begin in the minds of men, it is in the minds of men that the defences of peace must be constructed.

— Anonymous

The turning points of lives are not the great moments. The real crises are often concealed in occurrences so trivial in appearance that they pass unobserved.

— William E. Woodward

Next to entertaining or impressive talk, a thoroughgoing silence manages to intrigue most people.

— Mrs. J. Borden Harriman

The mutual confidence on which all else depends can be maintained only by an open mind and a brave reliance upon free discussion.

— Learned Hand

Two other parts of a speaking situation—the *setting* and the *occasion*—need to be considered in addition to the *audience*, which was discussed in the preceding chapter. An audience at a political rally, for instance, comes together in a setting of optimistic enthusiasm, with a speaker's stand, chairs, microphones, press and TV sections, etc., and also on an occasion, such as to nominate a candidate or whip up enthusiasm for a campaign. An audience at a dinner meeting of a club comes together in a setting of food and friendly conversation; the occasion might be a regular meeting or the appearance of a guest speaker.

Studying the setting shows you that communication does take place somewhere, not in a physical or psychological vacuum. In what formal and informal settings do speakers find themselves? What should speakers know about the setting (and the effects of the setting on an audience) so they can make their speeches more effective?

Different occasions call for different speaking approaches. Whether the occasion involves only one other person or a mass of people, the occasion will affect what the speaker does and how the audience responds.

The audience, the setting, and the occasion constitute the speaking situation speakers face as they prepare their communication and deliver it. An awareness of how these factors interact to make communication more or less effective will be useful to you both in your informal communication and also in public-speaking settings and on occasions when you face more formal audiences.

☐ THE SETTING

You in the Setting

You are someplace when you communicate. You may be in an informal setting, like a living room, the front seat of a car, a dormitory room, or a booth in a coffee shop. You may be in a more formal setting, such as a classroom, an office, a club room, or a banquet hall. No matter what the setting is, it will have an effect on your communication.

USING YOUR SENSES

You will be more effective in speaking if you can establish a variety of channels for communication. Your voice should be heard. Your face, with its expressions (or lack of them), should be seen. Your bodily gestures should reinforce the message you're trying to get across. Your receiving apparatus (your eyes and ears) should be tuned up so that you can catch the feedback from those whom you are addressing; in other words, be ready to see and hear the effect you are having so that you can adjust your message accordingly. All these points imply that you can be more effective if you make use of a variety of senses.

To See or Not to See   People can talk better when they see each other. Telephone conversations have three basic limitations that are part of that setting. First, you cannot hear all the tones produced by the other person because of the "flattening" of the frequencies in the actual transmission. This makes it more difficult to hear subtle inflections, to detect shades of meaning, or even in some cases to recognize a speaker's voice or mood. (For example, it is sometimes hard to tell whether a person is crying or laughing at the other end of the line.) Second, you cannot use gestures and facial expressions to support your spoken language (for example, indicating width or height with your hands or shrugging your shoulders). Third, you cannot get visual feedback from the other person. Without feedback, you can't tell whether a listener is displeased, agreeable, scornful, bored, uncertain, or confused. That information would guide your face-to-face conversations. Because of these limitations on our communication, we tend to exaggerate our speaking inflections over the telephone. If you try talking in a normal tone, using a normal range of vocal inflections on the phone, you will find that the other person has difficulty understanding you or thinks that you sound bored. Lacking normal visual support, we tend to overplay our vocal apparatus to compensate for this lack.

Speaking on the radio has a similar limitation. A radio announcer must use only voice to transmit much of what would be present in a face-to-face conversation. If you watch a television announcer, you can see how much of the impact is due to facial expressions and gestures. Any speaker who must do without the visual part of a message, such as the radio announcer, must work extra hard to make the voice compensate for the loss of the visual dimension.

Keeping in Touch   In dyads (one-to-one communication encounters) and sometimes in triads (three-person groups), the sense of touch may be used more than in larger public settings. Watch how often a speaker touches another person to make a specific point. You may put your arm around someone to express confidentiality, show affection, or enlist help. You shake hands when greeting others. You may also hold another person's hand while saying something sympathetic, expressing solidarity, etc. Have you seen a speaker who pokes a finger in the chest of another to emphasize a point? It is common to tug at another person's sleeve or gently take hold of an arm to get attention. All these moves are possible in the close setting of one-to-one communication—at parties, on the street, in casual conversations, and during personal discussions or arguments.

What We Don't Talk About   Although we may avoid talking about our sense of smell in our association with others, a great deal of advertising urges us to make ourselves and our surroundings smell good. "Buy this perfume," "Avoid bad breath," "Get twenty-four-hour deodorant protection," "Rid your kitchen of unpleasant cooking odors," and "Make your house smell like the great outdoors" are all olfactory suggestions. There must be some reason why we buy all those products to make ourselves and our homes inoffensive. It might be important to realize that our sense of smell (however it may offend us to talk about it) is a variable in our one-to-one communication effectiveness.

HOW CLOSE TO GET

Part of the communication setting is "interpersonal distance," or how far you stand or sit from another person. Books have been written, studies have been conducted, and much research has been done on this subject—proxemics, or how close people like to be to each other. This varies among people, among cultures, according to the situation, and so on, but it becomes an important part of the communication setting. For example, when you go to apply for a job, do you pull your chair up close

When you talk to a friend, do you sit closer than you would to a stranger? *(David Strickler/Monkmeyer.)*

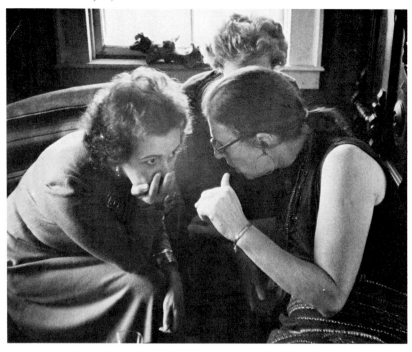

to the edge of the interviewer's desk, or do you keep your distance? When you talk to a friend, do you sit or stand closer than you would to a stranger? How do you feel if a person you hardly know sits very close to you while you talk about some neutral topic like class assignments? Would you feel differently if that person were a close friend telling you a secret? Do you feel that somebody crowds you when trying to sell you an item in a store?

The subject of proxemics is too broad to be covered in this book although there is a longer discussion in Chapter 3 under nonverbal communication. However, you should be aware of your own feelings about how close you like to be to others when you talk with them. Remember that other people also have the same kinds of feelings, but they may not have exactly the same distances measured out that you do. Watch for their reactions and try to adjust to them. Remember, though, that you are also giving others nonverbal indications when they get too close or are too far away for communication.

WATCH YOUR TIME

Time is also part of the setting. This factor operates in several ways. For example, we usually take turns talking—it is *my* time to talk, and then yours. If the other person talks a lot more than you do, you probably are conscious of it. That speaker is taking up some of *your* talking time.

Time also enters the area of communication settings in terms of punctuality for dates, for interviews, and for appointments. When you and a friend promise to meet at a certain hour, you have agreed to share time with each other. If your friend is late, this indicates something about how much effort was made to spend the time with you, or it shows that other factors interfered with your friend's being on time.

You also need to know when to leave. If you are being interviewed and the interviewer says, "It's been good to talk with you," that is a sign your time is up. Other remarks like "You'll be hearing from us," "I don't think we have any more questions," or "There are some other applicants waiting" are signals that the interview is over—your *time is up.*

If you are sensitive to how long someone wants to talk—especially in interview situations—you can give signals yourself that you are ready to terminate the interview: "I know you are busy," "If you don't have any more questions, I don't think I do," or "You were good to take the time to see me" indicates your awareness of the time dimension.

Other people appreciate your consciousness of using their time. In our culture, time is a *commodity* in the business and professional worlds, and thus it is a significant dimension in most official one-to-one encounters. You can improve your adaptation to the settings you find yourself in by being aware that time is important to any audience.

Interviews as One-to-One Settings

There are many types of interviews. You may have information that another person wants, and this results in an interview; for example, a famous entertainer or public figure is interviewed for a magazine article or a TV program. Any of us may be associated with news and become the topic of a news interview—for example, if you become a candidate for a public office, if you witness an accident, or if you want to help promote a fund drive or entertainment activity. Or you may be interviewed by a roving reporter interested in comments of an "average citizen."

You may sometimes be an interviewer. If you approach a librarian for help in finding a particular book, you are interviewing. If you ask for directions to another part of the city, you are an interviewer. If you become interested in another person and start asking about background, hobbies, favorite records, etc., you are an interviewer.

Most of us at one time or another take part in a job interview, a setting where we either are asking questions of an applicant for some job or duty or are in the position of being asked questions. Job interviews are one of the most common interview experiences. Some skill in handling yourself in such a setting will pay off in better impressions on the other participants in any interview. The principles of human communication apply in these situations. Talking to another person about a job is a special case of public speaking.

ONE-TO-ONE SETTINGS: APPLICATIONS

CAN YOU EXPLAIN IT TO A STRANGER?

Each country or culture regards certain sports very highly, and these differ from culture to culture. Soccer is even more popular in Europe than football is here in the United States. Europeans will tell you that football (which they may think is much like rugby) is very slow by soccer standards. At the same time, attempts to develop the popularity of soccer in the United States have been only partially successful.

A typical American watching a cricket match in England believes that it must be the most boring game in the world, ranging in activity somewhere between chess and amateur bird watching.

Latin Americans share the Spaniards' interest in bullfighting, which is illegal in the United States. What the American tends to see in the bullfight is the torture and killing of a defenseless animal; what the Spaniard sees is the stylistic ritual of a man risking his life in a hand-to-hand encounter with a massive and symbolically important animal.

1   What sport that is popular in another country would you like to know more about? How could you find out about it? See whether you can find persons

from that culture who can explain it to you. How do they make that explanation? Notice the kind of things they say about the sport. Do they compare it with the sports you already know about?

2 One stereotype about women is that they do not understand sports. Have some women in the class explain to the rest of the class how a woman might learn about a sport she is unfamiliar with. What questions would she ask? Of whom would she ask them? Does it embarrass a man when a woman asks questions out loud during a football game?

3 Try to work out in a group discussion how you would go about explaining a game to a person who has never seen it played. You must explain the general purpose, the rules, the strategies, the scoring, and who wins and under what circumstances (for instance, in golf the low score wins, while in bowling the high score wins). Then role-play a situation in which your group is responsible for telling another group how to watch a sport with which they are unfamiliar.

THE INTERVIEW SITUATION

Sally is applying for a part-time job at a branch of the Smythe department stores. She has an appointment with the local manager, but first she must see the personnel director. Both these store officials are men. Sally has done some homework on the jobs available in this particular store, and she knows that there are two openings. One is in the camera department, for which she is not at all qualified, and the other is in the toy department. The store has a training program and will give Sally several weeks of on-the-job instruction on store policies and operating procedures, but they will not give her any training for the particular department she will be in. They assume a certain amount of knowledge and ability on the part of the employee in the area of assignment. The personnel manager has a small office with a desk and two chairs, but he prefers to use the interviewing room, which contains a table and two soft chairs. The store branch manager has a larger office with an impressive desk and a sofa and easy chairs. Sally will be interviewed by both men. (Turn to figure on page 148 illustrating the three rooms.)

1 How will the personnel director respond to the application in the setting of the interviewing room (Figure A)? How will Sally respond? Will these relationships change in the setting of the office of the personnel director (Figure B)?

2 Is the setting of the branch manager's office the same as the settings used by the personnel director? (See Figure C.) How would you feel in this office if the branch manager continued to sit behind his desk? If he came around the desk and sat in one easy chair while you sat in the other? If he offered you a cigarette? A cup of coffee? If you saw ashtrays in the office, would you ask permission to smoke, or would you simply light up a cigarette?

3 How is the setting changed if the branch manager asks the personnel

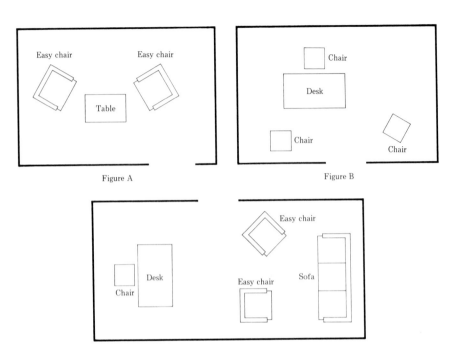

Figure A

Figure B

Figure C

director to attend the interview along with Sally? Where do they sit (in Figure C) in relation to one another? Should Sally wait to be asked to sit down? Should she pick a place and sit down, or should she wait to have a place indicated for her? Does this practice change if the applicant is a man instead of a woman? Who controls the setting—the man whose office it is or the visitor?

Groups as Settings

The number of people gathered together and their physical arrangement make up an important factor of setting. We have been discussing the one-to-one situation where two people are in contact over a desk, over coffee, or over the phone. In this section we shall consider the larger groups that get together in face-to-face encounters and what we expect will happen in those settings. While we shall describe different groups in discussion situations, this will not be a complete survey of group discussion as a method or as a speaking activity. We are concentrating here on the setting as it involves a group of people gathered to talk.

In Chapter 4, about the audience, we wrote about the reference groups people use to evaluate messages. Another reason for studying groups is that people tend to react differently when they are with other people from the way they react when they are alone. You would

"I'm afraid, Stanley, this party's like what they say about Mars. We may have chemistry, but we do not as yet have biology."

There is a distinction between groups and collections of people. *(The New Yorker.)*

probably react differently to a candidate making an acceptance speech if you watched alone on your TV, from the way you would react if you listened to the same candidate at a rally of a thousand supporters.

But there is a distinction between *groups* and *collections of people* (like mobs and rallies). The major differences lie in a combination of factors including (1) the kind and amount of interaction taking place between the people involved, (2) the presence or absence of shared goals, (3) the development of norms, (4) the development of roles, and (5) the feelings of the people involved. (Check back to Chapter 4 on reference groups and audience analysis.)

GROUP GOALS

Groups vary in many ways according to their stated goals. A group of friends getting together for a party (a social goal) is different from a group of committee members meeting to solve a problem or make a policy decision. What's different is the kind of communication (very informal at the party) going on, the norms that will develop (no drinking during working hours for the committee), the roles people will play (the life of the party may be the most quiet member of a working committee), and the feelings generated through all the communication taking place.

This implies that the factors which distinguish a group from a collection of people are all pretty much interrelated, and that when one factor changes, the others will be affected. Naturally, not all parties are informal, and not all working groups are formal. But knowing something about the *goals* of a group may help you to make some predictions about its other characteristics.

GROUP NORMS

Norms are the rules for behavior, the dos and don'ts of human situations. People in groups always develop a system of norms that establish the context in which interpersonal communication will occur. Norms may be formalized—for example, laws, rules, regulations, or by-laws of an organization. They may be informal or implicit, such as those relating to the kind of language tolerated in groups, modes of appropriate dress, and who sits where at a meeting, in class, in the living room, or at the dinner table. Norms reflect what a group considers to be appropriate behavior, and they are developed through interaction of the group members. Much of this development is neither explicit nor conscious.

GROUP CONFORMITY

Once norms have developed, tremendous pressures are exerted among the group members to abide by these norms. People who deviate from the norms are often pressured by other group members to conform to the acceptable pattern. For example, some Wall Street executives always wear conservative clothes and carry a briefcase to the office. On Saturday and Sunday, their attire may be quite different and may be dictated by the norms of other groups they belong to—golf partners, family, church, or whatever. The pressure to conform to all these groups is quite strong, and the persons who deviate will probably be the subject of a lot of communication intended to make them fit the mold. These who persist in deviating from the commonly accepted norms of a group may find themselves rejected by it. If they consistently wear the ''wrong'' kind of clothes at work, they may be fired for not presenting an appropriate image. Some organizations prohibit beards, sideburns, miniskirts, and pants suits, and even dictate the length of a person's hair. Deviants must literally shape up or ship out. Less formal groups, like an executive's golf partners, may not be able to fire nonconformists, but they may make fewer and fewer dates to play with those who flaunt the country-club norms of dress or other written and unwritten rules.

If your desire to belong to a particular group is very strong, you will feel the pressures to conform more strongly. You may pay a higher price for nonconformity. However, total nonconformity is not really possible. You do not live in isolation, but belong to a myriad of groups. You may choose not to conform to one group, but end up conforming to the norms of another. Total nonconformity would be possible only if you lived completely alone. But in our complex modern society, we are involved with family, school, church, friends, teams, age groups, coworkers, and political or social groups, for example. Being alone is difficult.

So for better or for worse, and depending on how much you can influence the norms of a group, you will conform to some norms. You may often shift your priorities in terms of which norm you can violate. Knowing that you belong to a certain group may not be enough to predict whether you will always follow the norms of that group.

If you are going to speak to a group, it will be helpful to know the kind of formal and informal norms they have set up for themselves so that you can (1) know how to behave with them and (2) predict how they might behave in relation to you.

GROUP SIZE

Another important factor in the study of groups is size. Size of a group may determine the amount and kind of interaction possible on the part of group members. The smaller the group, the more opportunity all members have to express themselves. In larger groups, there is likely to be a formal leader. Large groups are also more likely to splinter and form subgroups, or cliques.

You know from your own experiences in school that a class with fewer than ten students is run differently from the way a class with twenty-five or a hundred students is run. Student-to-student communication as well as student-teacher communication will be quite different in these instances.

As a speaker addressing a group, you should consider the factor of size and your mode of presentation should be adapted accordingly.

Informal Groups

Some informal groups are the cocktail party, the picnic outing, the barbecue, and the birthday party. These are arranged for the purpose of enjoyment. The setting is therefore very informal and generally centers around a table of food or drink, with people moving about freely, discussing anything they please, playing games, and focusing on having fun rather than on being informed or persuaded or taking action on an important matter. There is seldom a concentrated effort to keep everyone organized. This kind of group activity usually involves a complex of small groups in interaction as subgroups.

Groups for Discussion

More formal groups come together to take on tasks, conduct discussions, present informational material to a larger audience, or share their

A group as setting: You react differently depending on a group's goals, norms, pressure to conform, size, and formality. *(Charles Gatewood.)*

respective expertise, biases, or wisdom. These different groups have special names, depending on what they do and what kind of physical arrangement is required to make them work.

GROUPS AS SETTINGS: APPLICATIONS

VOTING WON'T ALWAYS DECIDE

A kindergarten class had been given a kitten to take care of for a few days as a way of teaching them about animals and their care. The children decided to name the kitten either Karl Kitten or Kathy Kitten, depending on whether it was a boy or a girl. No one knew. The class was divided between those who wanted to give it one name and those who wanted to give it the other. The teacher did not know the sex of the kitten and was at a loss to settle the argument until one boy raised his hand and said, "I know how we can tell whether it is a boy kitten or a girl kitten." The teacher, with some hesitation, told the boy to continue. He said, "It's simple. Let's take a vote."

1. Do you think that children of kindergarten age would believe that taking a vote is a good way for groups to determine the right or wrong of an argument? Does taking a vote determine who is correct in a group discussion?

2. How often do we use an inappropriate method to settle a dispute? Will a count of votes determine the sex of the kitten? Will assurance from a friend

help us pass a test, even if we don't study for it? Will reading the promotional material about a particular product or listening to the claims of a high-pressure salesman give us the most useful data on that product?

3   How would you direct the kindergarten children to determine the sex of their kitten in a more accurate way?

WHAT RULES SHOULD YOU FOLLOW IN SPEAKING?

An official of the Airways Facilities Sector (A.F.S.) in southern Texas sent a letter to all employees saying: "It has come to my attention that a language other than English is being used during official duty hours. This language has been used in the presence of persons or officials who speak only English, and this practice has caused some concern and misunderstanding among those who do not understand the language."

Some employees complained to the Federal Aviation Administration about the letter, and that agency promised an investigation to make sure there were no infringements on anybody's right to speak to others during informal conversations or while not engaged in official activities.

1   Have a group in the class discuss the kinds of situations in which such a letter might have become necessary. Did the A.F.S. official have a responsibility to write this kind of letter to all employees? What started this chain of events, which ended up with an official writing a letter? Who complained in the first place? Was that complaint reasonable?

2   Have a group in the class discuss the reactions that the employees who spoke "a language other than English" might have had when they received this letter. Why did the official letter not refer to the language by name? Are there different reactions to the names for the Spanish language in that region—names like Mexican, Tex-Mex, or Chicano? Does the letter imply a patronizing attitude toward those who speak another language?

3   Role-play situations in which speaking a different language would be upsetting to those around you who did not understand it. You might want to role-play the situation just described, or select another situation in which official business is being conducted, and there is also informal conversation going on among employees.

BUZZ GROUPS

These are the least formal of all because they are usually formed without much notice. They depend on the members for expertise rather than using outsiders. These are the groups suggested for discussion in the "Applications" sections. They are also the groups you will find assembled together in open meetings, conferences, or larger seminars. Often there is a preliminary report or speech by a main participant. The audience then breaks up into small groups to discuss the points made by the speaker or the problems raised. How these groups are formed may vary widely, depending on the physical setting of the meeting area.

If you want to form a buzz group, try to have no more than ten and no fewer than five members. Give them a place to meet and permit them to get into a face-to-face setting. Make sure the various groups are not so close together that their discussions interfere with the talk going on in other groups. If your setting is an auditorium or a place with fixed chairs, one way to form face-to-face groups is to use the "Phillips 66" system, named after its originator, J. D. Phillips. It involves three people turning to face three others (forming a group of six). The discussion is usually limited to six minutes. This overcomes the difficulty of trying to get people together who are firmly planted in immovable chairs—simply ask three people in one row to turn around and talk to the three people behind them.

Buzz groups usually have a topic to discuss. They sometimes need a moderator, recorder, or reporter to keep a summary of the group's deliberations if they will finally be called on to report to the major group on their conclusions or recommendations. The buzz group is common in large organizations, which need smaller groups for gaining consensus, for deliberations on problems, for recommending courses of action, or for simply exchanging information. The members of the audience are the expert, not a speaker who gives them one version of the truth.

AN ASSEMBLY

This gathering does not have the benefit of an expert outside leader to guide the audience in its deliberations. The Assembly of the United Nations has some of these characteristics, since it elects a moderator or chief executive periodically from its membership. An assembly may have difficulty if it is (1) too large to permit many persons to speak within a limited amount of time, (2) fragmented by opposing camps that have little chance to organize their statements and responses, (3) emotional rather than objectively intellectual or factual, (4) hampered by dissension and lack of order or mutual respect for opposing views, or (5) made up of people whose information, knowledge, or preparation in the subject or in the principles of discussion varies greatly. This kind of group usually has a very formal set of rules to guide its deliberations, such as by-laws, constitutions, and rules of order. The Congress of the United States is an example, and so are many law-making groups.

A FORUM

Not all scholars of group discussion will agree that the forum is an actual discussion group. In this group what the audience has to say about the issue seldom makes any difference to the leaders' presentation or conclusions. The setting of the forum consists of an expert or group of experts facing an audience and presenting one or several points of view on a topic. The audience then asks the speakers questions, but the continuing responses from the experts usually defend their statements rather than open up discussion of the issue. In a *lecture forum* the expert speakers address the audience from one point of view, while in a *debate forum* speakers from different sides of an argument give their respective points of view. A forum is usually on a specific topic, such as music, history, or taxes.

A COLLOQUIUM

This combines the features of a forum and a round table. Experts are present to guide the statements and deliberations of a group that is functioning as a discussion group by itself. A physical setting for this kind of discussion might be a table of discussants on one side of a room and the experts as passive observers or occasional speakers at a table on the other side. A moderator in between would keep the discussion going and help the experts enter the discussion when they wanted to. A colloquium discusses complicated, scientific, or highly specialized topics.

A PANEL

A group of well-informed or expert speakers, the panel will usually be at a table or on a stage facing an audience. They make presentations of informational material, and the audience reacts either *during* the discussion in an audience-participation panel or *after* the discussion in an audience-reaction panel. This kind of discussion is less formal than the forum because the presentations are not usually prepared as speeches. Group members depend on the give-and-take of audience reactions to implement the opening remarks by the panelists. The panel's success depends greatly on audience participation. For that reason the physical arrangements must encourage the two groups—panelists and audience—to interact. This may be accomplished by placing the groups closer together than in more formal speaking arrangements, by having microphones available to the audience as well as the speakers, and by having a moderator limit the length of the questions and answers. You often hear panel discussions on such topics as drugs, abortion, youth, and education. Each involves persons with some special interests in the topic, although not all may be "experts."

A SYMPOSIUM

This is a more formal panel discussion in which the panel members are experts who present prepared papers (or abstracts of papers) on various aspects of a topic. The information they present is usually not up for discussion, but in recent practice a question-and-answer period is usually arranged. However, questions are usually asked for the purpose of clarifying points rather than probing alternative views. The success of this presentation depends on the expertness of the panelists rather than the give-and-take of panelists with the audience. For that reason a more formal setting can be tolerated and in fact may be important to help establish the general nature of the meeting.

A CONFERENCE

This can be an extended symposium, or a series of meetings that people attend to be instructed rather than to work out solutions to problems in group discussion. However, in another sense a conference is a way of pulling together experts to work at solving a problem or arriving at some course of action for solving particular problems. The first definition covers meetings of professional associations, groups of clubs, individuals from the same business or profession, or national societies. The second definition includes things like conferences called by a sales manager so that salespersons can work out a promotional campaign for a new product; a conference on water pollution called by a city; a conference on mental health called by a state governor, or a conference on drugs called by the White House. Settings for these meetings can become very complex, depending on how many days the meetings go on, the numbers of people involved, and the kinds of presentations to be made, which often include a great amount of visual-aid material and multimedia resource presentations.

A ROUND TABLE

The round table requires a physical setup that permits easy interaction arrangements, such as a group seated at a table together. This setup implies that a round-table discussion group cannot be very large. It must also be small enough so that each member can talk fairly often; this is a very conversational group. Because of its size and the nature of its topics, this group can come up with recommendations for actions or conclusions to be given to others.

A SEMINAR

This is an instructional setting. It should include an opportunity for give-and-take with an instructor because of its small size and the setting, in which participants sit (around a table or in face-to-face informal arrangement). However, not all seminars are treated as round tables by all instructors. Seminars held in a setting of auditorium speaking appear to be a contradiction in terms, although they are sometimes called by that name.

A COMMITTEE

This is a special group for two reasons: (1) it is an offshoot or a subgroup of a larger organization, and (2) it is assigned to do a specific job. It must come up with specific recommendations or otherwise deliberate and

A committee, deliberating informally, is assigned to do a specific job. *(David Strickler/Monkmeyer.)*

report back to the parent group. Committees are ordinarily small (from three to ten members) and function either as standing committees, in which case they are permanent parts of an organization or a club, or as ad hoc or special committees, which are appointed only for a special job and are disbanded when they have finished. A standing committee, for example, might be the executive committee or the nominating committee of an organization, while an ad hoc committee might be a group appointed to arrange a party, to seek a new meeting place for the club, or to raise funds for a special purpose.

Deliberations by committees are usually informal, although it may be necessary to keep minutes or otherwise abide by the rules of the parent organization in their discussions. Settings for these committees will be any situation in which the group can conduct its business, and this may involve moving to different places. A committee chairperson is important in this group, and in reporting back to the larger organization the committee becomes a very formal symposium to the larger audience.

GROUPS FOR DISCUSSION: APPLICATION

Think back over the past few weeks. Using the categories of discussion groups listed in this chapter, record how many different times you may have been in, watched, listened to, or had some contact with any of these kinds of groups. (Estimate the number, write it in, and give an example of each.)

Discussion Groups	I've been in	I've seen or heard
Buzz groups		
Assembly		
Forum		
Colloquium		
Panel		
Symposium		
Conference		
Round table		
Seminar		
Committee		

One against Many

As we have progressed from the more informal and more limited speaking situations in which the speaker either has a one-to-one relationship with the audience or is a participant in a group, you can begin to appreciate the variety of settings available for speaking. In this section we shall deal with those settings in which a single speaker is addressing a larger group of people. You will find this situation in large lectures, public ceremonies, and gatherings of supporters to hear a leader espouse a cause.

WHAT THE SPEAKER NEEDS

If you are the speaker and you have been asked to address a large audience, what factors do you need to control? You should be sure there is a place from which to speak. Many groups invite speakers to address them without settling on places for them to speak from. If you are asked to speak to a group that does not normally invite speakers, such as a bridge club or an organization of professionals such as engineers, doctors, or lawyers, you need to establish what your speaking position will be. This may be a part of the room set aside as a speaking area, a raised platform in an auditorium, or the head table at a large banquet. Be sure you arrange to sit where you can be seen and heard by all members, preferably not in the middle, where you will have to turn constantly to see everyone.

After you have established what your speaking position will be and are sure that you can be seen and heard, learn whether your visual aids can be seen and whether the proper equipment will be provided. Try to follow this checklist: (1) Is there a lectern from which I can speak? (2)

Where can I hold my notes? (3) If the room is large and the audience is scattered, is there a public-address system? Is it working? Is it adjusted to my height? (4) Is there a screen for my slides or film? Can it be arranged so that everyone can see it? (5) Is there a projector? (6) Where do we plug in the machines? (7) Is the projector working, focused, and ready to be turned on? (8) Will I be using other multimedia aids such as sound recorders that will require outlets, testing, and checking?

How many meetings and presentations have you seen spoiled by visual aids that don't aid? How do you respond to a speaker who says, "I know some of you in the back can't see this thing I'm holding up here, but it is the Declaration of Independence engraved on the head of a pin and is really quite remarkable." How do you feel about a speaker who has to admit that there was not time to check the film or the slides or the projector and that "I brought the film of *Lepidoptera* instead of the one on pro football, but if any of you in the audience would like to stay to see the butterflies instead of the Los Angeles Rams, I'll be glad to show it"?

WHAT THE AUDIENCE NEEDS

When you know that you will have a suitable place to speak from, find out what is being done to meet the needs of the audience. Is there ventilation and temperature control? Is there noise control? Is there a way to control the distraction of late arrivals or early departures? Are there enough seats for everyone? Are there too many seats? Too few? Are there ushers? Is there some formal arrangement for opening and closing the meeting—such as using a moderator—so that the audience will know when to do what? If there are to be questions from the floor, are microphones positioned in several places in the room? If not, you may have to repeat each question that is asked before you begin to answer it so the audience will know what was asked.

No Distractions   When the audience is listening to you, they should be comfortable physically and alert psychologically. A stuffy, warm room will make them sleepy. A room that is too cold will distract them and make them anxious to leave. However, noise is the greatest distraction. It can come from inside the room—people talking to each other, people moving in and out, food being served during your speech, or noisy air-conditioning equipment or other machinery. Noise can also come from outside—open windows or doors left ajar permit noises from the hall or the kitchen or the street to come in and make it difficult for the audience to hear you. A member of the sponsoring group should be responsible for such audience comforts, or else you may ask someone to help you arrange for them.

Time   Time is another important consideration. Your presentation should start on time, and it should surely end on time, even if you have to cut your speech short. An audience waiting for you to finish is no longer an audience—it is a jittery thoroughbred at the starting gate waiting for the race to begin. The length of time you can expect an audience to listen depends on your topic, your ability, their interest, and many other things. The attention span of adults is now estimated to be less than thirty minutes for uninterrupted listening, and for many groups it is less than that. If you cannot get your message across in that time, you need a change of pace (some visual aids or other startling approaches) every so often in order to keep the audience's attention. Time, therefore, is an important factor in the setting. If you begin when you are supposed to, end when you should, and don't abuse their patience in between, an audience will appreciate your efforts.

Light   The setting also includes lighting, which needs to be controlled if you are using any visual aids. If not, remember that a soft light in the room with a strong light on you will help focus attention on your performance. If the room is to be darkened, make sure that there will be a light on the lectern so that you can see your notes.

ONE AGAINST MANY: APPLICATIONS

SPEAKING TO A CONVENTION GROUP

You have been asked to give the major speech at the annual meeting of the local Home Builders Association, which sponsors a seminar and several scholarships on the campus each year. You are to determine the topic of your speech, which will last about twenty minutes and will be given after dinner. Dinner will be preceded by a cocktail hour and thus is not likely to begin on time. Your speech will follow a program of awards, which may run long because many people are receiving certificates from the association. You will also accept the scholarship on behalf of the college, and so you will get up twice. The meeting is three weeks away. Your speech is ready. You need to know about the setting and how you can adjust to it to make a hit with your audience.

1   Remember that we are concerned with the *setting* right now. What will you, as speaker, ask, and of whom, about the evening so that you can anticipate any difficulties? Get together with some of your classmates in a buzz group and try to figure out what things can go wrong and how you can prepare for them.

2   You are a member of the program committee and want to make this a great occasion for everyone. You are pleased that this speaker has been arranged for, and you want to make it easy for the guest speaker to give a good presentation. You get together with a few of your friends in the Home Builders Association who are on the program committee to figure out how

you can make the meeting go more smoothly than the one last year, when the speaker had only five minutes to give the main speech because everything ran so long. Besides that, the projector didn't work, so that the pictures of the award-winning home designs couldn't be shown, and many members of the audience were walking around all the time, making it hard to hear. Also, some people left just after receiving their awards, thus causing more disturbance. The waiters continued to clear tables all during the program, and noise from the kitchen drowned out the speaker on one side of the room. Your group should come up with some plans to improve the setting of this event for the sake of the audience and the speaker.

3   Several of you should get together to discuss the annual meeting of the Home Builders Association as members of the audience there last year. Did you enjoy yourselves? What caused you to miss out on part of the program? What annoyed you about the setting or the speaker? Can anything be done to make the event more enjoyable this year? Was it too long last time? Was the room too hot? Too cold? Too noisy? Too packed? Come up with a list of suggestions to give the program committee on how things could be made better.

THE VISITING SPEAKER

Durwood Ruesse, a noted poet, is coming to campus. You are in charge of his appearance at the Wilson Auditorium, which seats 100 people. You expect a crowd about half that size to attend the lecture since it is being given on a night when most students will be off campus, and you also anticipate a mixed crowd of students and town people. The program is four weeks away, and you want to make sure that all is ready. You write to Mr. Ruesse, telling him you are in charge of his appearance on campus and inquiring whether he needs anything special set up in the auditorium.

1   Have one of the class members assume the role of Mr. Ruesse as he receives your letter. He should talk with several other members (a buzz group, perhaps) about the kinds of things a poet might need for a lecture. Suppose he has just written a new book of poems, some of which depend for their effect upon the way the words are arranged on the page. Will he want an overhead projector and a screen? Will he want some background music for the reading of his poetry? Will he want transcribed excerpts from the work of other poets whom he admires or dislikes? Will he want questions from the audience? Will he want to smoke while he talks? Will he want to wander around among the crowd rather than standing on a raised platform? Will he want a public-address system, or will he insist that the audience be within a few feet of him? Will he object to the auditorium setting? Will he want a conference with the English teachers after the session? Is he susceptible to colds and thus must speak in a room in which the temperature is set at 80°F? What kinds of things will you transmit back to the program chairperson?

2   As chairperson, anticipating what a poet might want, will you make

arrangements not only to secure the hall for that night (have you ever gone to a meeting and stood around for half an hour while somebody looked for the key to the room?) but also to make sure that the people who attend will be a good audience for this poet? What arrangements will you make without asking him? You should discuss with a small group of close friends various ways to make this a successful occasion by improving the *setting* as much as possible.

3 What might go wrong during the actual performance, even though you have made all the provisions the poet requested? Have a buzz group made up of class members discuss possible mishaps (call them "X factors") that might occur in spite of all your preparations. According to "Murphy's law," which is widely quoted in organizational circles, "If anything can possibly go wrong, it will." Is there a way of anticipating what might go wrong during the evening and of making some effort to correct them in advance—such as unlocking the doors at least half an hour before the performance, testing the lights and the sound ahead of time, and making sure that any other equipment is working?

☐ THE OCCASION

You are part of an occasion when you communicate. You're affected by the mood of the occasion, but you have a chance to influence the mood as well. When you speak at a local club meeting or at an awards dinner for the neighborhood Little League team, you will be part of that occasion. The audience is already selected, and the setting is prescribed. We are now adding the *occasion* as a special part of the speech situation for you to consider.

Getting in the Mood

Mood is one factor to discuss in understanding an occasion. Mood is a temporary, general feeling or attitude or inclination to think, feel, or act in a particular way. Often it is thought to be negative in character; we speak of "moody" people, for example, or of being in a "blue mood" or "ugly mood" or "violent mood." We seem to have more expressions about bad moods than about good ones. Nevertheless, mood should also be thought of as part of a positive atmosphere for speaking.

The mood of the occasion you take part in will depend on whether the members of the audience expect pleasant or unpleasant results from your speech. Are you announcing a new company policy that gives everyone a Christmas bonus, or do you plan to announce a cutback in employment? Are you telling your friends that they all just got an "A" in a course, or are you reporting that they all flunked? Are your friends complaining about an increase in tuition, or are they discussing exciting vacation plans?

Not only the content of your speech but also the way you speak will be affected by the mood of the occasion. If people are getting together for a serious occasion, your speech should be quiet and solemn. If they are getting together to give each other a lift, your speech could be louder and inspiring. Many occasions are designed to develop a certain mood in an audience—and a predisposition is already there for the audience to behave in a certain way. For instance, if you plan a pep rally before a big game, you know what is expected of the speakers and of the audience.

For other occasions the mood may be less well determined in advance. Many clubs and organizations are hosts to speakers of different kinds, ranging from humorous speakers to learned lecturers to serious, view-with-alarm orators. The audience needs to adjust to the different moods created by a variety of speakers. Total moods are not entirely predetermined; not all the members of the audience are likely to be in the same mood. Some may have had a bad day, and others an extremely happy one. For a general crowd that can absorb almost any mood for a short time, you as the speaker are in charge of the occasion. You may give a serious speech on the dangers of water pollution, or you may talk about the funny errors that appear in newspaper headlines. You may appeal to the generosity of the audience by asking for donations to an orphan's home, describing the sad plight of orphans, or you may talk about hunting polar bears in Alaska.

The speaker is not in charge of the occasion when an audience is gathered for a specific purpose that determines its mood—a memorial service for a deceased friend or the celebration of an anniversary, for example.

AUDIENCE ATTITUDES AND MOOD: APPLICATIONS

DID THE KID BREAK THE MOOD?

Two women are leaving a symphony concert and are discussing an event that occurred during the performance. The first woman says that she was annoyed by a young mother and her child who were sitting in the balcony and disturbed the people around them. The child was about four years old, and the mother seemed in her early twenties—"sort of a hippie type," according to this woman. She said that she would not have taken a child that age to a concert and that the young mother showed a total lack of consideration of others.

The second woman said that the noise the child made really hadn't bothered her. Surely it was good for a child that age to be exposed to fine music. The mother seemed to prefer bringing the child to the concert rather than not going at all—what if the only reason she brought the child was that she had been given the tickets by someone else and could not afford a baby-sitter? The mother was very attentive to the music, and the second woman suggested that the first should be glad to have what she called a "hippie type" attending such a concert instead of the other kinds of activities she must think such people attended.

1   What kinds of assumptions about children, concerts, and young mothers does the first woman seem to have? The second?
2   What kinds of assumptions do *you* have about children attending concerts and their young mothers who take them?
3   How would your assumptions have affected your enjoyment of the concert? If the woman who brought the child were a friend of yours, would you be able to talk to her about the occasion, supposing you had overheard the two women talking? It would be interesting to role-play a situation in which you (a friend of the young mother) were in a position to tell her what you heard these two women say. How would you describe them? Would your description be accurate, or would it be colored because of your friendship with the young mother?

EXPECTATIONS OF ACCEPTANCE

Joe, who has a degree in social work, has been assigned to a summer job in the Inner City Recreation Association (ICRA). Joe comes from a middle-class family and knows a great deal about how playground equipment is put together; he has built many different outdoor playthings. He has come to the ICRA meeting with some well-thought-out ideas for playground equipment that could be set up inexpensively, and he immediately begins to tell the parents and volunteers that he will take care of getting the things together and that the children will enjoy them. One parent objects to the use of playthings—children should be given a chance to exercise more normally, by playing ball, for example. Another parent says it is not likely that the youngsters will spend any time using the equipment. One volunteer says he does not understand the equipment and how it would be used. Another volunteer says she wonders what age groups the things Joe is proposing will appeal to. Another volunteer complains that the kids will have the equipment torn apart in a few hours. At this point Joe gets upset and says that with proper encouragement and supervision, the equipment will be useful and will not be wrecked if the volunteers just do their job.

1   What hidden agendas did the members of this meeting have? What kinds of preconceived ideas has each person brought to the meeting? Does the meeting actually start when the group gets together, or does it have a history of some kind that has to be taken into consideration?
2   Does Joe make a basic error in knowing his material and not his people? Should he make a more serious attempt to find out about the people in ICRA and their children before he decides what kind of equipment they should have? Even if he will finally recommend that exactly the same things be placed in the playground, could he have used a better procedure?

3 Role-play this situation. It might be useful to have alter egos behind Joe and some of the other members of the meeting (to speak their inner thoughts) to make sure that these hidden thoughts will be made clear to the audience.

4 What outcome would you expect from this first meeting? Will Joe have to make the biggest adjustment? What would you recommend to Joe if he were your friend?

Informal Occasions

Many informal occasions take place because you choose to speak to others—like a rap session in the dorm room to talk about the last football game, a meeting of a campus club, or discussions about whether you like or dislike an instructor or how you are doing in a course. Such occasions produce a personal conversation. You expect to be relaxed and informal and to talk on the level of your peers. The mood will depend on whether the group has sad experiences to talk about or happy ones. Things you say will be spontaneous, not rehearsed. What you say will fit what you think the mood of the group is. Have you ever seen a cheerful person rush into a roomful of students who are lamenting the loss of a football game or the flunking of an exam? The appropriateness of what you say on such an occasion will determine whether the others will label you as normal, weird, far out, or acceptable, for example.

You also may not always be ready to communicate. In Chapter 1 we discussed times when you are not interested in communicating. Remember that even in those instances, you do communicate something—if only your unwillingness to talk. In an informal occasion you have a choice to remain silent. This is not true when you are called on to be the speaker at a more formal occasion—and it is then that you must make your best assessment of what the occasion calls for.

Formal Occasions

A speech used on one occasion may be not at all appropriate for another. You would not expect to hear a humorous, entertaining speech at a funeral or a solemn eulogy at an office Christmas party. What appears to change from one occasion to another is the reason the people got together. Thus the audience and its readiness to hear a message depend entirely on the occasion.

You may be giving a report to the class. On this occasion, you will try to be informative, clear, and instructional. Or you may be asked to speak for a political candidate at a rally. In that case you will want to be enthusiastic, entertaining, upbeat, optimistic, laudatory, colorful, and even emotional.

In order to establish the mood of your speech, the content, you

The audience and its readiness to respond to persuasion and information depend on the occasion. *(Ron Sherman/Nancy Palmer Photo Agency.)*

need to understand the occasion. Even if the occasion does not suggest a subject, it can give you some guidelines for asking questions. Why are the people meeting? What is the significance of this meeting? Why am I a speaker? Who will be there? What do they expect? How long should I talk? What kind of language can I use to be most effective? How should my delivery affect the occasion—should I use a quiet voice, or should I shout?

THE ACCEPTANCE OF AWARDS AND THE PROPOSAL OF TOASTS

One of the most common serious speaking occasions is at an awards ceremony. Another is giving a response on behalf of your club, your team, your class, your family, or a group you represent. Toasts are made at weddings, anniversary parties, and many social events. There are probably more speeches made on those occasions every year than in any other category except for political speeches in an election year. Every banquet of honor for any club or group will make a presentation to recipients, and they will respond. Very familiar situations range from introducing the club's new officers to the annual display of awards for outstanding motion picture work (the Oscars), for television (the Emmys), or for recordings (the Grammys). Beauty contests like the Miss America Pageant or athletic events like the Super Bowl are also occasions when awards are presented and accepted.

OTHER CEREMONIAL OCCASIONS

Because our communication society is full of rituals and rites of associations, there are many other kinds of ceremonies that call for speeches. Dedications of buildings and historic monuments and commemorations of events such as national and local holidays are occasions for speech making. The Fourth of July speeches of the past century were the highlight of a local speaker's career. Commencements have become occasions where a speech of some importance is delivered to the graduates and their parents before the awarding of diplomas. The basic characteristic of ceremonial speeches is that they are designed to inspire more than persuade, to reminisce more than inform, and to invoke lofty motives and philosophy rather than call for action.

CEREMONIAL OCCASIONS: APPLICATIONS

PRESENTING THE AWARDS

The awards-day committee has decided to sponsor a dinner for those people who are receiving scholastic, athletic, or leadership awards during the second semester. On the insistence of the sponsors of the groups giving awards, it has been decided that only one recipient of each kind of award will give a response when the awards are presented. The occasion will take place during parents weekend, when some visitors are expected on campus and when the college is interested in promoting interest among parents in its programs. There will be three most-valuable-player awards given, and one speaker will respond for all three recipients. There will be four scholastic awards, one for a member of each class—freshman, sophomore, junior, and senior. Two leadership awards will be given—one for the student most active in campus affairs and one for the student who has done the most for campus organizations. The date is set. Recipients of the awards have been chosen. Now a master, or mistress, of ceremonies must be selected for the evening, and the three respondents chosen: one for athletics, one for scholastics, and one for leadership.

1   The class should form three different groups, each involved in a part of this occasion. Group A should select a moderator and give instructions on the kind of introductions to be made. Group B should select the three respondents to awards and instruct them on how to make their speeches. Group C is the audience. It will work out some ideas on what kind of person the moderator should be and what kinds of responders would be appropriate. They also should work out what kinds of speeches or introductions should be made and what mood should be established by the talks.

2　Did all three groups agree on the selections of people and what they should say? Did they agree on the mood of the occasion?

3　Which of the three groups would have the most influence on the mood of the occasion? Do they interact to form a mood?

THE CLUB SPEAKING ASSIGNMENT

Jim was invited by a member of the Townies Club to come to their headquarters off campus in honor of the fifteenth anniversary of the founding of that group. His friend assured Jim that it would not be dull—no speeches or anything like that—but that the club was proud of its record for growing membership and growing influence on campus and intended to pledge many new members at a future meeting.

Jim went to the fifteenth anniversary party, assuming it was a fairly solemn occasion. He found out it was a big beer bust. Jim was dressed up, and the members of the Townies were in casual clothes. He arrived a little late, and some of the members who had been imbibing a little heavily were shouting at each other, tearing down the signs that said "Townies Club—Fifteen Years of Service," and throwing around the flowers they had received from a local sponsor.

A week later, Jim's friend asked him to give the welcoming speech to the ten new pledges the Townies planned to induct the following weekend. Again, the friend assured Jim that this was an important occasion because the members wanted to impress the new pledges. Jim agreed to give the welcoming speech which would be about five minutes in length and would follow the ceremony of induction.

1　Assume you are Jim. What more do you need to know about this occasion? Have an informal discussion with others in class about the ambiguous situation Jim is in after having seen the serious occasion of the fifteenth anniversary treated so casually. How do you think Jim might expect the induction of the pledges to turn out? How would someone advise Jim to proceed?

2　You are Jim's friend, and you think that the pledges should have a very serious, sober induction into the club. Assume you are leading a group of officers of the club in a discussion of ways to make the occasion more serious than the anniversary celebration. How do you proceed?

3　Assume you are one of the new pledges to the Townies Club. What would you expect the occasion of the induction to be like if you had attended the fifteenth anniversary party? Get together with a group of other "pledges" to work out how you should act and dress and what you should talk about at the induction party. What did you talk about at the anniversary party?

PERSUASION OCCASIONS

We spend a certain amount of time trying to convince others about our beliefs. You may be a manufacturer addressing a group about your product. You may be a politician arguing your party's stand on the issues and urging voter support. You may be a representative of a chamber of commerce pleading for new street-lighting system or a parent arguing for more crossing guards at the schools. You may be a fund raiser pleading the cause of the Red Cross, the March of Dimes, the United Fund, or the alumni association. All these speech purposes must have an appropriate occasion. It will be useless to try to persuade members of the Kiwanis Club to buy aluminum pots. You do not pick a chamber of commerce meeting to raise money for some child to go to summer camp, but it would be a good occasion to raise money for civic improvements.

Many occasions are called for the specific purpose of hearing speakers present their cases. On those occasions not only is it *all right* for speakers to openly admit they are trying to persuade, but they should also be sure to point out to the audience that the occasion has been called for that reason. There is nothing more phony than speakers in persuasive situations trying to pretend that they just happened to drop by and just happened to be prepared to talk about their favorite causes. The persuasive speakers should be frank and open about their purposes and make the best use of the occasion. They should also make clear what action they want the listeners to take or what support they expect to receive.

INFORMATION OCCASIONS

In the classroom, in front of professional groups, at conferences, and at club meetings of many kinds, the occasion involves information exchange. Usually speakers who have some kind of special information or knowledge are invited to tell the group as much as they can about a subject in a given amount of time. The group may have gathered to hear the speaker, but may also have other business of its own to conduct. Clubs and professional organizations do, however, regularly invite speakers to talk about subjects ranging from aardvarks to zebras and from Alcoholics Anonymous to Zen. A speaker on these occasions must be aware of the items listed in Chapter 4: the educational level of the audience, their interests, and their age levels; who has spoken to them recently and on what subjects; and how much time they have to listen.

Any day of the week, across the country, there are service clubs and local and regional professional groups getting together to hear speakers at lunch or dinner meetings. Many of the speeches are given by people who are experts in their own fields but poor public speakers. For example, the chief engineer in the new atomic energy plant is well informed about the company's antipollution measures, but in talking about them uses technical jargon and turns off the audience. The analyst who conducts family-therapy sessions without any communication pause, finds herself tongue-tied before the luncheon club, even though the audience needs her psychological wisdom. Opportunities to give informational speeches are numerous if you have any special knowledge or skill to talk about. These types of speeches have earned a bad reputation, however, because of the difficulty speakers have in preparing a lively, interesting, and appropriate speech. That is a characteristic you can do something about. Knowing a subject well is the first step, but being able to bring your knowledge to life on an informational occasion is a real challenge.

ENTERTAINMENT OCCASIONS

If you can do magic tricks or make a good humorous speech, the groups mentioned above may want you to perform at their meetings. They like to spice their quest for information, knowledge, and intellectual growth with a little fun and amusement. On some ceremonial occasions audiences are more interested in being entertained than in being uplifted, persuaded, or informed. Speakers for the entertainment occasions must, as in the other cases, analyze the audience as well as the occasion to make sure their level of humor, cynicism, or satire is appropriate, recognizing that there are many kinds of "entertainment" occasions. A group of conventioners may call for broad slapstick, but at a banquet for retired ministers gentle satire would be more appropriate.

Pure entertainment is not always demanded by the occasion; an audience wants to be entertained, but may also want some philosophy or

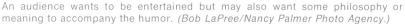

An audience wants to be entertained but may also want some philosophy or meaning to accompany the humor. *(Bob LaPree/Nancy Palmer Photo Agency.)*

meaning to accompany the humor. Very often, the audience on such an occasion will accept humor or tricks as a means of getting across a more serious point.

FORMAL OCCASIONS: APPLICATIONS

CHECK THE OCCASIONS

In the following list of speaking situations, fill in the blanks to indicate whether you *have been* involved as a speaker in such situations and also whether you think you ever *will be*.

Kind of Occasion	In the Past			In the Future		
	Never	Seldom	Often	Never	Seldom	Often
Acceptance of awards or proposal of toasts	___	___	___	___	___	___
Other ceremonial occasions	___	___	___	___	___	___
Persuasion occasions	___	___	___	___	___	___
Information occasions	___	___	___	___	___	___
Entertainment occasions	___	___	___	___	___	___

WHAT DO YOU LIKE TO DO?

Of the occasions listed (acceptance of awards, persuasion, imparting information, etc.), which would you *most enjoy* taking part in as the speaker? Why?

_____

_____

Which would you *least enjoy* taking part in as the speaker? Why?

_____

_____

THE EULOGY OCCASION

The following eulogy for a fallen leader might apply in the case of any number of people who have died for a cause. It might be delivered by a loyal follower after the assassination of a leader, for example.

The work he began was not finished. The cause he died for is not itself dead. The thousands of his loyal friends will carry on both the work and the cause. Only the tragedy of the death is finished. Such tragedy is known only a few times in our history—as in the death of a Lincoln by an assassin's bullet, so eloquently immortalized by Walt Whitman in his poem "O Captain! My Captain." The imagery of Whitman is as true to our leader as to Lincoln—the ship surviving the buffeting of the waves and storms, just as our cause has survived the storms of public misunderstanding and designed mistrust. Who will be the Whitman to speak for our fallen leader? Whose voice will join with my feeble pleas to rise up with new vigor—with new faith—with greater strength to meet the challenge which he had advanced for the benefit of us all? I want to hear you speak—to carry the message—to give witness. Who will speak for him whom the assassin has taken from us? Who among you has a voice?

1 At what kind of occasion might this eulogy be delivered? To what kind of audience? Friendly? Dedicated? Angry? Sad? Describe the kind of mood which might be present for any of the "fallen leaders" listed in the next question.

2 Discuss with others in a small group which one of the following persons this eulogy might have been about: (a) Robert Kennedy—political leader, Democratic presidential possibility; (b) Martin Luther King—civil rights and religious leader; (c) George Lincoln Rockwell—head of the American Nazi party; (d) Malcom X—Black Muslim leader; (e) John Kennedy—President of the United States.

3 Working with a group, suggest some additional remarks to be made by the speaker. One person in the group could be selected to respond to ". . . who will speak for him? . . ."

■LOOKING BACK

I. Setting is the surroundings you are in when you communicate, and it relates very closely to the other factors of communication, such as the audience and the occasion.

II. One-to-one settings are common in our informal communicating. Some settings—such as the telephone and radio—limit the senses we can bring into play to achieve effective communication.

  A. In one-to-one situations you should try to make use of all the appropriate senses, including sound, sight, touch, and even smell.

  B. The job interview—as a specific example—is an important one-to-one situation which you are very likely to face, and it involves some very distinct rules for making use of the setting as controlled by the interviewer.

    1. Psychological distance, or proxemics, is important, as discussed in Chapter 3.

2. You, as the interviewee, need to be aware of the setting, what it demands of you, and what it permits you to do.
3. Time is an important feature of this setting.

III. Different groups make up special settings in which certain kinds of rules of speaking, listening, etc., apply.
   A. *Informal groups* are usually assembled in a setting that includes food, drink, or entertainment.
   B. *Formal groups* are more likely to be gathered for the purpose of accomplishing tasks, solving problems, conducting discussions, presenting information, or sharing expertise.
      1. Buzz groups are informally organized discussion groups such as those you would have in class. They are often assembled spontaneously, sometimes for the purpose of getting a specific job done in a certain amount of time.
      2. An assembly is a gathering of people who want to do their own thinking and probing; there is no expert to serve as a leader or resource person.
      3. A forum consists of a group of experts facing an audience and giving some points of view, generally on one topic. The audience may ask questions, but not for the purpose of changing the minds of the experts.
      4. A colloquium involves a group of discussants on one side and a group of experts on another. The discussion goes on without intervention by the experts, except to clarify points or add information.
      5. A panel consists of experts who give their opinions and then are asked questions by an audience.
      6. A symposium is a more formal panel that often does not encourage questions; its purpose is to give information to others.
      7. A conference may be an extended set of people, symposia, or meetings, or it may be a special gathering to solve a problem (a business conference, for example).
      8. In a round table, all persons present are encouraged to participate in a face-to-face situation. It is much like an assembly, except that there are fewer people, and the setting is more intimate.
      9. A seminar is a didactic setting in which information is usually given by an expert (such as a teacher) to listeners (students, for example), and presumably there is a chance for give-and-take discussion.
      10. A committee is a special group assembled as representative of a larger group to work on a specific project or accomplish an assignment.

IV. A setting in which one speaker addresses a larger group is common in education, business, community affairs, and public affairs.

A. Speakers must be responsible for certain things in the setting that will increase their effectiveness in reaching the audience.

B. The audience requires certain things, such as a lack of distractions and a way to ask questions, and these should be taken care of by some representative of the organization sponsoring the event.

V. The occasion cannot be separated from the audience and the setting except as an exercise in analyzing it for your own purposes as a speaker.

A. Occasions affect what you do as a speaker.

B. Occasions may create audiences and dictate settings.

VI. Informal occasions may occur any time you are willing to talk.

A. Mood is the important factor in looking at informal occasions.

B. Mood relates to audience expectations of the occasion.

VII. People gather on formal occasions for a specific purpose.

A. Acceptances of awards and proposals of toasts frequently provide you with an opportunity to perform briefly in a special role. Ceremonial occasions are reflections of society's communication rites and rituals.

B. You should begin your speech on persuasive occasions with an honest admission that you are there to convince your audience, and you should end by asking for their cooperation.

C. The person who has special knowledge or information to share with others speaks on informational occasions; however, speaker effectiveness may depend more on speaking ability than on what the speaker knows.

D. When speaking on entertainment occasions, a mixture of humor or a light approach with a bit of philosophy may be best.

PART TWO

PART TWO

In this part we shall appear to concentrate on you as a speaker of communication messages. Often, however, we shall refer to you as a listener to those messages. It is very important to realize that you are not only the producer of speaking messages but also a consumer of many such messages each day. This part describes how to prepare effective, ethical messages for a variety of situations. At the same time you need to learn how to avoid being taken in by unethical or irresponsible messages sent to you by others in your world; to understand clearly their meanings and their implications—whether these communicators are your close friends, your professors, your parents, your boss, a politician, a radio or TV commentator, or an advertiser.

You will notice that when we discuss different kinds of speeches, such as those intended to inform or persuade, we

YOUR
COMMUNICATION
MESSAGE

are very conscious of the speaking situation. The kinds of speeches you can give also involve you—what you know, what your interests are, what you can do.

In these ways, the communication message is an integral part of the continuing activity we call communication. The message is not a grab-bag package to be handed out at any old time or unwrapped for any occasion. It is a carefully tailored, thoughtfully designed, and specially prepared gift for that audience, in that setting, on that occasion from you as an individual.

As you continue to study about outlines, research, proof, and all the other aspects of the communication message in this part, don't forget the suggestions given earlier about delivery, audience adaptation, and how to adjust to settings and occasions. They are all part of the intelligent preparation for, the final success of, the communication message.

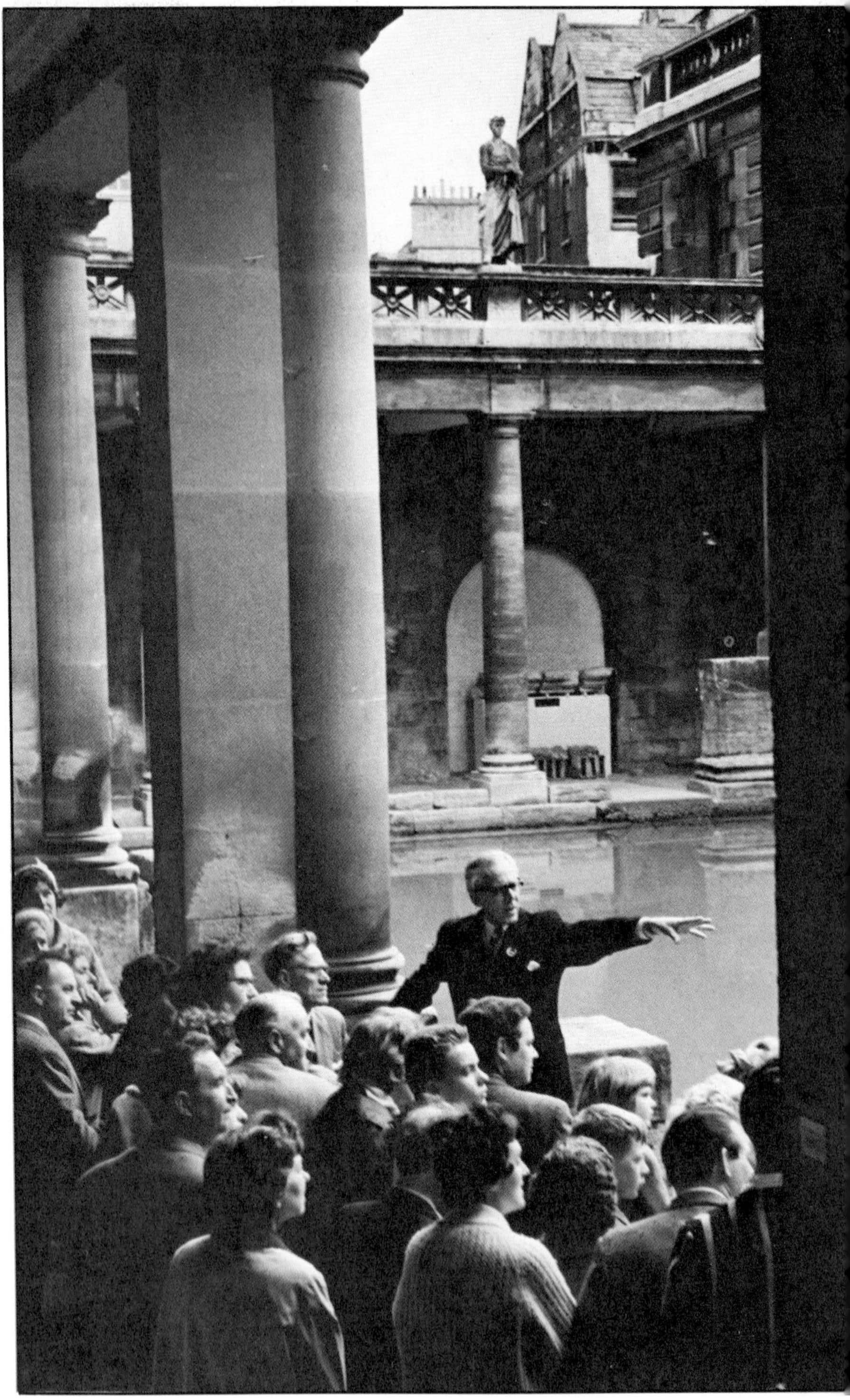

(Robert Mottar/Photo Researchers. Inc.)

CHAPTER 6
SPEECH SUBJECTS AND TYPES

Everything is funny as long as it is happening to somebody else.
— Will Rogers

Man consists of body, mind, and imagination. His body is faulty, his mind untrustworthy, but his imagination has made him remarkable. In some centuries, his imagination has made life on this planet an intense practice of all the lovelier energies.
— John Masefield

An idea isn't responsible for the people who believe in it.
— Don Marquis

You are in front of an audience in a given setting and on a definite occasion. You are going to speak *about something*. You don't just speak "speech" the way you figure arithmetic or calculus. Your message has a topic. You are concerned about what to say. Unless you pick a good subject for your speech, you will not stimulate your audience and probably will not be very interested yourself in either preparing your message well or delivering it well. You will be embarrassed when the audience doesn't like your message, and you probably will have communicated it badly.

In much of your communicating, the subject is chosen for you. If a friend asks you how to clean a carburetor, how to check out a library book, or how to apply for student aid, the subject is set. You can begin preparing your message on the basis of the question. If you have been asked to speak before a political club, the subject will probably be politics. You can start putting together your message with that in mind. If you are planning to persuade your friends to vote for your candidate, you can proceed to make an effective persuasive message.

You also choose the communication messages you listen to. For example, you can decide whether to go to a lecture on alpha waves and transcendental meditation, to go to the movies, or to stay in the dorm and talk to your roommate. You may prefer a lecture on modern poetry to a TV program on wildlife in the Amazon jungle. On the other hand, you often have little choice about the subject you will hear about, as when you are in class or attending a dinner meeting of a club or a business or professional organization.

Think about those listening occasions on which you heard subjects that were of interest to you, and you can select interesting topics for your own message. Your communication will result from your choice of subject, whether in the formal settings of speechmaking or in day-to-day encounters with friends.

☐ SELECTING THE SUBJECT FOR YOUR MESSAGE: GENERAL CRITERIA

Your relationship to your audience is very closely tied to the subject you choose. In general, you should select a subject that will interest your audience because it is new to them, is close to their lives, is familiar to them but capable of being treated in a new and fresh way, and is concrete or specific enough so that they can follow your arguments. Your message will be appropriate for your audience and the general situation if you can relate it to the audience's curiosity, their lives, or their sense of the familiar without giving them the same old stuff. Think about the people you like to listen to. They seem to talk about things that are part of your life, but the more new twists they give their communication, the more interested you are. They talk about what you want to hear. The same rules apply when you choose a topic or subject for the message you will communicate. Some more specific suggestions follow.

Choose a Subject That Interests You

If you try to talk about something that bores you, you are likely to bore your audience. On the other hand, if you pick a subject that interests you—one you can get excited about—you will transmit that enthusiasm to your audience.

Keeping in mind that a good subject should be interesting, concrete, acceptable to the audience and the occasion, and original, you need to evaluate yourself to determine what you can talk about confidently. You will be surprised at how many interesting things have happened to you and at how many things you know about and can share with an audience. Take a look at (1) your abilities—what you can do well, what you have had practice in, what unusual things you have accomplished; (2) your background—where you have lived, whom you have known, what events you have participated in; (3) your interests—things you would like to learn more about, things that catch your eye when you read or your ear when you listen, activities you would like to become more proficient at; (4) your knowledge—what you know a lot about or special information you may have; and (5) your experiences—unusual things that have happened to you and would be of interest to an audience. It might be helpful to make a list of things under each of these categories. Your abilities might include carpentry, playing the guitar, swimming, and scuba diving. Your background would consist of such items as the size of your family, your childhood, and whether you moved a lot because your father was in the military. Interests would include things like CB radio, reading, music, and sports cars. Your knowledge would be in areas like a foreign language, community events, and famous recording artists. Experiences would include such things as campaigning for a political candidate, being lost in the woods, and spending a vacation abroad.

In a chart like the one below construct a list of subjects for yourself. You will be surprised at how many topics for speeches it suggests. These are only an indication of how many subjects for speaking your own experience can provide. The next step is to adapt these subjects to the audience according to the additional criteria given.

Abilities _____ Intellectual
           _____ Physical
           _____ Social
           _____ Professional

Background	_____	Place of birth
	_____	Education
	_____	Family origins
	_____	Neighborhood
	_____	Religion
	_____	Politics
Knowledge	_____	Professional
	_____	Hobbies
	_____	Personal
Interests	_____	Professional
	_____	Hobbies
	_____	Sports
	_____	Intellectual
	_____	Travels
	_____	Friendships
	_____	Foods, cooking
	_____	Pets, animals
Experiences	_____	Physical
	_____	Emotional
	_____	Wins, losses
	_____	Persons, places

Choose a Subject That Fits What You Want to Do

Ask yourself: "Why am I speaking to this audience?" If you want to persuade them to do something, then your general purpose is persuasive. Once you know that, you must consider (1) your specific purpose (to get the audience to contribute to the United Fund or join the Red Cross, for example) and (2) any hidden purposes you may have. Later we shall discuss in more detail the purposes of our communication messages, but first it will be useful to consider the possibility that your message has a *hidden* or unspoken purpose besides its *stated* purpose.

If your specific purpose is to get support for the United Fund and your general purpose is to persuade, at the same time you may want to give a speech that will make the listeners elect you to chair the drive next year—that's your *hidden* purpose. Although your general purpose in speaking is persuasive, you might also be interested in having the professors in the audience perceive you as a deep thinker; this is your hidden purpose. A great many speeches have some measure of open and hidden purpose; you can watch for this in your own speeches as well as those of others. If you concentrate on the hidden purpose, you may fail to achieve either one, but if you do a good job with the open purpose, you are likely to succeed at both.

Choose a subject that fits the situation: What is appropriate for the setting and occasion? *(Chie Nishio/Nancy Palmer Photo Agency.)*

Choose a Subject That Fits the Situation

This includes, by our earlier definition, the audience, the setting, and the occasion. We have already indicated that the audience expects the subject to be interesting, concrete enough to grasp in the time given, and acceptable to the tastes of the majority of the members. The subject should also have some degree of originality, or the audience will feel they have heard it all before. We indicated earlier that some of the factors to consider when analyzing an audience include (1) the number of people to be addressed, (2) their age and thus the attitudes they can be expected to have, (3) their sex, (4) their educational and informational level (their background in the subject), (5) their socioeconomic status, and (6) their affiliations, such as with clubs, professional groups, religious groups, community organizations, and other associations. In addition, the audience will have an attitude toward the speaker and the subject matter, and they will also have an idea of what is appropriate for the setting and the occasion.

The speaker should know what the reason is for the gathering—the *occasion*. Is it an annual affair? If so, what happened last year? Is it a local meeting of a larger group? If so, what happened at the recent meetings of the bigger groups? Is it a special ceremony for a religious, cultural, political, educational, or social purpose? Does the intellectual or emotional tone of the subject fit the *mood* of the occasion? You don't talk about bloody surgical operations at a banquet meeting, nor do you present a learned paper on baroque music to the annual meeting of a chamber of commerce.

The *setting* includes the time of day and the amount of time you have to speak. Advice given earlier is worth repeating: Do not exceed your time and do not begin your speech late. The physical setting will affect the amount of audience participation you receive. In a very small, seminar-type room you can't act pompous or be distant in your approach. If you are going to speak in a large auditorium without audio-visual facilities, you obviously can't show slides of French impressionist paintings. For a radio speech you must rely only on your voice, while a television address should make use of visual aids as well as your own moves.

Choose a Subject That Can Be Covered in the Time You Have

Tracing the history of World War II in a ten-minute talk would be difficult, but you could give an adequate speech about one war hero or one battle in that amount of time. Speeches on very technical topics require more time, as do those dealing with complex processes or events. An informative speech that must provide much background and detail cannot be given quickly, nor can you persuade an audience to support a cause unless you have enough time to convince them of its importance and to tell them what you want them to do. The beginning speaker usually has to practice before being able to estimate accurately how much material can be covered in three, ten, or thirty minutes. Thus you should choose simple topics for your first speeches, because you will have a better chance of staying within your time limit and won't have to rush breathlessly through the presentation.

Choose a Single, Well-defined, or Simple Subject

Resist the temptation to say everything you may know about your topic. Don't give an exhaustive lecture on sports cars if the subject is the latest model of the Mercedes 450 SL.

Most beginning speakers overestimate the amount of material they need for a brief speech. As a result, they talk too long—generally without being aware of how long they actually were speaking. Practice will help you estimate more accurately how much you can cover in three minutes or ten minutes. You will probably find yourself limiting your speech content to simpler and simpler subjects as you grow more accustomed to the fact that you do really have a lot to talk about, and realize that it takes you longer to say it than you would have guessed.

☐ PURPOSES OF MESSAGES

Just as you will speak *about* something, which is why you are studying the communication message, you are also delivering a message for a *reason*, and that is your *speech purpose*. Traditionally, speech purposes have been categorized according to what response they are planned to elicit from the audience. Speeches are usually made (1) to inform, (2) to persuade, or (3) to entertain. More categories could be added, or the third category (entertainment) could be subdivided into speeches of praise, speeches to inspire, demonstrative speeches, courtesy speeches, etc. For the sake of simplicity, we shall add only one more category, (4) ceremonial speeches.

Informational Messages

When the primary purpose of a speech is to provide a learning experience for listeners, it is classified as informational or instructional. Conversations about how to fill out an application form or about the historical significance of a campus landmark are informational messages. So are speeches given by your instructor on the meaning of Faulkner's imagery, evidence presented in court, instructions to new factory workers about fringe benefits, and the comments of radio and television newscasters. The purpose of this type of message is to make the audience comprehend what the speaker has to say and to retain it.

GIVING INSTRUCTIONS

Instructions involve a how-to-do-it message. These may vary in complexity from how to pick up a heavy box without getting a hernia to how to build a television set from components. Much of our communication involves giving directions or instructions, and we can think of many examples of how these messages fail and cause all sorts of humorous or tragic consequences. You get lost trying to follow the directions to a friend's house and discover that she said *East* First Street and that you went to *West* First Street. Often, assignments given orally in class are

Explaining for better understanding is an important component of informational messages. *(Ron Sherman/Nancy Palmer Photo Agency.)*

subject to misinterpretation. A drugstore clerk's advice on how to use chemicals on a lawn to kill fungus needs to be very specific in its warnings on the dangers of these preparations to animals.

EXPLAINING FOR BETTER UNDERSTANDING

Messages of explanation are usually given under the assumption that the audience is only partially informed, or badly informed, on an issue, an event, an activity, or a philosophy. The speaker whose message is designed to let you in on the secrets of the CIA or who can provide you with the deeper meanings of existentialist poetry is giving a message of explanation. Music critics, drama critics, and interpreters of the political, social, or economic scene might be placed in this category. Lectures on many subjects are also included in this group. Speakers at conferences on special subjects—from undertakers to electron microscopists— engage in giving and receiving messages to inform.

MAKING A REPORT

Most organizations have a secretary who prepares minutes and reads them at the next meeting as an informative report. The difference between the minutes of a neighborhood social club and those of the annual meeting of General Motors stockholders is only one of degree, not purpose. Both messages are designed to do the same thing: report the activities of an organization, whether a professional group or club, or for the benefit of a special or general audience. Reports may be concerned with the progress of a project or group, with the financial standing of a company or club, with a committee action or recommendation, with a public event, with the path of an impending hurricane, or with a private in-depth study for marketing, political, educational, or civic purposes.

INFORMATION: APPLICATIONS

GIVING INSTRUCTIONS

Remember the story about the centipede, that many-legged worm, who was asked by an ant which leg he moved first? The centipede, who really didn't know which one went first, started worrying about it and then stumbled all over himself trying to figure it out. If someone asks you how you put on your coat, can you explain the process in simple terms and in the proper sequence? Have you ever thought about it?

1   As an exercise in giving instructions—or a speech to inform—try to instruct another person in the simple act of putting on a coat. Assume that the person has no experience with coats and does not know words like "lapel," "sleeve," "buttons," etc.
2   Try this exercise first with a group giving instructions to a single person. Start with the coat on the back of a chair and the subject standing next to it. The subject cannot anticipate your directions or instructions since this will be an entirely new procedure in his or her life. The subject will do only what you say—nothing more and nothing less. Your group can take turns giving instructions, or you may work together to figure out which kinds of things to say first, then next, and so on.
3   How do members of your group react to one another during the order-giving process? Can you agree easily on what should be said to the subject?
4   Try this exercise with one person giving instructions to a stranger. Then try it with the audience ready to accuse the person instructing of having made a mistake every time the subject does something wrong.

INTERVIEWS

Several years ago a farmer living near Dexter, Michigan, came to national attention when he and his son saw a "glowing ghost ship" in a swampy area near their home. It looked like a cigarette glow at first, the farmer said, and then it lit up; the "thing" had a greenish-white light on one end and a white light on the other. He said it looked like a car except that it hovered about 8 feet off the ground and stayed there until the son said, "Look at that horrible thing." Then it just took off into the darkness without a sound.

Among the people asked to come and investigate the phenomenon was a university professor engaged as a consultant for the Air Force. He said, "I don't want to give the impression that I'm puzzled. I'm sure this has a perfectly natural explanation, but I don't know what it is." Meanwhile, the farmer said he definitely did not believe in flying saucers or UFOs (unidentified flying objects), but he said very firmly: "I saw what I saw and there's nobody can tell me different."

1   Being interviewed by (a) the press, (b) the neighbors, and (c) the Air Force experts on this subject made the farmer a "public speaker" whether he intended to be one or not. Imagine how he would describe the scene to each of these groups. Would he talk differently to his neighbors from the way he might talk to newspaper, television, or radio people or to the Air Force consultant?

2   Divide the class into three interviewing groups: (a) the farmer's neighbors, (b) representatives of the press from all over the state and region, and (c) representatives of the Air Force, including a professor of astronomy and some high-ranking officers. What would you like to know from the farmer? In other words, what are you like as an audience when he becomes the speaker? What would you expect to ask? How would you ask the questions? Have the groups compare notes on what questions they would ask the farmer and how they would ask them. Have a member of the class or the instructor serve as the farmer for the interviews. If there are differences in the interview exchanges, what accounts for those differences?

3   In groups for discussion (four or five members of the class) try to develop a list of occasions when you—as normal, ordinary, everyday people—may be called on unexpectedly to inform or instruct others. The farmer in Michigan had the role of informational speaker thrust on him as a result of the observation he made; are you likely to have to become a speaker for some impromptu audiences in your lifetime? See whether your group can develop an imaginative list of the situations you might face. Be creative!

Persuasive Messages

Within the category of speeches to persuade we can distinguish those to achieve a change or reinforcement of attitudes (to convince) and those to bring about an action (to motivate to act). All messages of advocacy— buy this shampoo, vote for this candidate, join this cause, believe in our mayor, accept this view of religion, follow our logic for social change— are meant to persuade. Either the advocate wants to have you, the listener, end up with the same kind of opinions, beliefs, and attitudes which the persuader has, or wants to get you to do something that is in the persuader's interest.

These may not be selfish interests. They may be presented as changes that can be for your own good—believe as we do and be saved,

In attempting to persuade an audience, you must make them believe that your idea will benefit them. *(Gail Myers.)*

know your own ethnic history, read more books, study at home, learn to speak better, understand crime and criminals, join the investment club. They also may be presented as actions from which both you and the person doing the persuading will benefit: drive safely, fasten seat belts, avoid overeating, stay away from drugs, strike for higher wages, boycott this store.

The audience is of primary importance in the message to persuade, because it is from the audience that the action or attitude change must come. The speaker wants something to happen to the audience. This kind of speaking occurs so often that we are probably not aware of all the attempts made to persuade us or of the number of times *we* try to persuade someone else. When you ask a friend to lend you class notes or a car, you are trying to persuade. When your friend asks you to go to the movies instead of studying, that's a message of persuasion.

Later in this book we shall discuss the format and style to use in persuasion, but first here are four suggestions for planning a message to persuade when you are selecting a speech topic.

BE COMMITTED TO YOUR STAND

If you are making a genuine attempt to persuade, you will be most effective if you believe in your idea. You must believe that adopting your position will benefit your audience and that it is important for your listeners to be persuaded.

FIND A CHALLENGING TOPIC

Any time you set out to persuade someone, it will involve a good deal of your energy as well as an emotional and intellectual commitment. For a speech of persuasion, you will have to do a considerable amount of research, planning, and gathering of information on your topic and probably on your audience. The topic ought to be worth the effort.

COMBINE YOUR KNOWLEDGE WITH AVAILABLE MATERIAL

Getting ready for a persuasive message will demand all your own intelligence and all the information you can gather together from external sources. In selecting a topic and planning for a persuasive message you ought to determine, first, how much you already know about the subject and, second, how available additional supporting material is.

LOOK FOR THE X FACTORS

In any speaking situation, some things can't be anticipated. These "X factors" can shake you if you are not prepared for some surprises. Remember that even if you plan every word and every move, there is a

To persuade or inform an audience, you need enough time to convince them that what you say is important. *(Don Koblitz/Editorial Photocolor Archives.)*

chance that something will happen among the audience or to you that will change the situation. Try to anticipate the kinds of approaches that would offer you the most solid ground and the least number of X factors or surprise objections.

PERSUASION: APPLICATIONS

SOME TOPICS FOR A "PERSUASIVE SPEECH"

Following are some situations in which you might find yourself at one time or another. These are all cases where persuasion is important in your communication.

1 You want your friend to stop dating the boy she is going with because you've heard some things about him that you think she wouldn't like.
2 You want your friend to go to the movies with you instead of studying.
3 You want your friend to help you move furniture to another friend's new apartment.
4 You want your friend to work for the campaign of a candidate for mayor (or commissioner, President, legislator, etc.).
5 You want your friends to work as volunteers in a drug program.
6 You want your professor to allow you to take an exam a few days early so that you can leave town.
7 You want your club to make a gift of $50 to help support a clinic.
8 You want the student government to provide a location and some financial aid for a day-care center for students with children.
9 You want the members of your church to work as solicitors for a campaign to buy a new organ (or new hymnals, new Bibles, a new pulpit, or a new furnace).
10 You want the student body to support a student radio station with their own personal donations and to work to raise money and get the station licensed and on the air.
11 You want the members of a political rally to nominate your friend as their candidate.

"ABSENT EXPERT" MESSAGES

Many speeches and newspaper articles use a subject gimmick that we shall call "the absent-expert speculation." A minister decides to talk about the current social scene and constructs a sermon on the topic: "What Would Jesus Christ Do about Teenage Drug Abuse if He Were Alive Today?" Or a speaker at a commemorative meeting of the Daughters of the American Revolution might ask "How Would George Washington Advise Us Today to Combat the Communist Menace?"

When you use "absent-expert speculation," you take another person's philosophy and apply it to a "present crisis" of some kind; this gives you an instant speech.

1   What kind of audiences will these speeches appeal to most? At what kind of occasions might they be delivered more often? What kind of speech-maker will be delivering them?
2   Working as a small group in class, try to construct an outline of a speech from the "absent-expert speculation" model. You may select any kind of "crisis" to comment on or problem to solve; then speculate on how some well-known person (who is not likely to be in a position to do anything about it) would go about handling it. Specify your audience and your occasion when you do the outline.
3   Working as a small group, make up a list of crises or problems that would be good topics for this kind of speech. Then make a list of people whose philosophy (or standards, values, or historical comments) you could evoke to match up with the items on the list.

Entertaining Messages

Like ceremonial speeches, entertaining messages are not intended to make the audience know more or do better or to reinforce their beliefs or cause them to take some action. They are for diversion. The listeners want to spend a little time being entertained, and that can mean being amused or simply having their attention diverted to an interesting topic for a period of time. Such messages should help the audience get pleasure, without obligating them to know or do something afterward. The audience expects a good time—from an entertaining after-dinner speaker or from the girl whose stories about her dates keep her friends amused and interested. In informal settings, such as a party, the storyteller is speaking to entertain even if only four people are listening. Showing home movies when the neighbors drop over is entertainment with visual aids. Nightclub comics are professional entertainers, as are lecturers who show movies about the natives of Outer Mongolia or the care and feeding of animals in the African veldt.

Entertainment is very difficult. Even if your purpose is to have an attentive, relaxed, calm audience without loud laughter or wild applause, you must know what the level of appreciation of your audience is. Logical discourse is not the purpose; the focus is on giving the audience a good time. To do this you must guess right about what will amuse or attract your audience. Your own skill at storytelling and description will make the entertaining message successful, but only if it meets the audience requirements and the situational demands of mood and appropriateness. Much of the difficulty in finding subjects for entertaining speeches stems from the fact that the beginning speaker assumes it is necessary to be funny. To entertain, you may talk about your more serious adventures or travels as well as the funny things in your life.

"They didn't laugh because you forgot to look cross-eyed
when you delivered the punch line."

(The New Yorker.)

ENTERTAINMENT: APPLICATIONS

SYMBOL SOURCEBOOK

An entertaining speech could be constructed from special reference books and other library materials. For example, *The Henry Dreyfuss Symbol Sourcebook* includes some 8,000 symbols that are in use throughout the world to guide people in their relations with one another and with the world they live in. You can construct an entertaining speech with examples from this book by showing how we respond to pictures much more quickly than to written words. Two of our early symbols are the plus and minus signs, which are almost universal. One symbol for "fasten your seat belt" has saved having to write it in several languages on airlines and in automobiles. Traffic signs are beginning to have a universal appearance—widely used in many parts of the world—and they do not need words to show that you should not make a left turn, that you should not park, or that you must stop. Symbols on restroom doors make it easy for people traveling in foreign countries to know which is the ladies' room and which is the men's room. In movies about the old West, you may see symbols on buildings indicating whether they are saddle shops or barber shops, for example. These were intended partly to help those who did not know how to read, and even today the extent of illiteracy in many countries makes it necessary to have symbols rather than written words to convey such messages.

1   From the material presented above, outline a brief, entertaining speech to

be given to (a) a class, (b) a group of small children, (c) a group of elderly persons, and (d) a group you know well and belong to.

2 Why does this speech seem more like entertainment than like one of information or persuasion? Could you turn it into an informational speech? How? A persuasive speech?

3 Find other kinds of sources of material for an entertaining speech besides the suggested one (library or book sources) and make up a sample description of what you would talk about. How about your own personal experiences as an important source?

TALKING ABOUT YOURSELF

You spend a good deal of time talking about yourself. You are quick to tell your friends what *you* think about a movie, a political figure, or a class. You will also jump at the chance to tell about how you were stopped for speeding, what you said to the cop, and so on—that was *your* experience. You may also talk at length to a person you have just met about how you came to choose this college or why you joined a particular group.

When we talk to others about what we know, what we own, what we like, or what we are capable of, we can exchange a lot of information with them and perhaps entertain and persuade them. It isn't even necessary to be an expert on a subject we talk about. For example, even if you have not won an Olympic ski medal, you can talk to a friend about the first time you put on skis and how you spent most of the day in the snow. You don't have to have made a hit record to talk about music with others.

However, when you begin to address a larger audience—more than just your friends and acquaintances—about some of your experiences, it may be necessary to single out the ones with more flair, more impact, and more unusual qualities. You can't just say you have a pet dog; you ought to tell about the problems you had training him to count to five by barking. You can't just tell this bigger audience that you were born in Poughkeepsie; you should make some point about being the first baby born in the new year, about being born in a taxi on the way to the hospital, or about being delivered by the only midwife in upstate New York.

When you talk about yourself to a larger audience, you will select more dramatic things to say than you might in your day-to-day communication with your friends. For instance, you will want to talk about things the audience is interested in—probably things you have in common with them. If you want to talk about your hobbies, they should be either very unusual (collecting beer cans) or very outstanding (the best stamp collection in the city). For example, a collector of our acquaintance has pull handles from nearly fifty public toilets in France, which makes that person an unusual collector. Everybody has a name, but you can make a good story out of yours if it has given you trouble (being mistaken for a boy if you're a girl named Bruce, for example). Almost everyone has pets, but a python or an armadillo will make a better speech subject than a dog or cat.

1 Construct the kind of messages you would exchange with a stranger who was helping you change a tire on your car. There are only two of you, and you have never met before.

2 Construct the kind of messages you would exchange with friends after you have seen a movie together. You thought it was great, and your friends thought it was awful.

3 Construct a speech a few minutes in length telling about something you own, have experience with, or can do. Pick a topic that will be familiar to your audience, and thus interesting to them, and develop your own unique report about it.

4 Develop a situation in which you present a very boring kind of message that describes only the most ordinary, drab, or common kinds of experiences or activities. How would an audience react to that?

5 Develop a situation in which you would construct a message that makes it seem that you do everything (swim, read, ski, fight, sing, make things, collect things, etc.) better than someone else does. Imagine the other person has said he comes from a town with the tallest buildings in the state; then tell him about the taller ones in your town.

Ceremonial Messages

Some writers, perhaps justifiably, put these messages in the same category with those meant to entertain. As was mentioned before, the audience listening to a ceremonial speech is under no obligation to do anything better, to take some action, or even to know more, once the message is over. However, ceremonial messages are easily identified, and they occur with such frequency that they deserve special mention.

Ceremonial messages range from the introduction of one friend to another, to the introduction of a visiting speaker at a formal lecture. They range from the honorific statements made about someone who is to receive an award, to the reply that person makes when handed the award, responding to the fine things the previous speaker had said. They range from speeches made at such special ceremonies as inaugurations, commencements, and funerals, to the unplanned and spontaneous acceptance of awards or honors or public notice after winning ball games, elections, door prizes, or beauty contests.

Speeches for ceremonial occasions are very seldom based on logic or argument. They are usually highly emotional and geared to the level of the audience involvement. Polite clapping will greet the speech of the retiring company treasurer who has just received a gold watch. Wild shouting will greet the remarks of the captain of the championship team in describing how they won the trophy. Although the emotion of *pride* is expressed by the audience, it is usually not considered appropriate for the speaker (the person receiving the award or the person's representa-

Ceremonial messages, such as an inspirational eulogy, are highly emotional and geared to audience involvement. *(Charles-Gatewood.)*

tive) to act proud—the tone must be modest and thanks must be offered to all those who had a part in the success.

In speeches of introduction, as a special case of ceremonial speeches, the important thing is to impress the audience with the appropriateness of this particular speaker for the situation. Like speeches of praise for honorees, these can be more flowery and flattering than most other speech forms can be.

Inspirational speeches fall in the ceremonial-message category. They are usually given at special occasions or for special audiences that enjoy the emotional uplift that a sermon, a eulogy, or a farewell can give them.

CEREMONY: APPLICATIONS

SAMPLE INTRODUCTIONS

Dr. Karl J. Pelzer, Chairman of the Council of Southeast Asia Studies at Yale University and Chairman of the Department of Geography at that institution, is an Asian scholar of world renown as well as a pioneer in Asian Studies programs in America. He has taught at the University of California at Berkeley, at Johns Hopkins University, and at Yale University. His tenure at Yale extended over a period of thirty years.

Dr. Pelzer has served various agencies of our government as a Southeast Asian specialist. His research interests in agriculture and pioneer settlement have taken him to many of the Southeast Asian countries for extended periods. He plans to spend 1977 in Malaysia, Indonesia, and the Philippines.

Holder of the Ph.D. from the University of Bonn, Dr. Pelzer migrated from his native Germany to the United States in 1935 to begin his teaching career at the University of California at Berkeley. In 1940 he became a naturalized citizen of the United States. Shortly after beginning his teaching at Berkeley, he married Elizabeth Allerton Clark of that city. The Pelzers have two daughters.

Professor Pelzer is the author of more than thirty-five publications, including books, journal articles, papers, and chapters of other works, and sixty reviews and review articles. His library of over 10,000 volumes, acquired from around the world, represents one of the finest collections of Asian materials assembled by a private individual in America.

The keynote speaker of this year's Distinguished Lecturer Series is Dr. Jerome Kagan, prominent educator, psychologist, and author. Since 1964 he has been Professor of Human Development at Harvard University. Dr. Kagan's primary research and professional interest have been in the field of cognitive and personality development during the first decade, and he has been awarded the Hofheimer Prize for Research from the American Psychiatric Association. He is a Fellow of the American Academy of Arts and Sciences and a member of the American Psychological Association and the Society for Research in Child Development.

Dr. Kagan's professional expertise is widely recognized, as evidenced by his positions as Consultant for the Department of Pediatrics, Massachusetts General Hospital; Editorial Consultant for *Child Development*, the *Journal of Experimental Child Psychology*, and several other journals; Consulting Editor for Harcourt, Brace, & World, Inc.; and member of the Panel on Educational Research of the President's Science Advisory Committee. He has also served on the Committee on Learning and the Educational Process of the Social Science Research Council.

Dr. Kagan has authored and coauthored numerous books and professional articles, among which are *Birth to Maturity* and *Change and Continuity in Infancy*, both published by John Wiley; *Child Development and Personality*, published by Harper & Row; and *Understanding Children*, published by Harcourt Brace Jovanovich. Most recently he has co-authored for Harper & Row Media *The Development of the Child Film Series*.

CONSTRUCTING YOUR OWN INTRODUCTION

You are going to introduce the speaker at a meeting. You want him to begin his own communication with the best possible relation with his audience, and you want to find the most appropriate things to say about him for the occasion and setting of the meeting. Are there some items you will emphasize and some you will leave out? His "resume" is as follows:

John Doe was born in 1923 in Clark, South Dakota. He attended the Plankinton Community College, South Dakota State College, the University of Oregon, the University of Iowa, and Denver University. He served in World War II in the South Pacific theater, where he earned a variety of citations for his administrative work with an Air Corps communications outfit. He was stationed on the islands of New Caledonia, Guadalcanal, and Oahu, and he rose to the rank of sergeant major. He has studied plant pathology, sociology, and museum science (at the University of Iowa, where he earned his bachelor's degree), and he earned both his master's and doctorate (Ph.D.) in psychology at Denver. He was also a teaching assistant at Denver. His dissertation was entitled "A Measure of Training Inhibition Related to Diet when Correlated with Appetite Variations in Nonhungry Rats." It was never published. He has lectured civic and industrial groups on the subjects of group discussion and decision making and has been consultant to various government agencies for the purpose of studying the fluctuations in employment stability. He is a practicing industrial and consulting psychologist. His office is in the Milam Building, Rooms 204-5-6. His home is in the Westward Park apartment complex, Apartment 6-B. His office phone is area code 618 442-4433. He has a wife and three children in college. His daughter Susan is a senior at Swarthmore, majoring in Far Eastern Studies. One son, Jeffrey, is a junior at Memphis State majoring in physical education and is a member of the outstanding basketball team. Another son, Samuel, is a freshman at the Milam Junior College and plans to major in medical technology. Samuel lives at home and drives a VW to school. The family also has a Mercedes 240 SL, which they like to drive with the top down when the weather permits, and a Vega station wagon. They belong to the Rolling Hills Country Club and the Milam Tennis Association. They have a membership in the University Club for eating and entertaining. All the family plays tennis, and son Jeffrey was all-city champion for two years before he went away to college. Among the speaker's other hobbies are photography, hunting, skiing, and sailing. His sailboat is a 470 class, and he keeps it at the Milam Lake Yacht Club, where he is also a member, and has won trophies for three years in the open-class regatta. He skis in Colorado every winter and has a condominium at Aspen, which the family occupies during the Christmas season. He also goes to Aspen in the summer for the music festival and a meeting of psychologists, so that he keeps his expenses related to business. He has had photographs published in the local newspaper and in several photography magazines. His camera equipment consists of a complete Hasselblad system with wide-angle, normal, and telephoto lenses; a 35-mm single-lens reflex Pentax, which also has a wide-angle and telephoto zoom; and a pre-Anniversary 4×5 Graphic View with a 6-inch lens. He has written a book entitled *The Stable Employee* and has published numerous articles in professional journals, including "Measurement System for Civil Service Turnover" in the *Management Journal* last January; this summer that same journal will carry his article entitled "Why

Are Shrinks Expanding in Industry?" In addition to those articles, he has published a research report in the *Journal of Psychology of Corporate Personnel* entitled "Eating Habits of Experimental Animals under Conditions of Stress" and another entitled "Obesity Related to Nervous Disorders." He has helped devise a system for assigning employees to their most effective places in assembly-line operations. He has been on a panel of experts to advise the governor on labor legislation and has served on the board of the state association for the study of the mentally retarded. He has been active in local and county groups working for promotion of health clubs as an alternative to drug use and overweight. He has also been a member of a commission to promote the humanistic studies of production personnel in industrial plants. He is listed in *Who's Who* and in *Directory of American Scholars*. His parents (now deceased) were of Midwestern origin. His father was a Pennsylvania Dutchman who emigrated from Pennsylvania to Iowa in the 1880s and later became a cowhand and moved to South Dakota. His mother's parents came from Trondheim, Norway, and settled in South Dakota, where the family had a tailoring business and a small farm. He has a brother and a sister, who each have four children and still live in South Dakota. His political leanings have been more Republican than Democrat, although over the years he has considered himself an independent and has so registered before every election. He grew up in the Lutheran faith and later joined a Presbyterian church in Milam while his children were small. He is a member of the synodical governing group of the local church and attends regularly. Among the kinds of employment he had had in his lifetime, he lists clerking in a J. C. Penney Store, operating a popcorn stand and working as a janitor in a movie theater, working as a free-lance photographer and studio assistant in a portrait studio, being a museum attendant and assistant to the curator of a natural history museum, assisting in the relocation of Sioux Indians in federal housing projects, and working as a psychologist with the Colorado state association for mental health and as assistant psychologist at the Canon City penitentiary. He later went into private practice.

1 Introduce John Doe to your club—a campus club or a social organization—when his topic will be "Handling Your Emotions in Conflict Situations."
2 Introduce John Doe to a class in physical education where he is going to be the guest lecturer on the subject of "Athletics versus the Drug Scene."
3 Introduce John Doe to the parents organization for the local school district when he will talk on the subject of "The Responsibility of Being a Parent."
4 Introduce John Doe to the faculty of the local college when he will be speaking on the general subject of psychological consulting.
5 Introduce John Doe for a speaking assignment at an organizational meeting of a minority group attempting to get a community center started in a storefront building.
6 Make up a situation in which you would introduce John Doe and make use

of some of his biographical material that was not significant to *any of the above* groups.

7   In every case, imagine you are a member of the audience and do not know John Doe. Do the things that are said about him make you want to listen to him? Have confidence in what he will say? Give an evaluation of the items that were selected by the introducer in each case. Did they make the introduction too long and dull? Too brief and sketchy? Did they present the speaker in an interesting way?

☐ IN GENERAL

Whatever subject you choose to speak about will be intended to benefit an audience in some way, whether you hope to make them feel good, to know more, or to behave differently. That audience may be as informal as one friend sitting beside you drinking coffee, or it may be as formal as a political caucus to select candidates for election to some office. At once you can see the relationships between the audience, the setting, and the occasion. At the same instant you should grasp the significance of the *message* to that audience, that setting, and that occasion. Whatever your reason for speaking, you will adjust your message to fit.

At some time during your life you can probably expect to be asked to introduce someone or give some kind of ceremonial speech. You will also be faced with persuading others, with informing others, and often with entertaining or amusing others. How you go about making those messages effective will be the subject of the next two chapters. You will have to organize your message into some kind of intelligible structure (Chapter 7) so that you can make sense out of what you want to say and so that your audience can make sense out of what they hear. You will also have to be conscious of your own use of supporting materials and persuasive and informative devices (Chapter 8).

A point that we cannot stress enough is that while you are thinking about the messages you are using, you must also be aware that others are sending messages to you. Our aim is not only to help you construct better messages but also to help you make more sense out of the messages which come to you from others.

TYPES OF MESSAGES: APPLICATIONS

CHECKLIST OF MESSAGE FREQUENCY

Think back over the past few weeks. How many times have you either *communicated* or been *spoken to* with messages of any of the four types listed below? In the blanks put check marks indicating the frequency of your either sending or receiving these kinds of messages.

	Sent by me			Received by me		
Kind of Message	Never	Seldom	Often	Never	Seldom	Often
Ceremonial						
Informational						
Persuasive						
Entertaining						

PERSONAL PREFERENCES OF MESSAGE TYPES

Which kinds of messages are you most interested in sending or receiving? When you have listed your preferences, compare your list with those of others. What conclusions can you draw from the similarities and differences you come up with? (Write these in the appropriate spaces provided: ceremonial, informational, persuasive, entertaining.)

These are the kinds of messages I would prefer to *send to others*:

1.
2.
3.
4.

These are the kinds of messages I would prefer to *receive from others*:

1.
2.
3.
4.

◼ LOOKING BACK

I. You will always be speaking about something.
   A. You don't just speak "speech."
   B. Look at your own listening habits to get ideas of what others enjoy.

II. Subjects should be selected with an understanding of the factors that make up a speaking situation.
   A. Choose a subject that interests you.
   B. Choose a subject that fits the situation.
   C. Choose a subject you can cover clearly in the time you have.
   D. Choose a subject that will do the job for you. It should answer the question: "What do I want the audience to do as a result of this message?"

III. You always will have a reason for speaking.
   A. Messages are not random.
   B. There may be more than one purpose for a speech.

C. There may be more than one result of a speech, even if the speaker did not intend it.
IV. Although different authors use different names and categories for the various speech purposes (message types), we shall divide them into four categories:
   A. Ceremonial messages, which occur on special occasions and are more likely to be emotional than logical. As in the case of entertaining messages, do not expect the audience to know more or act better as a result, although ceremonial messages may be highly inspirational and give the audience an emotional lift.
   B. Messages of information, which are intended to either instruct or inform an audience so that it will know more or do something better when the speech is over.
   C. Messages to persuade, which are designed to convince an audience or move them to act.
      1. Convincing may consist simply in reinforcing an audience attitude or in making a present belief even stronger.
      2. Convincing may involve changing a belief or attitude.
      3. The actions the audience takes as a result of your message may be covert or quietly carried out, or they may be overt and open.
   D. Messages to entertain, which do not necessarily have to elicit a lot of laughter.
      1. They can provide a diverting time for the audience.
      2. The audience is not expected to know more or act differently after the speech is over.

CHAPTER 7
ORGANIZING YOUR SPEECH

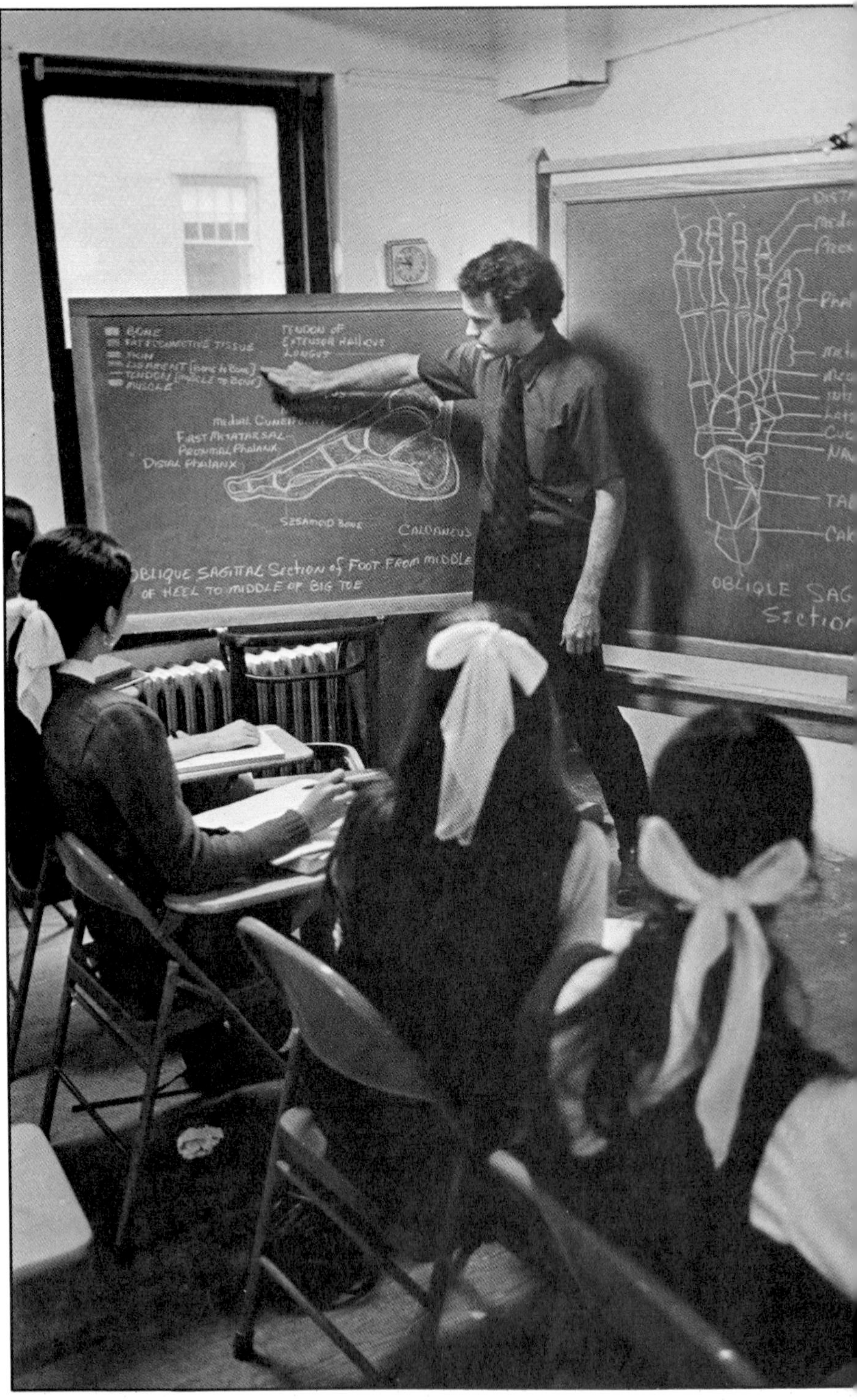

(Charles Gatewood.)

CHAPTER 7
ORGANIZING YOUR SPEECH

The dissenting opinions of one generation become the prevailing interpretation of the next.

— Burton J. Hendrick

It took me forty years on earth
To reach this sure conclusion:
There is no Heaven but clarity,
No Hell except confusion.

— Jan Struther

I have observed with wonder so many intellectual and literary fashions that I have come at last to rely positively on one conviction alone. No idea is so antiquated that it was not once modern. No idea is so modern that it will not some day be antiquated. . . . To seize the flying thought before it escapes us is our only touch with reality.

— Ellen Glasgow

☐ HOW THE PARTS OF A MESSAGE GO TOGETHER

The Structure of a Speech

This chapter sets up the steps to take in organizing the speech and getting it ready for delivery, including the difficult parts of a speech and how they fit together.

A well-organized structure will benefit you in your preparation and delivery and will help your audience follow what you are doing. Out of the chaos that is our communication world, we try to create order by simplifying the complexities of living. Organization and order are means to simplification. By putting things (like the parts of your speech messages) together with a well-defined pattern so that you can follow it and your listeners can too, you can make some very complex ideas quite simple. In fact, one of the qualities of a good message is the conversion of ideas which may be disorganized, complicated, or fuzzy into organized, simple, and clear concepts.

Organizing the speech, studying the structure, and going through the steps involved are not just classroom exercises. There's a very real communication advantage to learning these steps and working on speech organization. Learning how to set up a speech structure will improve your communication effectiveness at three places in the communication sequence: (1) when you are getting ready to give your message, (2) when you are actually delivering it, and (3) when you are getting results from your audience at the end of it.

Getting Started

If you are assigned a speech topic, you proceed from that general topic to get the message ready. On the other hand, you may be given an assignment to "speak to the Chi Delt dinner." In that case you have to start with the question of what to talk about. Both of these situations involve looking at your audience. (See Chapter 6.)

> What do you want to have happen to them as a result of your speech?
>
> What interests do they have? What things can't you talk about to them? (The taboos or "sacred cows").
>
> How much do they know about things you might want to talk about?
>
> What are they concerned about? What worries them?
>
> What do they think is worth talking about or listening to?
>
> How big will the group be?
>
> What do they do for a living?
>
> Are they men only? Women only? Mixed?
>
> Are they a closely knit club or a loose collection of people

without a specific purpose in being together except to hear this speech?

To get answers to these questions, you may talk to someone who knows the group, you may investigate the group yourself by means of some kind of questionnaire or scale, you may get a small group of friends together and check out what you all know about this audience, or you may rely on the advice of the person who has arranged for you to talk.

When the program chairperson for the Campus Forum approaches you and asks you to speak at their next meeting, you are likely to ask, "What about?"

You may get the following answers: "Well, it is our spiritual-revival meeting, and we want a talk on religion." "You are opposing the new library hours, and we would like to hear your arguments." "Anything you want to talk about. We need a freshman to give this next lecture."

By now you know that there is no single way to start speech preparation. Selection of your subject and analysis of the factors involved in your speaking are so intermingled that you would have trouble sifting them out. Procedures most often recommended include going through these steps to narrow your focus and to get under way.

SET THE GENERAL PURPOSE

If you were to ask: "What do I want to have happen to the audience?" the *answer* you would give is the *general purpose*. The general purpose is stated in the infinitive form (using the word "to"): I want my speech *to inspire*; I want this talk *to persuade*; I want my speech *to inform*; I want this speech *to entertain*; I want this speech *to honor* (someone or something); I want this talk *to convince*; I want this message *to instruct*.

FIND YOUR GENERAL SUBJECT

Your general subject is the major category of what you are going to talk about, chosen after analyzing your own abilities, the audience, the setting, the occasion, and your speech purpose. It should be stated very simply. General subjects would include education, politics, religion, atomic energy, war, transportation, hobbies, heroes, and motion pictures. If the general purpose answers the question, "What do I want to happen to the audience?" the general subject answers the question, "What am I talking about?"

MAKE YOUR SUBJECT SPECIFIC

You know you cannot cover—in the time you have and with the resources you can pull together—a subject as large as education or politics. Your job here is to get a manageable subject out of the general

To get started set a general purpose, find a general subject, then make both specific. *(Maurie Rosen/Black Star.)*

subject in terms of what you can find out about it and can tell about it, and what the audience will hold still for. Education as a general subject can produce such specific subjects as improved reading skills of children, spending for higher education in America, or high school dropouts. Politics as a general subject can be narrowed to working for a candidate, getting out the vote, or corruption and honesty in local government.

PULL OUT THE SPECIFIC PURPOSE

At this point you need to identify the specific purpose (based on your general purpose) and relate it to your specific subject. For instance, if you originally intended to inform an audience and have picked education as your general subject and college dropouts as your specific subject, then your specific purpose might be to inform the members of the County Teachers Association of the trends in college attendance during the past few years.

For the specific purpose you must add to the general purpose the answers to questions like: "About what?" "Who?" "How?" and "Under what conditions?" It is stated in the infinitive form, as is the general purpose.

SUMMARY

Before you begin to develop the speech itself, you must settle on a speech subject that is specific enough to do the job for you. That means you need to get a general subject to fit your general purpose and then develop your specific subject and be able to announce your specific purpose.

In an example the progression looks like this:

General purpose: to inform
General subject: education

Specific subject: reading in the elementary grades
Specific purpose: to give information on methods of teaching reading to parents of kindergarten children in the local PTA

General purpose: to persuade
General subject: voting

Specific subject: getting out the vote
Specific purpose: to encourage all registered voters to exercise their franchise on election day

General purpose: to entertain
General subject: pets

Specific subject: the crazy things some pets do
Specific purpose: to amuse the audience with stories of animal activities

Write the Topic Sentence

This is the core sentence, the basic idea, the central idea, the subject sentence, the basic proposition, the thesis, the central theme, or the core concept. The topic sentence you construct should be a statement of the unifying idea. The specific purpose tells what you want to happen to the audience, and the topic sentence tells what the speech is about. It must be stated positively. It must be simple, concise, and complete and must contain only a single idea. It gives a very specific answer to the question: "What are you talking about?"

Here are some sample topic sentences based on the subjects that are stated with them. Reading them will give you an idea of how to construct topic sentences of your own.

General purpose: to inform

Specific purpose: to give information to the parents of the kindergarten in the local PTA about the reading programs

Sample topic sentence: "The best educational results are obtained by a combination of phonetic and visual approaches to reading."

General purpose: to persuade

Specific purpose: to get members of the local party caucus to give money or time to help with the campaign
Sample topic sentence: "Each of us has an obligation to support our candidates for political office by giving money or doing work."

General purpose: to honor

Specific purpose: to pay tribute to the coaching staff of a championship team
Sample topic sentence: "No one has worked harder to achieve a winning season than the coach and the coach's staff."

ORGANIZING A SPEECH: APPLICATIONS

GETTING THE MESSAGE TOGETHER

The scene is a department meeting in a banking institution. After the usual agenda items were taken care of, the marketing officer, Don, began a discussion of the features of the bank's new computer services.

Don: Let's try to name some of the features of the computer services. (Silence)
Don: (trying again) Come on, now, we wouldn't offer this service if it didn't have any features. Name one, Louise.
Louise: Well—there's—well, I guess the saving of time is a feature.
Don: Good. Now let's name some more.
Carl: I suppose accuracy is one.

And the group proceeded to name confidential processing, convenience, timely reports, completeness, alphabetical listing, complete service descriptions, etc.

Don: All right. Now let's translate these features into benefits.
Carl: What do you mean by that?
Don: Features have to be translated into benefits because it is benefits that appeal to people. Always speak in terms of benefits to the customer—not features—because people don't give a damn about features. They want to know how it will benefit them.
Sandra: Sure, don't you see, Carl, we have to talk in terms of benefits so the customer can better understand what our service will do for him.

Carl: I still don't see the difference. It seems to me that a feature can do the same thing as a benefit.

Sandra (leaning forward): No. Features are what our service provides, and benefits are what the customer receives. Does that seem clear enough?

Louise: I can see the distinction you are trying to make, but it seems to me that these two things are interrelated and can't be listed separately.

Don: Yes, they are closely related, but I think we can distinguish between them.

Carl: I don't see what good this is doing. We all know what we're talking about, and it is impractical to go on listing benefits and features if they are the same thing.

Sandra: But, Carl, they're not the same thing.

Don: Hold on, Sandra. It's getting late. Why don't we think about this and consider it again next week.

1 Essentially, this group was constructing a message for the customers of a bank. The things they were doing were not too much different from what you would do in getting together a speech. What were they planning to achieve with their message? Did they all understand what they were trying to achieve?

2 Get some class members to pick up this conversation the next time this group gets together. Review what went on before. See whether the persons who did not understand the previous time are still confused. How do you try to explain? Role-play or have a group discussion about this group as it tries to develop the message.

3 Suppose the group had decided at the end of this first session to turn the job of writing the message over to *one member*. Role-play your group (or have a discussion) as if it had decided to assign the preparation of the message to one person. How do you proceed to select that person?

4 If you were the person selected to get the message together, how would you proceed from there? Would you get more data? From whom? How would you construct the message if you planned to speak to the gathering of the bank's clients at their annual meeting? What kinds of things would you want to include in your message?

WRITING A TOPIC SENTENCE

In the following examples there is a chance to practice writing topic sentences. Given this basic information, what would a sample topic sentence be like?

General purpose: to entertain

General subject: sports
Specific subject: humorous spectator behaviors

Specific purpose: show how crazily some spectators behave at sports events
Sample topic sentence: _____

General purpose: to persuade
General subject: mental health

Specific subject: treatment of mental patients as outpatients
Specific purpose: improve attitudes about mental patients
Sample topic sentence: _____

General purpose: to persuade
General subject: education

Specific subject: value of a high school diploma
Specific purpose: convince students not to drop out of high school
Sample topic sentence: _____

General purpose: to inform
General subject: laser beams

Specific subject: use of lasers in light transmission
Specific purpose: acquaint others with potential for laser networks
Sample topic sentence: _____

☐ GATHERING MATERIAL

When you have decided on the subject, you must begin to draw together the raw materials that will give your argument strength and also limit the extent of your message. Investigation may turn up less information on the subject than you had hoped to find, and in that case you will make adjustments in your speech plan.

The range of investigation is wide. You may sit and think about a subject and pull together your own thoughts or feelings (for example, an impromptu response to a speech honoring you for a surprise award), or you may do very serious research in libraries or in original laboratory situations. You may simply skim a magazine article for ideas for an entertaining speech, or you may dig deeply into many serious documents for an informational speech. You may go back through hundreds of pages of naturalist journals to prepare an entertaining speech on desert wildlife, or you may interview many fellow students or leading citizens for a persuasive speech on air-pollution control.

Whether you are talking about things you know from personal experience or things you know from having consulted other sources, you can report only on what you know and remember. Unless you have developed some form of acquiring information in an organized way, you

Unless you acquire information in an organized way, you will not be ready to pass it along to others. *(Hugh Rogers/Monkmeyer.)*

will not be ready to pass it along to others. Just sitting and letting all the sights and sounds of your world wash over you like waves will not prepare you for communicating with others. You must be conscious of how you received the impressions and information you have. This will enable you to make better use of your abilities to collect information. If you have trouble remembering, you should develop the habit of taking notes, of making outlines, of setting up card files, or of otherwise writing down things your own memory cannot store perfectly for you.

Where to Get It

No speaker ever became famous from rushing into a library, skimming through some material on the shelves, and dashing off a speech. For good public speaking, as well as for good communication on an informal basis, the more you know, the more interesting you will be to others. Your whole life has been a preparation for any speech encounter you have—whatever you know now will be part of your communication with others. Your intellectual and emotional background will be part of your delivery as well as part of the content of your speaking. You are already a speaker. You can be a more effective one if you continue to learn about what is happening in your world from whatever sources you choose, depending on the audiences you will face. Here are some ways you can get information, either for your own casual conversation with others or for use in a more formal speaking situation.

FROM YOURSELF

Everything that has happened to you in your lifetime has become a part of you. You are the sum of your own history. You are unique. There is no one else exactly like you in what you know, think, feel, and have experienced. You are the product of all you have read, heard, and been told about, as well as what has actually happened to you. All this put together gives you a considerable wealth of material to talk about and resources to draw on to substantiate your points. When you use yourself as a source of information, be aware that you have a tendency to look very personally at the things you "know" from your own experience. You may distort your information if you rely only on your own perceptions, without checking some outside sources. (Remember the maps and territories in Chapter 3.)

FROM PERSONAL EXPERIENCE

You have had firsthand experiences that you could develop into a speech, such as answering the telephone at the local crisis center. A meeting of the City Council becomes more alive to you if you have an opportunity to participate in city government by giving testimony on some issue. Visiting ghetto schools will give you better data than you can acquire by reading about them. Spending some time in a public housing project will give you insights into what it's like to live there. Working as a volunteer in the Salvation Army, the Red Cross, or one of the hundreds of other social service agencies that exist even in relatively small communities will provide you with personal experiences that you can incorporate into your speech. These experiences, gained specifically because you want to talk to others about them, will increase your communication effectiveness. Since you know more deeply about a firsthand experience, you will have a greater variety of more interesting and vital things to say, and you will be better believed than if you were only a casual observer.

FROM RESEARCH

Informal kinds of "research" provide good resource material for speaking. You might decide to try a new recipe, test the braking power of a car, or measure the contents of some canned goods to see whether the weight is as stated on the label. Contrast these with the very formal and highly rigorous experimentation of a chemist or physicist. Very formal research is reported primarily to other professionals in journals, symposia, professional meetings, etc. You could try conducting simple experiments of your own to obtain data to talk about. However, don't make too strong a claim for your data if you have not carefully designed and controlled your research. Advantages of even very elementary

Everything that has happened to you in your lifetime has become a part of you and provides a wealth of material to talk about. *(James R. Smith.)*

research are that you learn more about the subject, you think about it more deeply, you are more inclined to organize it well, and thus you benefit yourself as well as your audience.

FROM COURSES OF STUDY

One way to get speech information is from the classes you are enrolled in or have taken. If you are taking a course in education and learn something interesting about teaching reading, you could share it with your friends as well as with an audience of parents at a local school. If you are taking a course in biology and have become proficient in preparing specimens for the electron microscope, this can become the subject for a technical talk for a class assignment or even an entertaining one—about what can go wrong or the mistakes beginners make. Information you acquire as you are taking a course is always available to you, but you can often present it best to an audience when you are still enthusiastic about the material.

FROM OTHERS

You can acquire information from others in person, by writing letters, or by telephoning. If you want to know when the library is open, you get that information by reading the sign on the door, by asking someone who would know, or by telephoning and asking the librarian. If you want to know what the Ajax Tool Company is doing about air pollution, you can write to their home office and ask them to send you a list of their antipollution projects, or you can arrange an interview with someone in their environmental-control department and ask your questions in person.

It makes sense to ask other people when they know more about a subject than you do, when they have an opinion you want to quote or have experienced something you would like to talk about, or when they are in a position to direct your information seeking.

There are some courtesies to observe during an interview that will help elicit better replies. You are the one asking the favor, and you should remember that in your approach. If you plan to interview someone seeking information or opinions you should review the list on page 219.

FROM MASS MEDIA

This source of information offers two great advantages to the speaker. First, the material is usually presented in an interesting way, thus giving some indication about how the speaker may adapt it. Second, the general population is already "tuned in," both actually and psychologically, to radio, television, movies, and popular magazines. You can gear your speech to your audience if you can base it on something you learned through the media, since the fact that it appeared there means that it must be of interest to a fairly substantial audience. For ideas, topics, information, critical analyses, and reports the mass media provide good, basic data. Newspaper editorials give you attitudes and opinions, while the news columns are more likely to contain more factual data. How often do you talk with your friends about a TV program you saw?

FROM THE LIBRARY

You will probably consult only a small amount of the printed material available. Libraries, fortunately, have very efficient means of cataloging and organizing the data they store. They also have a large number of books dealing specifically with sources of information. The *Reader's Guide to Periodical Literature*, for example, is devoted exclusively to reporting what is published in magazines and journals. *Books in Print* tells you the titles, authors, and topics of all books currently in print and available. Specialized indexes and compilations are only part of what an outstanding library will offer. Card-catalog listings by subject, by author, and by title will help you find the books you want. In addition, libraries have listings of general magazines, special magazines, professional journals, and atlases; biographical listings; lists of quotations; lists of audiovisual aids; and guides to materials available in different types of libraries.

The library is an important source for materials to support, clarify, and reinforce your message. *(Arnold Hinton/Nancy Palmer Photo Agency.)*

GATHERING MATERIAL: APPLICATIONS

WHERE DO YOU GO FOR THE INFORMATION?
Think of topics that would normally be associated with each of the following sources of information about a speaking message. In other words, what subjects for communication would you usually research in each of these following resource areas?

From personal experience (for example, a visit to the Head Start program on the West Side)

_____

_____

From your own reserach (for example, growing a garden in a window box)

_____

_____

From courses of study (for example, the ancient Greeks as public speakers)

_____

_____

From others (for example, antipollution practices of the Ajax Tool Company)

_____

_____

From mass media (for example, newspaper attitudes about price controls)

_____

_____

From the library (for example, a report on recent research in transactional analysis)

_____

_____

_____

OBSERVATIONAL DATA AND INFERENTIAL DATA

Where and how do you obtain the knowledge you have of the world around you? How do you collect your own personal data? How do you make sure they are good data?

To tell the difference between observation and inference, it might be useful to look at two different kinds of measures—a yardstick and an IQ test.

A yardstick measures inches, a standard distance already established and agreed upon. At one time the basic measures were the knuckle of a hand, the distance around a wrist, how far a man could step, or the length of a foot. These were all difficult to standardize because not all people are exactly the same size. Now standard weights and measures have been established; you can expect the measurements you make with a yardstick to be duplicated by other persons under different situations and at other times.

An IQ test measures a person's responses to a series of questions. The selection of what to test for (recognition of words, recognition of shapes, memory ability) is difficult. In addition, answering the questions (unlike reading the simple sequence of numbers on a yardstick) depends on the ability to read and to respond to symbolically phrased questions. There is also the rather questionable application of this type of test to the measurement of things (such as "intelligence") that may be called something else ("learning ability," "academic potential," etc.).

1   In trying to determine how the symbolic world works for us, we need to discover which of our instruments or devices are really capable of producing objective data and which are capable of producing only inferences. In a group discussion, you should draw up some comparisons like the one above (comparing a yardstick with an IQ test) based on the kinds of data that will be produced. (An example to start you out: While rowing a boat, you may "feel" that both your arms are pulling with the same force, and if you judge where you are going on the basis of this feeling, you may end up far away from your mark unless you turn around and look. That way you are using direct observation to check on the things your muscles tell you are happening. As another example, think of things that are sold by the pound, yard, quart, etc., and things that are sold on the basis of how they look, without any objective measurements or weights to use as a guide.)

2   Have several groups come up with kinds of measurements that will produce observational, or objective, data and with measurements that will produce inferential data.

HOW TO INTERVIEW

1   Tell specifically who you are; give your name clearly.

2   Tell who or what you represent (a school, newspaper, or department, for example).

3   Explain what you would like to find out. Try to have a list of questions written out. Some people want to see such a list before giving an interview.

4   Explain honestly what you intend to do with the information (use it in a speech to the chamber of commerce, write a report for class, etc.).

5   Follow the interviewee's suggested method of crediting the source of

information ("a reliable source," "an official of the company," the person's name and office, etc.).

6   Estimate how long it will take to conduct the interview. Most people who are important enough to be asked for opinions or information are busy, and they will appreciate knowing how long you will take. Don't overstay your appointment.

7   If the interviewee is interested, tell which other people you have talked to or intend to talk to.

8   Ask questions that require definite, specific answers. It helps to have them written out before the interview, even if the interviewee has not asked to see them in advance, because having them in writing will help you keep on the subject and stay within your time limit.

9   Do not ask embarrassing questions unless that is the specific reason for your interview. In that case you may expect either nonanswers or hostile replies.

10 Let the interviewee answer the questions—do not lead or suggest answers that you would like to hear, and do not project your own opinions on what you hear. Beginning interviewers often ask questions in which the answer is implied, or they ask a question and assume they know what the answer will be before the other person has a chance to reply. Be alert to the answers the other person gives—both verbally and nonverbally— and do not make up your mind in advance as to what those answers will be.

☐ HOW TO COLLECT MATERIAL

Any material you are collecting will be used to support, to clarify, and to reinforce your message and to make it more informative, more believable, more persuasive, and more enjoyable to your audience. It will be useful to you only if you can remember what you collected and will have authenticity to your audience only if you remember where you found it. Vague statements like "I read somewhere recently . . ." are not nearly as acceptable to an audience as specific references, such as *"Time* magazine reported in its July 15 issue . . ." or "According to Dr. Paul Campbell, the expert in space medicine, in his book *Man in Space . . .*"

What to Collect

As you are developing the support material for your speech, you will have to decide what to collect and what to forget about. Only those things which you are quite sure you are going to use in your speech and which are directly related to your central idea should be collected. You can overcollect; you can get so bogged down in collecting material that

Interviewing others whose opinions may shape your message is a useful way of acquiring information. *(Charles Gatewood.)*

you will not be able to sift it out when you put your speech together. However, don't use that as an excuse to come up with only one or two references. Make sure you are really seriously looking for material and not just wandering through back issues of *National Geographic* or *Readers Digest.*

Some items you may want to collect are descriptions, definitions, examples, quotations, statistics, anecdotes and stories, comparisons, contrasts, visual aids, fables, new uses of words, events of historical significance, testimony, legal judgments, and poetic or particularly catchy phrases.

What you collect must relate to the topic you are speaking about and, equally important, must relate to the audience.

Writing It Down

Keeping your notes clear, concise, well organized, and accurate will be of great value to you when you put the speech together. Nothing is more frustrating than finding a quotation among your notes and being unable to locate the source. In those cases you must either go back and do the research over again or resort to the weak and hackneyed, "As one writer has said," which neither convinces nor impresses an audience. To avoid the difficulties of partial information, you should (1) write down the accurate quotation and (2) carefully note the source, including the person who made the statement or wrote the article; the place in which it appears; and the date of publication and other appropriate bibliographical data.

Book Reference: INTERNAL COMMUNICATION

"If one human lived alone, without contact with other people, the chief concerns of this person would be internal."
G. E. Myers and Michele Tolela Myers, *Dynamics of Human Communication*, 2d. ed., McGraw-Hill, New York, 1976, p. 95.

Magazine Reference: LIVING TOGETHER

"If all the people in the world who are lonely were to walk into the streets at the same time, the houses and apartments of this entire nation would be emptied in a matter of minutes."
E. A. Billings, "The Lonely People in Our Society," *The Midwest Religious Review*, vol. 13, no. 4, p. 77, Oct. 10, 1972.

Interview Reference: SENTENCING PUSHERS

Judge Smith has made a practice of giving the greatest sentences permitted ("maximum penalties under law") to any drug pushers who have come to him after conviction for sentencing. He does so because he believes they should be "kept away from uninfected youth as long as is legally possible." (Direct quotation checked for accuracy.)
Personal interview with Judge J. G. Smith in his chambers in Superior Court Building, April 15, 1973.

Correspondence Reference: POLLUTION CONTROL IN STEELWORKS

Even though "millions have been spent by most major and all the minor steel companies," there has been little success in completely eliminating the problem of fly ash in the communities surrounding the plants. This is primarily because "mechanical means of capturing the fly ash have not worked out in practice as well as in theory," and the ash bags continue to be "only about 60 percent effective."
Personal correspondence with Hiram Smith, Coordinator of Waste Control Programs, Alloy Steel Co., East Alton, Illinois. Letter dated August 7, 1973.

If you follow these forms to collect data, you will be in an excellent position to support the accuracy of your quotations in your oral presentation, in a written report, or in a digest of your speech for a printed assignment.

WRITING IT DOWN: APPLICATION

HOW TO KEEP GOOD NOTES
1   Be neat and orderly. Pick a style for recording your notes and stick to it.
2   Use cards (like 3- by 5-inch file cards) or slips of paper all the same size. This will make it easier to keep them in order and will be helpful when you want to rearrange your materials.

3 Put only one piece of material on a card. Resist the temptation to put several quotations or statistics on one card just to save space.

4 Use headings on the cards so that you can locate the substance of the material without having to read the whole selection.

5 Make sure you copy the quotation exactly as it is written if you intend to use it verbatim.

6 For long quotations or examples that you intend to refer to but not quote in their entirety, make an accurate summary, an outline, or a list of items you have picked from that longer resource material.

7 If you summarize or paraphrase the original material, be sure you indicate that on your card so that you won't present it as a direct quotation later.

8 Make sure you have included all the bibliographical material you would need to direct a doubting listener to the source.

Read Widely on the Subject

If you devote all your time to one side of an issue, you may miss an important point that your opposition could use against you. Thus, especially when planning a persuasive or informative speech on a controversial issue, you need to read up on both sides of the argument. This will prevent you from being inadequately informed about your subject and from delivering seriously biased, distorted, or prejudiced information. Your audience may have more information about your subject than you do if you limit your investigation to only one side, and you may appear naive, uninformed, or even stupid to them. You need to know what others are saying about your topic in order to muster up an intelligent persuasive or informational speech. You do not have to present the opposing position on a subject, but you should at least know when you begin to argue or instruct, what your opponents know or what your audience may have in mind.

☐ ORGANIZE IT—AGAIN!

The first time you began to organize your speech, it was to determine your purpose and to begin gathering material and putting it together. Now you will begin to develop (1) the normal parts of a speech, which—quite logically—are called the *introduction*, the *body*, and the *conclusion*; (2) the outline of the speech and the kinds of items you will be covering in your presentation as you have sifted through your material; and (3) the kinds of proofs, stylistic devices, arguments, strategies, and appeals you will use in the final delivery.

In this section we shall take a preliminary look at the parts of the speech and give you some advice about outlining. The next chapter is devoted to the act of putting the speech together and to the strategies which you will use and which will be used on you.

The Body Comes First

It may sound strange to work on the middle part before you work on the beginning, but it is often best to do it this way. Once you have collected some material to work from, begin to figure out which main points you will include in the speech.

Write out your main points. These are derived from your central idea and will be the major headings of an outline you may do later. These are the most important things you want to say to the audience—the general statements of what you want to prove to them or tell them. They should all be of the same order of importance (and will be preceded by Roman numerals—see the outline below), and they should not overlap or duplicate each other. When you write them (and when you are saying them), they should be brief, vivid, clear, important to your message, and sure to capture the interest of your audience.

ORGANIZE THE SUBPOINTS

These are preceded by capital letters with subnumerals under them. These are the materials you have collected and organized to support the main points. They give strength to your persuasion, clarity to your instructions, and substance to the bare-bones material of the main points.

FOLLOW A UNIFIED PATTERN

For your speech to be effective, everything you put into it should ultimately relate to the central idea. Only when you present your materials in a consistent, comprehensible, logical, unified, and coherent pattern or order can you be sure that your audience will follow you easily and learn from your speech what you want them to learn. Although patterns will relate to your speech purpose, twelve common ways of organizing your information are listed and briefly described on the following page.

Plan the Introduction

The main purposes of the introduction are to introduce yourself and get some favorable attention from the audience and also to introduce your subject and arouse interest in it. If someone has been assigned to introduce you to the audience, part of this job will be done for you. It is

TWELVE WAYS TO ORGANIZE INFORMATION

1 Chronologically. Many recipes are given in this fashion: "First you add a cup of water. . . ."

2 Spatially. For example, "*A* is connected to *B*" in a certain way. You might use this when describing how a machine operates.

3 Topically. This is classification by topic, such as animal, vegetable, mineral; or land, sea, air.

4 In ascending or descending order. Here you go from the larger to the smaller or vice versa, as in phylum, class, order, genus, species; city, county, state, nation; or letters, words, phrases, sentences, paragraphs.

5 Causally. You show that this happens because of this; if this is done, then you can expect this consequence. For example, "If you vote Republican, then you can expect . . ."

6 In terms of problem solution. Start with a problem, develop possible solutions, and select the most useful or logical one.

7 By the process of elimination. Begin with a lot of possibilities and show how all but one are inappropriate: "Thus only through economic sanctions can antipollution measures succeed."

8 By repetition. Use the same form or statement or argument as a basis for each successive point; for example, "We need the United Nations because it gives us a forum; we need the United Nations because the world needs a focus; we need the United Nations because the world is a family."

9 In order of increasing difficulty or complexity. Here you would go from atoms to molecules to solutions or from cows to livestock to farm animals to agricultural assets to the economy.

10 Using indirect sequence or the withheld proposal. You save making the conclusion or proposal until you have developed all the arguments or the possibilities.

11 In pro and con order. Here you attempt to present both sides of an argument—first one and then the other. There is currently little agreement among speech scholars about which argument (either the first or the last presented) carries the most weight with audiences. Scholars use the terms *primacy* (for those arguments presented first) and *recency* (for those presented last), and there are occasions when one works better than the other. One solution is to present your strongest argument first and then review it briefly after presenting the major part of the speech in a persuasive situation.

12 In terms of the climax. You lead up to the punch line, as when telling a story. When you organize information in terms of an anticlimax, the shorter and weaker points are made later, with the most important part coming early in the message.

helpful to have another person tell the audience about your accomplishments and say why they should listen to you. You should do the following things in your introduction.

GIVE CLUES ABOUT WHAT WILL FOLLOW

The introduction will give the audience some idea of what to listen for. You will usually present the topic or the central idea or at least imply it, unless you are using a reverse-order, anticlimax, or indirect-order pattern.

ESTABLISH THE CONTEXT OF YOUR MESSAGE

You may want to suggest what you expect might happen as a result of your message, to announce in general what things you will not be discussing, and to give the audience an idea of how long you will speak or how many points you expect to cover.

DEVELOP CONFIDENCE AND EASE

This is the time to become comfortable with your audience. Work for a confident and modest tone in your approach to the audience, and they will respond.

DON'T APOLOGIZE

If you are unprepared, don't apologize in advance for it. "Unaccustomed as I am to public speaking . . ." has become a cliché, but speakers still use variations of it. Don't apologize as a way of making yourself look superior either; your audience will be quick to perceive phony attitudes.

AVOID TRITENESS

If you are going to establish yourself as a real person, try to get a fresh opening for your speech. "I don't want to take more than a few minutes of your time . . ." is trite. You must also try to keep your language suitable for your audience. Don't sound as if you are addressing Congress when your audience is your speech class. Remarks about the wonderful audience, their wonderful club, their wonderful good deeds, and the wonderful meal are bound to turn off all but the most susceptible egoists. Keep your appreciative comments honest, modest, and brief.

INTRODUCTIONS ARE IMPORTANT ENOUGH TO WRITE OUT

Even if you are giving a speech without notes, it is helpful to write out and practice your introduction. Write some sample introductions for any speech and practice them with a friend or by yourself to see how they sound.

DON'T THINK YOU HAVE TO START WITH A JOKE

There is really no reason to start your speech with a humorous remark. "A funny thing happened to me on my way to this meeting . . ." has become a cliché. It isn't necessary to use a joke to get your audience in a relaxed mood. If you feel you have to begin with a light touch, relate your remarks to something that happened to you during a previous speech or something that went wrong when you were being introduced—the person who introduced you may have mispronounced your name, for example. You have heard speakers add immediacy to their speeches and an engaging beginning by use of the "running joke" such as a waiter who has been spilling things all through dinner, or a member of the audience who keeps getting phone calls. If you feel you must start with something funny, make sure that it will be funny to your audience, that it relates to your appearance there or your message, that it isn't so long that it interferes with the rest of your introduction and your speech, and that it doesn't give the audience the mistaken impression that you are there to give a humorous speech if that is not your purpose.

ESTABLISH YOURSELF AS WORTH LISTENING TO

You may want to remind the audience of your qualifications to speak on this subject, or in fact, to be present as their speaker. In as simple a setting as coffee conversations, you can hear the speakers establish their credentials: "I was an only child and I sure know what it's like to . . ."; "I drove a Yamaha for six months, and . . ."; "I went out for tennis when I first got on campus . . ."; "Last semester I had ol' prof. Whoosis for calculus . . ."; "I eat here every day, and . . ."; "Nobody goes to more movies than I do, and . . ."; "How many of the rest of you have ever been in a drunk tank overnight?"

In formal settings you may have a title or some other signs of credentials to establish your right to speak. If you are introduced by another person, it is that person's responsibility to help establish your right to be there and the audience's responsibility to listen to you. If that introduction is not done well, or at all, then you must reassure the audience about yourself. Without boasting, you must qualify yourself either as an expert because of what you have done or been, or because of the extensive study you have made of the topic. "My three weeks on a working ranch in Wyoming gave me a healthy appetite and a healthy respect for the life of the cowboy." "As a manager of a rock group last summer I learned a great deal about the recording business." "Traveling with a political candidate before the election gave me insights into . . . ." "Metric changeover cannot be more confusing than my experiences with

The introduction: Establish your topic as worth listening to. *(Hugh Rogers/ Monkmeyer.)*

monetary systems in six countries. . . ." "Even three years in law school did not prepare me for . . . ."

You need not only to establish your credibility but also to arrest the attention of the audience. A good introduction should do both, quickly and clearly.

ESTABLISH YOUR TOPIC AS WORTH LISTENING TO

We have already emphasized that audiences are interested in themselves. Topics that concern them will be listened to; those remote from them will not. Early in your introduction, you must assure the audience that it is to their advantage to hear you. You will make them feel better, know more, act more effectively, or somehow be better off for having listened to you. Will you make them healthier, happier, wealthier, or wiser? Will you give them an emotional experience or an intellectual one? Often these advantages to an audience are not specifically stated. If you are giving a speech in a speech class, and the class is being graded on attention or has to evaluate your presentation, the advantage is already established. If you are attending a public lecture on how to make money in the stock market, the speaker is not likely to spend time telling you that you are interested in making money. A ceremony for honoring a winning team does not need to convince the audience to hear the coach speak.

On occasions when you believe the audience needs convincing to be involved in the topic, you can approach them with a variety of devices. Most are designed to answer the implied question "So what?" An audience to be *informed* needs to believe that knowing will be good for them; an audience to be *persuaded* must be capable of making a change or being affected by your topic. An audience to be *entertained* must be favorably involved with the topic you select—a society against cruelty to animals will not take kindly to a speech about your exciting deer hunt; humorous experiences in foreign countries frequently dredge up stereotypes and ethnic humor not acceptable to all audiences.

ESTABLISHING YOUR TOPIC AS WORTH LISTENING TO: APPLICATIONS

APPEALS FOR FUNDS

At one time or another an organization you belong to will want to raise funds for a worthwhile project. As a member of many different kinds of organizations or as just a plain citizen you will come in contact with efforts to raise money for causes—the United Fund, Christmas Seals, and the March of Dimes, for example. Persuading people to give donations means asking them to part with their money in the hope of receiving (almost always) intangible gains. Yet millions of dollars are given to various causes each year, and foundations and charitable funds are established for the sole purpose of supporting good causes.

1. Prepare, alone or working in a group, an appeal for funds for some kind of project or cause (a class party, a gift for a sponsor, a scholarship fund, a research grant, a new library, or a day-care center, for example). Who is your audience? What motive do you appeal to? What kind of language will you use? If you are giving speeches about this effort to potential donors, how would you construct the speeches?
2. Find examples of appeals for donations in newspapers and magazines, in TV or radio advertising, or in the mail you get. What motive do they appeal to? From the way the message was set up can you analyze the way the person thinks who is trying to get you to contribute?
3. In a group discussion, share with others the way you feel about giving money to causes. Make distinctions as you will—remember that you may like to give to poor people but not to a church; you may want to contribute to an alumni fund for scholarships but not to a hospital building fund; you may give generously to the United Fund but not at all to the March of Dimes. What makes the difference in your attitudes about giving? What messages will generally induce you to make a gift?

Monroe's Motivated Sequence was developed by A. H. Monroe, speech teacher and scholar, to encourage a progressive system for analyzing and handling problem solving and persuasion. A similar pattern was earlier proposed by another speech teacher, H. L. Hollingworth, who suggested that the speaker could develop his material into the same general five parts. Both systems are helpful to a public speaker as an option, particularly in persuasion, available to planning and constructing and finally delivering and analyzing the public communication.

Monroe suggests this order:

1 Attention—getting an audience tuned
2 Need—what problem is there to be solved or attacked
3 Satisfaction—what can be done about the problem; an explanation
4 Visualization—imagine what things will be like after a solution
5 Action—how the audience (and speaker) can go about making the solution happen

Hollingworth's pattern was nearly the same:

1 Attention
2 Interest
3 Impression
4 Conviction
5 Direction

Earlier much the same reflective thought system had been described by John Dewey as:

1 Recognition of the problem
2 Description of the problem
3 Discovery of possible solutions
4 Evaluation of solutions and acceptance of the best one
·5 Plan of action to implement and test the preferred solution

All these sequences[1] may be used in constructing a persuasive argument or in problem solving. Often they are applied to group problem-solving situations, and the steps are recommended. Some difficulties in making an effective persuasive speech (and in solving group problems) arise when the process is distorted; for example, when a speaker spends the entire time developing description or analysis of the problem and does not provide a

---

[1]Monroe proposed his system in *Principles and Types of Speeches*, Scott, Foresman, Chicago, 1949. Hollingworth's system was stated in his book *The Psychology of the Audience*, American Book Co., New York, 1935; and Dewey's thought processes were suggested in *How We Think*, D. C. Heath, Boston, 1933.

workable solution or ways in which the solutions can be implemented by either a speaker or an audience.

SOME DEVICES FOR OPENINGS

Although the introduction will take up only a small part of your speech, it sets the tone for your relation with the audience and their acceptance of you and the topic. Devices to get attention have been classed by some teachers in the categories of notes, quotes, and anecdotes.

Notes would include such devices as rhetorical questions and startling or challenging statements ("How many of you have never ever told a lie?" "By tomorrow one of you in this audience will be in an auto accident."), notes about the subject or the occasion ("Using the term 'nuclear' in the way I will tonight would have been impossible fifty years ago." "For the tenth time you have asked a citizen to talk to you on Founders Day, and for the first time you will hear a dialogue."), or some kind of consequence or reward. ("By attending this meeting you have proclaimed yourself an enemy of several American traditions." "You will certainly benefit in your pocketbook today, if not in your own soul.") Figures and statistics are in this group.

Quotes are, of course, those borrowed statements which either fit the occasion or fit the subject matter of the speech and have been said so well and so succinctly by others that you have difficulty improving on them. Quotes should be brief and related to your speech. Your sources must be appropriate—quoting a Democratic President favorably to a Republican audience is not acceptable, nor is it useful to quote a bigot or a bigoted statement to a group known for its openness and lack of prejudice.

Anecdotes offer the widest variety of material. Stories about what has happened to you or to others in similar situations may catch the audience's attention. Fables, newspaper clippings, wise sayings of children, jokes, puns, may all be in the attention system of an audience. Your challenge in making illustrations like these, as in the other devices, is to be sure the audience can relate to the story you tell—that it is something within their possible experience.

Develop the Conclusion

When you have sorted out your supporting material and have developed a pattern for your speech and the introduction, you are ready to prepare the conclusion. It should provide your audience with a satisfying and effective culmination of your remarks. Depending on the purpose of your speech, your conclusion should enable you to urge action, summarize your orders or instructions, restate your philosophy, leave the audience with a positive feeling, repeat your illustrations, or have an introduction come full circle. Here are some general suggestions for developing the conclusion.

NO NEW DATA

The conclusion is not the place to introduce a new argument or bring up an additional point of information. This is when you refer back to other points you have made for emphasis.

DON'T APOLOGIZE

This is no time to point out to the audience that you have run over your time limit, that you have left them confused, that you have not had time to develop all your points, or that somehow the job you did was inferior. Stop on a positive note. Say that you enjoyed being there, and don't bring up any shortcomings in your speech that they may not even have noticed.

END WITH STRENGTH

A strong ending does not consist of a statement such as "Thank you, ladies and gentlemen." End with a point relating to your own talk, making use of that moment to tie it all up. Make it sound like a conclusion.

DON'T BE TOO ABRUPT

If possible, signal your audience that you are about to conclude your speech. They have to adjust to your stopping, just as they had to adjust to your starting. Too fast a finish will leave an audience unsatisfied and tentative. Your conclusion should be smooth, and its tone should be as much as possible like that of your speech to make it seem like a part of the message.

CHECK YOUR CONCLUSION

Test your conclusion by asking these questions of yourself: Does my conclusion help the audience be where I want them at the end of my speech? Does it help finish my presentation rather than leaving an audience dangling about what I intended them to know, to feel, or to do? One very important suggestion is to look at the introduction (or beginning) of your speech and then check your conclusion to see if you should make use of some of the same devices you used in the introduction—did you start with a quote which could be a summary as well? Did you tell an anecdote at the start of your speech which you need to return to at the end? Can you issue a challenge to the audience? Can you confess or declare that you will take a certain action or adopt a certain belief, and invite the audience to join you? As in the introduction, you may want to look for notes, quotes, or anecdotes which will finish your speech with strength and purpose.

Make the Speech Hold Together

You have probably heard speeches that seemed to be made up of disconnected paragraphs or unrelated parts. Such problems are due to poor *transitions*. Once you have written the body, the introduction and the conclusion of your speech, you must make them flow together so that they don't sound as if they were put together by complete strangers working in different rooms.

The bridges you make between these parts of your speech—most importantly, between different points within the body of the speech—will make it move forward evenly, like a basketball rolling across the floor. Unless you give such attention to your transitions, your speech may resemble a football being dribbled down the court.

The most commonly used transitional phrases are the ones like "And for my second point," "And then," "In conclusion," "Now for another thing," and "That reminds me of another story." If those sound familiar to you, is it possible they will sound altogether *too familiar* to your audience? If you can be a little more imaginative, your audience will appreciate it. In addition, your paralanguage (the stress you put on words, the rate of your speech, the loudness of your voice, the pauses you make, and the way you stand and gesture) is another means of making a smoother transition between parts of your speech.

If one part of your speech leads logically to another, you may want to use transitional words such as "because," "therefore," "for," and "since." You may want to interject a warning to your audience that they are about to hear a story: "Let me explain with this example." You may want to let them know that you have some figures to give them. You should connect examples and illustrations to the main idea of your speech. Too often a speaker will suddenly begin quoting statistics or making comparisons without warning the audience what is coming. A timeworn but simple formula for effective speaking is contained in the advice that you can make your message more understandable if you can tell your audience you are going to tell them something, then tell them, and finally tell them you told them.

DEVELOPING THE PARTS: APPLICATION

The two candidates for a seat on the school board in the city of Metropolis have come up for interviews and will make public appearances before civic groups and educational gatherings. Following are the general profiles of the candidates.

Ernest Willson is a six-year veteran on the Metropolis school board and has the backing of the Metropolis Educational Advancement League (MEAL). He is a physician, fifty-five years old, and black. His children are grown, but all attended school in Metropolis. He serves on several state committees concerned with education and urban affairs. At one time he was backed by the Southern Christian Leadership Conference (SCLC), but now there is some confusion as to whether the SCLC is supporting Willson or his opponent. The local director has not made it very clear where the SCLC support is going.

The opponent is a young lawyer, also a native of Metropolis, aged twenty-nine, and also black. Her name is Susan Jarritt, and she is running as an independent, since she did not get the backing of the MEAL group or the open support of the SCLC. She does have the support of an organization she helped found a few years ago, the Metropolis Black Citizens Association (MBCA), which seems to represent the younger elements in the community.

On the issues in this campaign, the two candidates have come out this way:

Busing: Willson says that busing is a fact of life and is being used as an argument against integration of the schools.

Jarrit is in favor of the concept of neighborhood schools and against forced busing. "Children should go to school near their homes."

Punishment: Willson favors counseling over corporal punishment in the schools.

Jarrit favors paddling youngsters, "not in junior high and high school, but certainly nothing helps keep order better in the lower grades."

Expulsions and Suspensions: Willson says that counseling is generally preferable to suspension—"There were 8,000 suspensions handed out last year, and 6,000 of them were to minority students. There is no reason to assume that such a figure represents the enrollment percentages in our city's schools."

Jarritt agrees that counseling would probably be of help, but would first want to establish the legal processes by which the suspensions and expulsions would be valid, paying particular attention "to the vastly ignored principle of due process."

Reading: Willson says that the early childhood program should be expanded and that reading should be taught intensively in all schools and at all levels. New experimental programs already begun should be continued.

Jarritt considers reading of primary importance. "No person graduating from the schools should be deficient in reading. It is the responsibility of the grades, each in turn, to present the reading materials and not to pass a student along unless he or she is at that grade's actual reading level."

1 Assume that you are going to introduce both of these candidates to a group of parents of students in Metropolis schools. A large number of people have come out to hear these two candidates, both speaking from the same platform—not in a debate but taking turns. Your job is to introduce both speakers so the audience will be acquainted with them as they get up to speak. What kinds of things will you say about them?

2 Assume that you are the master of ceremonies at the preelection dinner meeting of the MEAL, the organization backing Willson. You are going to introduce Willson, who will give the main speech at the meeting. What do you say about him?

3 Assume that you have been selected to introduce Jarritt for a preelection television speech. You will have about five minutes in which to give her a good strong introduction; the time is being paid for by the MBCA, which Jarritt helped found. Plan your introduction.

4 In a group discussion, develop persuasive speeches for each of these candidates. What kinds of points should they make? Are there issues other than those mentioned on which a stand should be taken? What will each candidate want to say about supporters as well as policies?

5 Assume that Willson is elected to the school board for another term. What does he say in his victory speech? In a group discussion or individually, try to work out the kinds of things he will say over television the day after the election.

6 Assume that Jarritt is elected. What does she say in her victory speech? Again in a group discussion or by yourself, work out what she will say in a television interview. Also work out what she will say to the school board at its first meeting when she is called on to say a few words—for about five minutes.

☐ OUTLINING MAKES SENSE

You will use an outline for many things. You can make one outline to prepare for your speech and another for presenting it. You can make an outline that gives your topics in the order in which you will present them or in a logical sequence as you will argue them. The simplest way to look at outlining is in terms of structure.

The *word outline* is useful when you have your speech very well in mind or when you are beginning to collect data and want to see how the order of your material and your speech organization fit together. The *phrase outline* gives you more guidance. Although the *sentence outline* is the most difficult to construct because of the time needed for preparation and the care you must take in properly relating the points, it is the best form for the beginning speaker to use because it offers the most guidance in message delivery. It is the closest thing to having a manuscript to speak from. You lack only your supporting data.

Three General Classifications of Outlines

Word outline
I. Health care
   A. Hospitals
   B. Nursing homes
   C. Outpatients
II. Physicians
   A. General physicians
   B. Specialists

Phrase outline
I. Delivering health care
   A. Through hospitals
   B. In nursing homes
   C. For outpatients
II. Physicians' role
   A. General physicians available
   B. Specialists involved

Sentence outline
I. Delivering adequate health care is a major problem in the United States.
   A. Hospitals are overcrowded.
   B. Nursing homes vary in their ability to serve their patients.
   C. Outpatients have difficulty getting services.
II. Physicians are taking the lead in expanding care.
   A. General physicians have begun making emergency calls.
   B. Specialists have formed cooperatives to serve larger groups of patients.

Outlining Principles

The key to good outlining is to establish the order of the symbols you will use and the appropriate indentions. Besides the suggestion given below, remember that there should always be at least two subordinate points—a single subpoint is very rarely found.

1 The rank of each point is indicated by its number or letter style.
   I. *Main points are indicated by Roman numerals.*
      A. *This subordinate point is indented.*
      B. *This level uses capital letters.*

1. *Another indention will show the next level of items.*
2. *This level uses Arabic numbers.*
   a. *Further indention occurs when needed.*
   b. *This level uses small letters.*
   c. *Remember that there must be at least two items on each level.*
      (1) *Further breakdowns of information are indented.*
      (2) *At this point you begin to use parentheses around the letter or number.*

II. *You continue the main points with Roman numerals.*

2. Subordinate points are indicated as shown in the outline above—by indention and the use of different symbols. The subject matter of the subpoints should be related to that of the main points, but less important in terms of value or content.
3   Coordinate points are preceded by the same kind of letter or number and have the same indention.
4   You should have only one idea per point. Keep it simple.
5   Each item should be distinct from the others and should not overlap a previous or following point.
6   There is an order of progression from one point to another. Your outline may be based on a sequence, order of importance, or a space relationship, but it should reflect a pattern or arrangement, as in the outline above, where all the points are related to outlining order and occur in sequence.

OUTLINING: APPLICATION[2]

SAMPLE OUTLINE (TOPIC OUTLINE)—FROM A STUDENT SPEECH
Title: Black English

I. Introduction
    A. Chinese dialect
       1. Northern
       2. Southern
    B. Subcultures in the United States
       1. Mexican-American dialect
       2. Social class dialects
       3. Black Americans
II. Difficulty in communication
    A. Unfamiliar to many listeners
    B. Black child reading problems
III. Black English versus standard English

[2]Sample outlines are from student work in the class of Frank Jarrett at Trinity University. The "Black English" outline is by David LaRue Murphy and "The Interesting Side of Washington, D.C." is by Cathy Cragin.

A. Rate of speaking
B. Sentence structure
   1. Unmatched subjects and verbs
   2. Function words and prepositions
   3. Adjective reversal
C. Special differences
   1. Dropped endings
   2. Flatness
   3. Word usage and adaptations
IV. Use of black English
V. Summary—conclusion
  A. Necessity for black English
  B. Adaptation to achieve a purpose

SAMPLE OUTLINE (SENTENCE OUTLINE)—FROM A STUDENT SPEECH

Title: The Interesting Side of Washington, D.C.

I. Monuments in Washington are famous, but were not interesting to me.

  A. They looked exactly like the pictures I've seen.
  B. I discovered more interesting things to do.

II. A city within the city is intriguing—Georgetown.
  A. When other places close, Georgetown remains open.
    1. Unusual shops stock items from all over the world.
    2. Restaurants are open late and feature foreign foods.
  B. Architecture of the city is classic and very well preserved.
    1. Attempts have been made to retain a consistent flavor of the buildings.
    2. Close-set structures are unusual and offer an interesting variety of well-kept façades.

III. Many tourists miss the great attraction of Washington theaters.
  A. Historical Ford's Theater is easy to find and still operating.
    1. All types of plays are presented today.
    2. A special historical exhibit is made of this place where President Lincoln was shot.
  B. Kennedy Center has a strikingly modern and elegant feeling about it.
    1. It is a four-story, glass, pale marble, and metal construction.
    2. Its interior is beautifully finished and furnished.
    3. Performances include all kinds of artistic events.
      (a) Dance performances range from classical to the most modern.
      (b) Musical shows and classical theater are part of the season.
  C. For the Shakespeare fan, there is the Folger Shakespeare Library with a model of the Globe Theater.

D. The Potomac River Theater Company plays from a boat and spectators sit on the bank.

IV. If you want to see a roomful of money, visit the Bureau of Engraving and Printing.
   A. It is actually a money factory.
   B. Visitors are carefully searched at the start and finish of a tour.

V. There is a five-sided crazy house there called the Pentagon, which is worth a visit.
   A. Gets its name from five sides and five floors.
   B. At first glance it reminds one of a bowling alley because it has no stairways.
   C. It is so spacious and vast that much of the communication is conducted by bicycle or on roller skates.

VI. In summary, you should consider visiting more than one Washington.
   A. Visit the traditional one with the monuments and parks.
   B. Also, you should visit a few of the unusual places.
      1. See the city hidden within the bigger city, Georgetown.
      2. See some shown at the many different theaters.
      3. Visit the Bureau of Engraving and Printing and watch your money being made.
      4. Go rollerskating at the Pentagon.

■ LOOKING BACK

I. Organizing a speech well helps the speaker make an effective presentation and helps the audience with their participation.
   A. The sequence of getting started includes:
      1. Setting your general purpose.
      2. Setting the general subject.
      3. Setting the specific subject.
      4. Pulling these together to state the specific purpose.
      5. Writing the central idea, or topic sentence.
   B. Gathering materials involves searching many sources for supporting information for your speech.
   C. Collecting the material in an organized fashion, including keeping neat notes, helps in the final work with your speech.
   D. After you have collected the material, you organize the speech for a second time.
      1. You develop the body, or the main part, first.
      2. Next develop the introduction.
      3. The final step is to develop your conclusion.
      4. Pay particular attention to transitions.

II. Outlining helps you organize your speech and put it together in logical order for delivery.
   A. You may want to use word outlines, phrase outlines, or sentence outlines.
   B. The order of symbols and proper indentions is important.

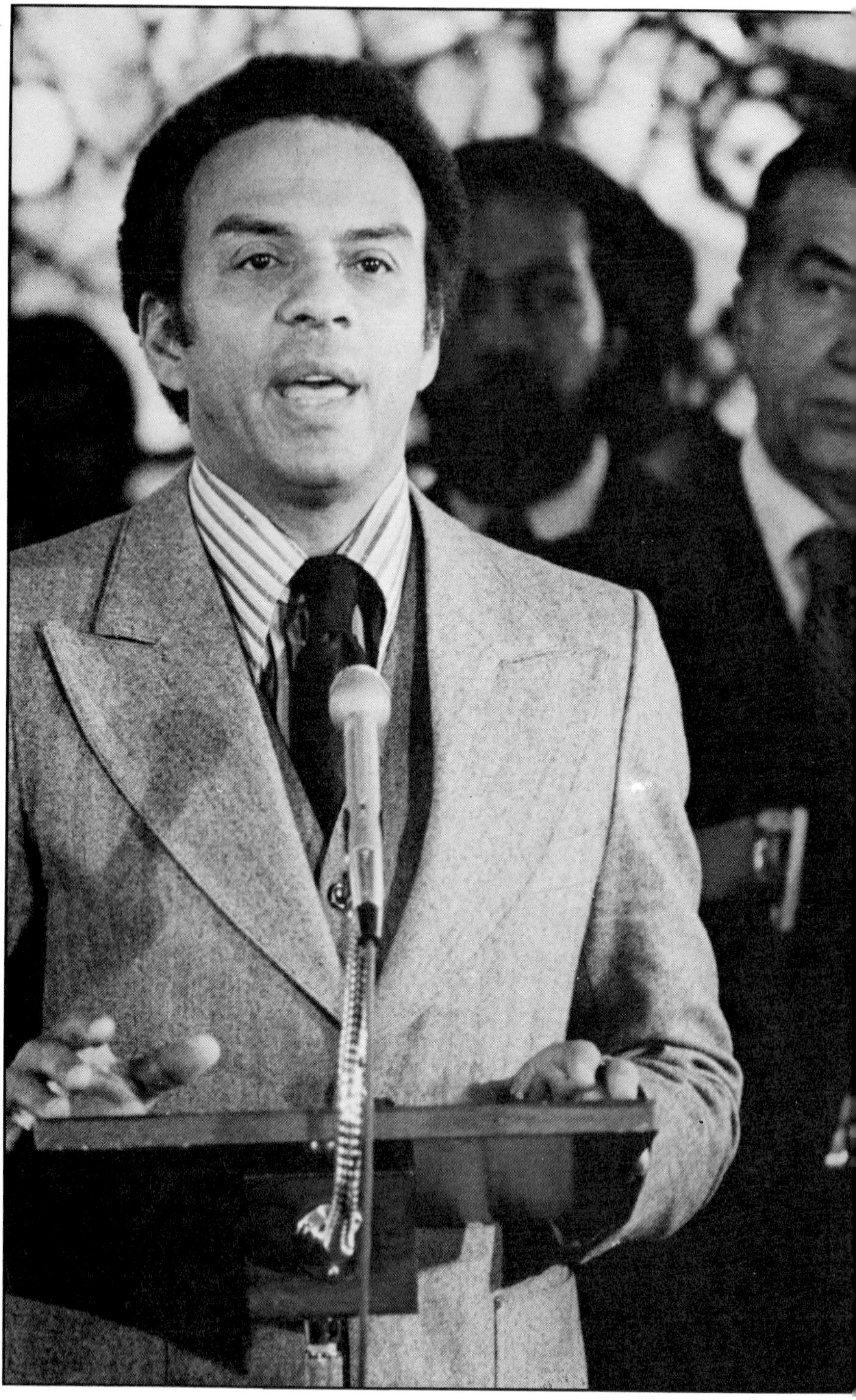

(United Nations/M. Grant.)

CHAPTER 8
SPEAKING STRATEGIES

In the United States, it is almost incon-
ceivable what rubbish a public man
has to utter today if he is to keep res-
pectable
— John Maynard Keynes (Lord Keynes)

An honest man, like the true religion,
appeals to the understanding, or
modestly confides in the internal
evidence of his conscience. The im-
poster employs force instead of argument, imposes silence where he
cannot convince, and propagates
his character by the sword.
— Anonymous

People who want to understand democracy should spend less time in the
library with Aristotle and more time on
the buses and in the subway.
— Simeon Strunsky

I n this chapter we shall discuss some of the strategies which are available to you as a speaker and which are also likely to be used on you as a listener.

In Chapter 3 you read about the slipperiness of words and the difficulty in establishing meaning. Much of what we include in this chapter on *message strategies* is related to communication misunderstandings, which occur either by accident or on purpose. By citing the ways in which reasoning and logic are used unethically on you, we are not suggesting that you adopt these strategies to use on others. Ethics and honesty are as important to a good speaker as are delivery and the material.

☐ PLAN YOUR PSYCHOLOGICAL STRATEGIES

You will need a certain strategy to achieve the kind of speaking effect you want. Moods of audiences are sometimes difficult to change—for instance, it may be hard to make a really grim audience respond to an entertaining speech. If a ceremony is very dull, the listeners may reflect this in their attention to your honoring an event or a person. Beliefs, attitudes, and opinions of persons in an audience are not easily changed, as you will find out when you seek to persuade. Even some relatively interested audiences can resist being informed or instructed if the message and situation are not right.

What Motivates an Audience?

Different writers have listed many different kinds of personal and human motives. One such system, Maslow's hierarchy of human needs, was discussed at length in Chapter 4, and is the classic list to which many other writers and researchers refer when they work with human needs. To review briefly, Maslow describes the basic needs as physiological, safety, social, self-esteem, and self-actualization. Maslow says further that these basic needs are hierarchical; that is, one need will not become important until the previous one is satisfied. Having friends, for example, does not become important until one's physiological and safety needs are met adequately. The important point to remember here is that according to Maslow, it does little good to talk to a hungry person about being respected because other needs must be met first. Respect will not be one of that person's motives. Similarly, people whose needs for self-esteem and self-actualization are satisfied may have little sympathy for those who are still struggling with more basic needs. During the Depression of the 1930s, President Franklin Delano Roosevelt's statement that one-third of the nation was ill-housed, ill-clothed, and ill-fed did not persuade millionaires to support the sweeping economic measures he proposed.

Motivational researchers and other social observers have developed lists of the forces that motivate people. Vance Packard, in his book *The Hidden Persuaders*, says that advertisers appeal to such needs as:

1 Emotional security—peace of mind
2 Reassurance of worth—ego and self-image
3 Ego-gratification—being recognized for accomplishments or being in the limelight
4 Creative outlets—feeling competent in artistic endeavors
5 Love objects—being popular with members of the opposite sex
6 A sense of power—leadership recognition, prestige, and authority
7 A sense of roots—belonging to a group or to an area
8 A sense of immortality—leaving a legacy to the next generation

Looking at human needs in a different system of categories, writers of advertising copy and public relations materials have listed four things that a persuader must appeal to if the message is to succeed. Some writers favor a subliminal approach, while others believe in a more open appeal.

1 Fear. Like Maslow's need for safety and shelter, this need motivates people to build houses, set up building codes, have police and fire protection, lock doors, buy smoke detectors, buy safety devices for cars, and maybe even give up smoking.
2 Hunger. The merchandising of foods has become a highly important part of our economic life in America. Some of the biggest advertisers are the food producers and the food-selling agencies. We also know what pills or cures to buy when foods disagree with us or when we "overindulge."
3 Sex. This involves our need to be loved, our admiration for youth and beauty, and our feeling of belonging when we can be attractive to someone of the opposite sex. Sex is used symbolically to sell much of the merchandise in our economy today.
4 Anger. Persuaders sometimes appeal by using things that upset our sense of right, offend our dignity, or go against our value system. They show cheating, lying, stealing, betraying others, or beating children—or whatever we can be taught to hate.

How Motives Are Used

Every need and desire of a listener represents an opportunity for a speaker. You should attempt to determine which needs are important to your listeners. In speeches to inform, you will talk about them because they are interesting to the audience. In speeches to persuade, you will make use of that concern to show how things can be better by following the position you support. In speeches to entertain, you can make light of these human concerns, satirize them, overplay them. In ceremonial speeches, you will know which philosophical agreements you can get from your audience.

USE OF AUDIENCE IDENTIFICATION

The principle of identification implies that the more closely you as a speaker can identify yourself and your topic with the audience, the better attention (and the better probable effect) you will get. A useful strategy in building such an identification is to show how you are like your listeners in important ways. You may belong to the same groups or have the same cultural, ethnic, geographic, or religious background. You may have had some common experiences or mutual friends. In substance, you should try to relate your motives and needs to theirs.

In *humorous* or *entertaining speeches* you should try to strike a common bond with your audience, or you will lose them. Remember that we are all embarrassed or amused by things in very much the same way, and we might like to shoot the rapids of the Green River on a raft or perhaps hunt lions in Kenya. Showing the audience that you have some fears and motives in common will help them accept you and to be interested or amused by what you say.

In *speeches to inform* you must connect with the needs and the motives of the audience so that they will listen to instruction or information. The

To succeed, a persuader must appeal to what motivates the audience.

(Bruce Anspach/Editorial Photocolor Archives.)

(Andrew Sacks/Editorial Photocolor Archives.)

(Louis E. Hartmen/Editorial Photocolor Archives.)

teen-ager who is learning to drive will pay attention to things having to do with cars because that is the immediate big interest; on the other hand, he or she may not be as concerned about becoming a prominent scientist in later years. Similarly, a talk about the prime interest rate or the availability of government bonds will be far more involving to a banker than is a discussion of hamburger stands or pizza parlors.

Persuasive speeches make use of all the motives that can be directed to an argument for or against an issue. If you are "one of them," they will tend to listen better than if they see you as a complete outsider. Identifying yourself and your issue with their motives must be done carefully. If you overplay this, you insult the audience. You can go too far with excessive name dropping of mutual friends, with farfetched relationships or associations, or with an implication that you "used to be just like them" until you changed. This last device is often employed by reformed smokers, political-party switchers, and self-made people. It must be used with great modesty and very sparingly.

Ceremonial speeches, on the other hand, can stand a degree of audience identification that would not be tolerated in a persuasive situation. The audience is gathered to honor an association or a relationship and expects to be reminded of it. One of the reasons for ceremonies is to get people together for a common emotional experience, and the process of identification becomes not only a motivating device but also a reason for being there.

MOTIVES: APPLICATION

HOW PEOPLE ARE INFLUENCED

Studies done at the University of California at Los Angeles by the Survey Research Center there have identified six ways in which people control one another. These basic forms of "interpersonal influence," according to Dr. B. H. Raven, director of the center, involve (1) reward, (2) coercion, (3) expertise, (4) legitimacy, (5) reference, and (6) information. -

Reward means that you get something good if you do what I want you to. *Coercion* (or punishment) is the opposite: Something bad will happen to you if you don't do what I want.

Expertise as a control mechanism rests on the argument that you should do what I say because I am smarter than you, have more experience, or am superior in any other way. *Legitimacy* as a basis of power over others is based on recognized facts: I have a right to do that—"I'm your father," "I'm the chairman," "I own the bat," etc.

Reference involves belonging to groups; I can ask you to do things and have you do them because we are part of the same family, team, or club, for example. The *informational* basis of influence involves controlling others by educating them: I can explain to you how to do something, and then you will do it.

1 In what kinds of situations are these control bases evident? Raising children? Police training? Schoolwork? Politics? Others?
2 Working in a class group, try to identify some person or group that uses each of these six means of control or influence. How do the persons in control try to let those being controlled know about their relationship? By talking? Gesturing? Wearing uniforms or other insignia?
3 In a group discussion, work out the ways in which these types of control can be expressed in speeches. How do speakers identify the kind of audience they can be effective with in using these bases of influence or control? Do they all work with all audiences? Why or why not?

Emotional Proofs

All audiences are, to some extent, susceptible to emotional appeals. A public speaker who can use the emotions is simply using what is already there. The speaker did not create the feelings in an audience; the people brought their feelings with them to the situation. For entertaining speaking, we understand that humor, curiosity, and drama can all involve the emotions. For speeches to inform, we can get attention and hold it when an audience is listening with more than simply intellectual curiosity. Persuasion can be accomplished by appealing to the emotions, as evidenced by the rhetoric at huge rallies in Hitler's Germany or the political bandwagon speeches at conventions.

Pathos can be used to give an audience at a ceremony the opportunity to openly engage in emotion. The fact that we all operate on both an intellectual and an emotional level is often obscured by our attempts to be objective, cold, and matter-of-fact. The use of pathos as a speaking technique for psychologically motivating an audience is both very old and very effective.

Apt pupil of Plato, tutor of Alexander the Great, teacher at Plato's academy, and author of the classic book on speaking, *Rhetoric*, Aristotle developed a number of concepts that are as current and useful today as they were in his lifetime (384–322 B.C.).

From the work of the Greek orators and teachers, we have selected Aristotle's to summarize the types of proof a speaker may use. His descriptions were roughly:

Ethos—proof based on the character of the speaker

Pathos—emotional proof

Logos—intellectual proof

The subject of the speaker's *ethos* was discussed in the chapter on the audience. Much of the speaker's ethos is bestowed by the audience rather than deriving from what the speaker brings to the occasion.

The items of *pathos*, or emotional proof, in this chapter are directly related to the teachings of Aristotle's rhetoric.

Logos, or appeals to the intellect or logic, Aristotle believed should include logical proof, deduction, induction, and analogy.

Aristotle had what we would call an "interdisciplinary" attitude toward the speechmaking of his day. He wrote that rhetoric is a composite art—drawing on law, politics, ethics, philosophy, scientific investigations, and what might have been called "psychology." Therefore, his system for making speeches reflected this broad base of knowledge, and the methods of proof covered the variety of human responses that can be expected in communication.

EMOTIONAL PROOFS: APPLICATION

HATEMONGERS ARE SPEAKERS, TOO

Following are some items about George Lincoln Rockwell, onetime leader of the American Nazi party, hatemonger, white supremacist, anti-Semite, and fanatical anti-Communist. These are all terms he used to describe himself because he wanted to create "a pretty rotten image of myself to attract listeners." His idea was that people would show up to hear "a monster." He didn't care why people came to hear him speak, just as long as they showed up to get his message.

Rockwell claimed that President Kennedy would not have been shot if the Nazi party had been in power in the United States because the assassin, Lee Harvey Oswald, would have been shot (presumably by Nazi party orders) the day he left the United States to visit in Russia in the years before the assassination.

"Sure, I'm a hatemonger. I don't see anything wrong with hating bad things like Communists and traitors."

"Anybody who ever did anything worthwhile in the world was a fanatic."

"I don't believe that Hitler tried to exterminate a race [the Jews]. If he had wanted to he would have, and they wouldn't have got over here to buy up all our real estate."

"Nazism stops communism. It wipes it out and annihilates it."

"Jews are a race. You can recognize them. Some people say they are only members of a religion, but you don't grow a long nose by going to church."

"People who are pushing for civil rights are using the Negroes. Every single Negro organization except the Black Muslims is led by New York Jews."

"I hope the civil rights bill passes, and they make it stronger, so every white girl has to have a date with a Negro."

"Our goal [of the Nazi party] is to gain power. We're the only [radical right] group openly trying to gain the White House." He estimated that there were 700 members at that time in the party nationally.

"The American Negro is an African, not an American."

"Colored people are still eating each other in some parts of the world. I do not hate the colored man. Personally I admire Malcolm X. I simply say the black man has not had biological time to mature like the white man has."

1 How does making himself "a monster" contribute to the persuasiveness of a speaker and a cause? Is that kind of reasoning valid or useful?
2 What propaganda devices and what faulty reasoning can you see in the statements quoted from Rockwell's public appearances? These were statements made at press meetings and in speeches to university students in the middle 1960s. Are these statements typical of hatemongers in any year? If these statements were made in a speech on your campus now, what response would the speaker get? Do you believe in letting this kind of person speak to university audiences? Why or why not? Get a group together to discuss the issue of whether a self-styled fanatic should be permitted to speak on a campus. How about other places, such as in the civic center of a community, in a local church, in a public auditorium, in a school building, in a private club, or at a dinner meeting of a service club? Who decides which messages are worth hearing and which are too dangerous to listen to?
3 Form a group to discuss the kinds of faulty logic used in the statements Rockwell is reported to have made. Do you find other examples of such messages being said today? By what groups? For what purposes? Are they effective as persuasive devices? With whom? Under what circumstances?

☐ PLAN YOUR INTELLECTUAL STRATEGIES

In entertaining or ceremonial speeches, you will probably have less occasion to use intellectual strategies than when you are speaking to inform or to persuade. The reason is that the "epideictic speeches," as they were classified by classical rhetoricians, are for special occasions that call for audience involvement on a more emotional level. Emotion or psychology can play a part in informational or persuasive situations. Audiences are subject to psychological appeals by the very nature of their being human. However, the model for the persuasive speech and the informational speech is much more rigorous and logical. It involves proof based on intellectual grounds, evidence, factual reports, or sound reasoning. Logical methodology is a science all its own, involving the principles of deduction, induction, and analogy to support or prove what you say.

Proof is the process of using evidence to secure belief in your ideas or statements. How you use the evidence, how good it is, and how it fits your statements (or propositions) are the subject of this section.

Supporting by Reasoning

Your own thinking must be conditioned to accept the processes and procedures of logical reasoning, or honest supporting of evidence. This is more than an exercise in proving what you say. It is a challenge for you to become more reasonable in approaching the "facts" in your world and the "inferences" that you may sometimes confuse with facts.

Using Deduction

This is the process of reaching a conclusion by moving from the general to the specific. Logically you would start with one kind of generalization, make a series of controlled inferences (or guesses), and end up with a specific conclusion that must be related to the original generalization. The deductive process usually involves a premise, a reasoning process, and a conclusion—the conclusion is the product of your deduction. If you are going to college and believe that this will help you get a good job, then your conclusion might be that you have a better chance of finding a good job. If you think you can't trust anyone over thirty, and your parents are over thirty, then your conclusion is that you can't trust your parents. If you are a college student and think that all college students have long hair and smoke pot, then you must have long hair and smoke pot.

Using Induction

The opposite process is involved in induction. You have some evidence about a group you have observed, and you have some knowledge about groups like the one you are observing. On that basis you can say that the things that happened in the particular case will happen in a general case. This is going from the specific instance to the general by way of inference. Induction is also used widely (and often not too wisely) to move from unknown causes to form a hypothesis. If you see something happen and can't explain it on the basis of what you have seen or already know, then you may decide that its cause was x—the x is your induction. Much of the knowledge we have in science was developed by induction—including the classic story of Sir Isaac Newton and the apple.

Sir Isaac wondered why the apple did not fall up instead of down, and he decided there was a force pulling it to earth—gravity was "invented" by induction.

Using Analogy

Much of our scientific knowledge was discovered by induction, but much of that same scientific knowledge is explained by analogy. When scientists first tried to understand electricity, they could not see a flow of electrons through a wire or really understand just what was going on. They began to describe those electrical processes in terms of something else they knew about that worked in a similar way. They took the language of water action: current, flow, resistance, and conduction. Analogy is the method of inference in which you reason that if two (or more) things agree with each other in some aspects, they will probably agree with each other in more. Similarities of form, sequence, size, color, actions, contents, or other parameters give us the basis for analogies.

Literal analogies are made by comparing things in the same categories, such as comparing cows and sheep as farm animals or high schools and kindergartens as educational levels. *Figurative analogies* compare things in different categories and consequently provide some of our most colorful inferences as well as some of the most difficult to develop with originality and accuracy. "Sending our tax dollars to Washington is like pouring sand down a rathole." "Watching a cricket match in England is as exciting to an American as watching paint dry."

Analogies are very useful in developing an understanding of similarities between things, but you must be aware that there may be differences that outweigh the similarities. In every analogy there will be similarities *and* differences. You may want to test your analogies if you intend to use them in an argument. However colorful and entertaining figurative analogies are, they are not reliable as proof. For that reason you must first check to see whether the analogy you are testing is figurative or literal. If it is literal, do the differences in the comparisons outweigh the similarities? Are the similarities relevant? Are they significant?

The Trouble with Inferences

Inferences are the guesses you use to fill in the gaps in your reasoning process. Our language permits us to make statements that make no sense in the real world, although they may be grammatically correct. "A unicorn is in the garden" is a perfectly good sentence, but unicorns are nonexistent, mythical beasts. Try these: "People don't like me because I'm fat" or "That professor hates me, so he's going to flunk me."

Let's be clear about "facts" and "inferences." Facts are those evidential things which you can measure and which have occurred somewhere, and may even occur again. An inference is a guess—an educated guess, you hope, but still a guess. When we make inferences and rely on them to guide our logic or our lives, we should recognize their limitations. We should be especially cautious when we are either getting statements from others about their inferences or passing on our inferences to others in the statements we make to them.

Statements of inference can be made any time, but statements of fact can be made only after observation.

Statements of inference can go beyond our real world and are limited only by our imagination, while statements of fact must remain connected to what we can observe.

Statements of inference can be made by anyone, while statements of observation (or fact) can be made only by the observer, unless qualified as "secondhand," "thirdhand," etc.

Statements of inference deal only with probability, while statements of fact approach certainty. They could be certain statements except for the human limitations on the observer's abilities to observe and then put the observations into words afterward.

Statements of inference can be made by the incompetent and uninformed, while statements of fact depend on the observer's competencies.

Other Forms of Support

Whether you are trying to impress, to inform, to instruct, or to persuade, there are times when you would like your message to be based on more than simply, "I believe this is so. . . ." You want to call on other sources. You want to expose your reasoning process so that others can judge how well you are making your argument. You want to call up the resources you investigated through reading, asking questions, watching, and listening. Here are some ways you may want to express the support materials you have collected.

STATISTICS ARE USEFUL

Although statistics can be helpful, they are deadly when used in large doses. No audience can (or wants to) listen to a lot of numbers, percentages, or ratios. Used sparingly, they can be helpful because the appearance of quantification is important for some kinds of audiences. Try to put your statistics into meaningful numbers; very few of us really understand what a million, a mile, or a pound actually is. "A half million cars produced each year in Detroit could stretch in a massive traffic jam from New York all the way down the Eastern Seaboard to Miami." "We spend $7 billion every year on education, and that would be enough money to give every American alive a new television set every year."

When you want to expose your reasoning process so that others can judge how well you are making your argument, use statistics, examples, and expert testimony. *(Dennis Brack/Black Star.)*

What statistics can prove is that something is so big, so important, or so objectively overwhelming that it establishes itself as proof. Large numbers are not proof in themselves. They must be related to the argument, they must be documented, and they should represent the most recent and complete quantified data you can pull together. Statistics by themselves do not prove anything. They can describe and they can help make a presentation impressive, but without your specific application of the data to your proposition, statistics do not stand as proof.

DEFINITIONS ARE OVERRATED

This device is greatly overworked by beginning speakers who think that they prove a point by reading a dictionary definition or who believe an audience will be impressed because the speaker has looked up a word. Definitions can distinguish one thing from others like it, can put a thing into perspective, and can explain exactly how the speaker intends to use a term. They are most useful if a term is unfamiliar, is being used in a special way by the speaker, is vague or abstract, is little used, or is so crucial to the speech that its meaning must be made absolutely clear.

However, when you use words in a special way, or when you think your audience might misinterpret your language, it is important to "define your terms," remembering that meanings are in people and not in the words themselves.

EXAMPLES MUST CLARIFY, NOT CONFUSE

These are selected by a speaker to illustrate a point being made. "For example," is a prelude to a clarification. If the example is more difficult to follow than the main point, it does not serve well. If it is not familiar to the audience, they will not accept it. If examples are briefly stated so that they do not overwhelm the speaker's point, they will be useful. Examples are useful to illustrate your arguments, but do not qualify as proof unless you can make them apply directly to your argument.

AUDIOVISUAL AIDS GO ON FOREVER

With the coming of cassette television and the potential for easy recording and playback, the expanded use of TV to support speakers is widely predicted. This technological aid will join proved systems, including tape recorders to bring actual sounds into the message, motion pictures to dramatize or illustrate difficult concepts or special ceremonial

Technological aids are new forms of support that help both speakers and audiences. (Gail Myers.)

effects, and slides and projectors of all kinds to illustrate or dramatize. Before these systems were available, we had chalkboards, posters, models, flannel boards, mock-ups, replicas, sketch pads, charts, and various other means that enabled a speaker to extend the efforts of the unaided voice with audio or visual aids. Multimedia presentations now utilize a variety of sight-and-sound equipment to reinforce a message.

QUOTATIONS AND EXPERT TESTIMONY ADD VARIETY

Literary quotations, poetry, slogans, epigrams, homilies, and bits of homely philosophy are not in themselves proof, however interesting and illustrative they may be. As support for descriptions or in ceremonial and entertaining speeches, quotations are very useful. Calling up the philosophy of great men or women or quoting well-constructed phrases adds variety and life to your speaking in those settings.

Expert testimony of authorities on various subjects may be offered to an audience as proof. Qualified persons who are acceptable to an audience have said or written many things that you can quote, honestly abstract, or paraphrase to give strength to your arguments. The expert should be established as qualified in his field—dentists are better sources of expert testimony on cavity-fighting toothpaste than television stars; your barber can tell you more about hair preparations than can a member of the New York Mets.

You should never simply string together a bunch of quotations to make up your speech. You must bring a part of yourself into the message. You should use quotations as supplementary material and not as the main substance of your speech.

In delivery, it is amateurish to say "quote" and "unquote" when you are reading or reciting quotations from other sources. If you want to make your presentation a put on or a parody of good form, then you may want to say "quote" when you start reading the material and "unquote" when you end it. But if you are serious about the quotation you want to present, avoid saying those words.

How, then, do you let the audience know that you are using someone else's words? How do you, in your speaking, make the sounds that approximate the little quotation marks we use in writing? Vocal inflections can do the job of the punctuation that is missing from your spoken words. Use a different tone of voice when reading; pause before you begin (and when you finish) the quoted material; make it sound as if you are reading it rather than just saying it. All these methods depend on voice control. In addition, you may have the quotation on a card or a sheet of paper—lift it up and very obviously read from it, or at least start reading. If you have it memorized, you can stop reading after a few words. Use movements to establish that you are departing from your own words and using the words of another. A combination of voice level, pitch, loudness, precision of pronunciation and enunciation, gestures, and even body movements will make it clear to your audience that you are using a quotation.

EXPERT TESTIMONY: APPLICATION

THE BABOONS DIDN'T KNOW THE STATISTICS

When the Los Angeles zoo designed their baboon cage, they included a moat across which the public could view the animals without bars or cages. Expert advice given to the designers and architects determined that baboons could not jump farther than 10 feet. Builders made the moat 12 feet across to be sure.

Very soon after the zoo was opened, three baboons escaped by leaping across the 12-foot moat and running out of the zoo. It took several days to recapture the baboons. Commenting on the events, an assistant zoo director was quoted by the Associated Press as follows: "We were informed when we placed the animals there that they could not jump more than 10 feet. Regrettably, it appears the baboons were unfamiliar with this data."

1　How do you explain the discrepancy between the verbal definition of a baboon's ability to jump and the actual performance? Did the zoo officials check their verbal maps with a territory? If the experts tell you that an animal can perform certain feats, are you inclined to believe them?

2　When you seek expert advice, is it important to test out that evidence in actual practice? Is it always possible? Is there a way to cover the possibility of error (like making the moat 12 feet to cover a 10-foot limitation), or do you simply build in to your planning some other extra margin?

3　Find other examples of statistics being cited to determine the outcome of future events. At one time there was a law against designing railroad trains to travel more than 50 miles per hour because "experts" predicted that the human body could not withstand speeds of that magnitude; and women were not permitted to take up the job of typewriting because the female physique was too fragile to tolerate punching keys for hours at a time. Can you find other examples?

SUPPORT: APPLICATION

SUPPORTING YOUR CASE

Find an example of each of the following forms of support in a news story; a newspaper, television, radio, or magazine feature; an editorial; or a magazine report. Indicate whether the message was improved by the use of this device, and in what way.

Statistics. (For example, a message about the consumer price index must necessarily use statistics to get its point across. How are they handled?)

Definitions. (For example, in a message about a special process used to control the attitude of the high-gain antennae on a space probe, what has to be defined?)

Examples. (For example, a message about some unfamiliar legal problem might use a reference to a simpler legal situation. How much do we already know?)

Audiovisual. (For example, messages about the weather usually include a map of the area. Does television really make full use of its visual potential, or is it radio with pictures?)

Quotations and expert testimony (For example, a medical authority discusses breakthroughs in cures for heart diseases. Is the expert really an expert or just somebody who wants to talk on television or have name in the papers?)

☐ MISUSING YOUR THINKING AND REASONING

We have already discussed some ways in which inferences can be misused; these included making leaps beyond the evidence you can verify and confusing facts with statements *about* facts. Sometimes you may very innocently get trapped in some of the means of faulty reasoning discussed in the following section. Sometimes you will be tempted to use some of them deliberately. Sometimes you will be the victim of another speaker's manipulation of these means. As you develop as an effective producer and consumer of speech messages, you will be better able to recognize these devices.

Fallacies in Reasoning

These are sometimes called *improper methods of proof, misuses of reasoning*, or *reasoning fallacies*. Whatever name is used, they are capable of misleading a great deal of thinking and believing. In the case of each fallacy, you can check to make sure you are not misleading others or are being misled.

HASTY GENERALIZATIONS

These are simply the generalizations you might make on the basis of very little evidence or very few examples: "Mexicans are lazy," "Americans are money-mad," "Democrats are liberal," "People are no damn good," for example. To check, ask whether the sample is representative

TABLE 8-1
Methods and Examples of Supporting and Amplifying Your Messages

Method	What You are Saying	Characteristics	How Used
Statistics	A Gallup Poll of parents and teachers showed that 68 percent of all parents and 60 percent of all teachers believed that an "ability to speak correctly" was the most important verbal skill to have. Americans work 2 hours and 45 minutes each day just to meet their federal, state, and local taxes. To provide for housing, a worker works only 1 hour and 26 minutes; while it takes 1 hour and 14 minutes for food and tobacco, 30 minutes for clothing, 19 minutes for recreation, and 21 minutes for medical expenses.	Make sure your figures are understandable. Using charts or other aids (such as blackboards) will help. If you use very large numbers, round them so you will say "about 42 million" rather than "42,314,602." If possible, use comparisons rather than just raw numbers. Controversial statistics need to have sources cited.	Can be used for proof if appropriately identified and attributed to sources which are legitimate and believable. Also used to enrich a speech, and to give an impression of scholarly research or of quantifiable evidence. In some speeches, using numbers and figures will give an impression of authenticity and seriousness to your message.

Definitions
  Of words
  Of philosophies
  Of points of view
  Of processes or
    systems
	When I refer to "accountability" in education I mean that teachers, administrators, yes, and students are subject to evaluation by a higher authority or organization.
	
	A major source of the controversy over Title IX and athletics is the meaning of equality. Equality may be measured in terms of opportunities, procedures, or results.
	
	The main solar collector is a simple sheet of copper painted black. Placed in the sun, it gets hot.
		What you set out to define should in the first instance be more complicated than the terms or expressions you use to define it; it should in the second instance be something which your audience might have a question about. Defining words or processes which they are already familiar with is a waste of your time and theirs. Be sure your definition has a purpose of clarifying your terms or points of view, etc.	Definitions can be used to limit the meanings of some complex terms or processes. You can use definitions to make a point, but they are not proof—even if you quote the dictionary as a source of meaning; all you prove is how the word is recorded in a book as a sample of its current usage. Definitions often precede longer explanations of philosophies or processes.

	Examples		
Literal analogies Figurative analogies, metaphors, similes, fables, parables, anecdotes, etc.	Playing a musical instrument is like riding a bicycle; you never forget the techniques once you have learned the skills. "A man never steps in the same river twice," Heraclitus said, "the man changes and the river flows."	Items to be compared must be alike in the important features; similarities must outweigh differences. Analogies should be clear, vivid, and easy to grasp: they should fit the point you are trying to make, and should relate to your audience and to the material you are speaking about.	Only specific and directly related instances or the most literal analogies can be used for proof. Others are to add richness to the speech, get attention, or clarify or dramatize: to capture or hold an audience.
Quotations and expert testimony	"We have nothing to fear but fear itself," said President Franklin D. Roosevelt as he led the nation out of the Depression. "When firmness is sufficient, rashness is unnecessary," said Napoleon. Aggression is an unusual means of achieving mastery, according to the chief psychiatrist at the State Hospital. Western world academics are concerned about the "falling standards" and an uneasy depression in educational opportunity, according to a major writer of educational topics, Malcolm Scully. The magazine *Change* reports that "humanities do not humanize and the liberal arts do not liberate."	Quotations must be from recognized authorities or those whose credentials can be established. Make sure the quote or testimony is based on firsthand evidence or knowledge. The testimony or quote must be from a person whom the audience not only knows but also respects, so it can have confidence in that expert's opinions or statements. Then you must quote accurately, honestly, and within context.	Quotes can add spice to your speech, get attention, condense some long and complicated ideas into a brief and pithy comment. Expert testimony or quotes accurately given can be offered as proof if you restrict the range of proof to that covered in the quote and within the expertise of the expert quoted. Often the use of quotes and testimony is directed to convincing an audience by weight of authority or bandwagon appeals. Use quotes sparingly and use brief ones; audiences are not thrilled by long readings of quotations or testimony.

of the whole population about which the speaker makes the conclusion. What about the exceptions or negative instances? Has the speaker cited enough examples to back up the conclusion? Is the speaker being honest about the sources? Can anyone ever say everything about anything?

AD HOMINEM REASONING

This means getting at the person. You attack the character or personality of the person who opposes you and in that way try to prove that you are right and the other person is wrong. This kind of personal abuse is often used in politics when issues have become so confused that voters are easily led to voting *against* a candidate rather than *for* a candidate. To check, ask whether the character of the candidate in question has a bearing on the argument. Do quirks in personality have any relation to the issue being discussed? ("Can a divorced man become President of the United States?" was a great question at one time, just as was "Can a Catholic become President of the United States?" This was an issue which defeated Al Smith but which proved to be ineffective in the case of John Kennedy.) What is the basis for the attack on the person? Does the attacker deal with facts or with gossip and rumor?

One very subtle form of *ad hominem* reasoning is to "damn with faint praise," or tell very little about a person, as if there were nothing else of importance to reveal. "Senator Smith is certainly a capable small-town grocer." "Considering his racial and educational handicaps, John certainly has gone far." "If I had not helped Elaine when she was really cracking up, she wouldn't be able to do even the most simple assignments today." Watch for these put-downs phrased as complimentary or supportive remarks. (We call them "talk-up put-downs.")

AD POPULUM REASONING

This is the popular appeal to the fears, greed, or prejudices of the masses. Hatemongers use this approach to stir up support for their campaigns against whatever religious, ethnic, geographic, social, or economic group they happen to be after. If one of our basic motivations is self-preservation, the demagogue can certainly appeal to our fear or biases to get support. Hitler's rise to power, based on the fear that the Jews were ruining the country, is a classic example of the use of this kind of reasoning. Any time a speaker can rally an audience to follow against the "enemy out there," it is probably this approach. To check, ask whether the threat is a real one or is imagined by the speaker. What is the evidence that the group of described events actually exist and will cause the consequences predicted. (Are we really being invaded by little green men from Mars? Is the end of the world coming on April 13?)

CIRCULAR REASONING

This is also called *tautology*, or the use of one unsupported statement to prove another. You reason in circles when you confuse causes with effects or simple variations happening at the same time. You can't prove that because one thing is happening, another thing is also happening. "Bethoven was a great composer because his music is considered immortal." "Slums are created by poor people living there." "The world is flat, and anyone who sails to the edge will fall off; we are sure of this because those who have sailed to the edge have never come back." To check, ask what support the original statement has and how it relates to the conclusion. Ask whether one thing happens because of the other or whether both of them happen because of some other forces not mentioned. Try to reverse the argument and reason the issue backward—if it reads backward as well as it does forward, then be suspicious of a tautology.

"RED-HERRING" REASONING

This name comes from superstition that a red herring dragged across your path will divert the attention of a wild animal following you. This device is often used by people who do not want to answer a question directly. A speaker will use this device to avoid discussing an embarrassing issue and instead concentrates on side issues easier to control. Press interviews are often subject to this kind of game: "Senator Smith, what is your opinion of the corruption being exposed in your party?" Smith's reply: "I'm not sure I understand what you mean by 'corruption in your party.' My committee has been totally dedicated to maintaining representative government, and you will see by the record that whenever anything important has happened in Washington, I have reported directly to the people, as I'm doing right now." To check, when asking questions of a speaker, determine whether the speaker is answering the question you asked or one the speaker chose to answer. ("That's the answer to another question; now, the original question I asked was. . . .") When listening to a speaker, see whether the speech strays from the original points to "prove" the case with irrelevant arguments about issues that are not central to the one being discussed.

"STRAW-MAN" REASONING

This is so called because the speaker sets up something that is very easy to knock down—like a figure made of straw. The idea is similar to "red-herring" reasoning—you pretend to be attacking the main issue, but you develop the argument on an issue you can beat. If you are trying to prove that education is wasteful, you would use a straw-man tactic by pointing out only the most flagrant examples of waste in educational programs and try to prove your argument using those. In arguing with political opponents, the candidates will take on only those issues where they are sure of their ground and which will make them look good—they will avoid their weaker issues. To check, as with red-herring reasoning, you need to know what the main issues are, and you must try to follow how the speaker avoids them. What phony issue can be developed to attract your attention away from the bigger issues and on to the ones the speaker can handle easily?

REASONING FROM SIGN

If you detect a sign of something, you can leap to any kind of conclusion. Clouds are a sign of rain; not all clouds produce rain, however. Walking in a weaving pattern is a sign you're drunk, but it may also mean you have had a blow on the head, you are ill, you have been taking a strong medicine, you are stoned on drugs, or you are practicing a balancing act. In the days of Senator Joseph McCarthy and the Un-American Activities Committee hearings, just belonging to certain organizations was a "sign" that you were a Communist and therefore a menace to America. Reasoning from sign becomes dangerous when you go beyond the actual relationship to establish a *word relationship*. You may also see things as related *on purpose* which are related only *by accident*. You may think some things are caused by signs that may be happening along with, or as a result of, other factors. To check, ask how dependable the relationships are that the speaker says exist. Do they happen often or seldom? Is the relationship accidental or a matter of cause and effect? For more discussion on mistaking causes and effects for coincidence (referred to as "concomitance"), see page 264.

POLAR REASONING

This two-valued orientation says that everything must be black or white, either-or, on or off. There are just enough cases of actual polar situations (you are dead or alive; you miss the bus or catch it; the light switch is on or off; etc.) to give one the idea that almost everything can be treated that way. But only in our verbal world can we divide some "contraries" (things that are different in terms of grade or degree) into actual "contradictories" (things that are either one way or the other). "You are for us or against us." (On what issues? How far? Under what circumstances?) "You are a loyal American, or you are a Communist." (What is "loyal"? Are there other things besides Communists and "loyal Americans"?) To check, ask whether there are really only two alternatives. Check to see who makes up the opposing categories. What are their reasons for setting up these groups? Look to see whether the things are polar opposites in the real world or only in the verbal world.

When certain issues become taboo and when speakers are severely limited in the arguments they can present, intimidation may be involved. At a supposedly "open" political convention, only certain candidates will be nominated. Groups who want to go in a different direction may receive delicate threats as to the political futures of those who oppose the favorite. Being told by a speaker to believe this way and act that way—"or else"—is simple intimidation. When a speaker uses a position of power or the threat of sanctions to achieve agreement, this is convincing by force. Force may be a good way to get quick agreement, but it is useful only as long as the authority of the speakers is strong. If they are deposed, they have nothing else to stand on. To check, determine how many things cannot be spoken about (the "sacred cows" or taboos) and how tolerant the speaker is of any argument. What consequences (threats) does the speaker say or imply will result if the audience does not follow orders, directions, or beliefs?

Miscellaneous Kinds of Faulty Reasoning

Many of the types of reasoning mentioned above involve either faulty analysis or faulty causal reasoning. Those two general types of reasoning errors account for most of the problems we have in being misled and in misleading others. By pretending that your own attitudes and biases are really proof, you are making an analysis error. ("You'll have to agree with me that college is really a waste of time." "I've been a Catholic all my life, and I can't see why anybody is worried about the Pope taking over America." "Cucumbers really disagree with me, and I can't see why they are classed as food.")

Other types of faulty analysis can occur when you take the word of persons who are not qualified as experts; this hurts your analysis of a situation. Also, setting up definitions of words or things so that they will fit your arguments, rather than using them in the usual way, starts your analysis with a strong bias.

It is easy to find reasons why things happen as long as we are just *talking* about them. It is harder to pin down those causes if we actually have to make the experiments or do the research that would prove, in the real world, that one thing causes another. "The movement of the trees is what makes the wind blow" seems like a perfectly valid statement if the observer sits and watches trees and sees that wind accompanies all tree movements. However, it switches cause and effect and is accurate only in the verbal world. "He's a college graduate—he doesn't know how to drive nails" may not express a complete causal relationship. "Poverty causes crime" may be incomplete causal reasoning, as is a statement like, "Old people are conservative because they are rich." Most of our superstitions and much folklore are based on poor causal reasoning: Does walking under a ladder bring bad luck? Does catching a bride's bouquet make you more likely to be married? Will dropping a knife or walking in the house through both the back and the front doors mean that company will arrive? Does stepping on a spider cause rain, or do we have to depend on atmosperic conditions?

There are many different kinds of faulty cause-and-effect relationships in the messages we give and receive. Try to check these out to make sure that there is a real relationship between one thing that happens *because of* another and not just along with it (concomitantly). If you take away the cause, would it still happen? If you look at the result or effect, can you be sure it happened for the reason you say it did?

FALLACIOUS REASONING: APPLICATIONS

Fallacious reasoning usually is in the following general categories. If you can identify the fallacy and make its nature clear, you can refute the arguments of the opposition and strengthen your own. Avoid committing these fallacies. Detect and examine them when they are presented by the opposition. While most of these fallacies are typical of formal debate, they occur frequently in our everyday communication.

I. Formal (Errors in Reasoning or in the Structure of the Logic)
  A. Causal reasoning (from cause (C) to effect; or effect (E) to cause):
    1. *Non sequitur*—C does not produce E (It does not follow . . .)
    2. *Post hoc*—E comes after C, therefore because of it
    3. Inadequate causation—insufficient cause to produce that result
    4. Counteracting causes—reaction to C prevents E
    5. Assumption—general cause assumed on evidence of E as a specific
    6. Other causes produce the same effect and have not been included or identified
    7. Cause will produce more evil effects than good
    8. Cause is only a sign or symptom of other causes
    9. Cause limited by time, space, conditioning factors, etc.
  B. Example (from the specific to other specifics and to general):
    1. Irrelevant examples used to establish proof
    2. Insufficient examples presented
    3. Examples not typical—too "selected" to give real proof
    4. Examples limited by time, space, conditions, etc.
    5. Lack of examples taken as proof ("You have not shown . . .")
  C. Analogy (only literal analogies serve as potential proof):
    1. Significant points of similarity lacking

  2. A difference that is critical but not mentioned or denied

  3. Analogy is noncumulative—does not add up to anything

 D. Structural weaknesses (organizational deficiencies):

  1. Internal contradictions and inconsequencies

  2. Argument in a circle—tautology

  3. Faulty synthesis and division—selecting arguments

  4. Extension or *ad absurdum*—making argument ridiculous

II. Semantic (Errors in Manipulation of the Meaning of Words and Ideas)

 A. Rephrasing and reconstruction of opponent's arguments

 B. Late definition—adjusting definition to fit arguments after defined terms had been set

 C. Refuting arguments not advanced—minor for major substitution

 D. Use of question-begging terms

 E. Use of assumptions in vague way—then shifting ground

 F. Ignoring questions and selection of issues that are "major"

 G. Reversal and turning tables—"You must prove . . ."

 H. Speculation and refutation of own speculation; guessing and relying on your guesses

 I. Questioning techniques:

  1. Dilemma—either error technique and limiting possibilities

  2. Forcing arguments on other issues

  3. Sidetracking and mousetrapping opposition

  4. Extension by demand for answers to minor points

  5. Challenging "practicality" or "intentions" or "motives"

 J. Appeals:

  1. To tradition

  2. *Ad hominem*

  3. *Ad populum*

  4. Ignorance of the real issues or opposite effects

III. Evidence

 A. Testimony:

  1. Opinion or inference for fact

  2. Biased material presented as objective data

  3. Out of context

  4. Time and space limited

  5. Vague assumption or indirect source

  6. Lay versus expert testimony

 B. Statistics:

  1. Selected and prearranged

  2. "Big Picture" not specific

  3. Floating mean; unrepresentative sample

  4. Time and space limitation

  5. Unverifiable figures

  6. "Trends" showing only a segment of a period

  7. Fluctuating base line

  8. Unreliable source

Enclosed in a package containing a sample tube of toothpaste is a small brochure entitled "Why Should This Toothpaste Have a Red Stripe?" The brochure itself is all about an exclusive, magic ingredient which kills germs. The question of why there should be a red stripe in the toothpaste is *never answered*. Reading the material leaves the impression that the red stripe is only an advertising gimmick.

An advertisement for a new magazine just being "born" has these words in big letters: "What does Blank magazine offer you?" This is followed by a long discussion about what a remarkable opportunity it offers to a person of distinction with an inquiring mind, an alertness to the changing world, a curiosity of great magnitude, good taste, and all the other attributes that an advertising writer assumed any reader of the advertisement would have. But nowhere in the ad was there a description of what would be in the magazine—and the question that was asked was never answered.

Two students are talking in a dorm room:

First student: "Hey, will you come to town with me to see a movie?"
Second student: "I've got a biology test tomorrow."
First student: "OK. Let me ask you this: Do you have a biology test tomorrow?"
Second student: "Yes—I just said. . . ."
First student: "Now, back to my question: Will you go to town with me to see a movie?"
Second student: "Yeah—I'll go."

1   We often ask questions that we have no intention of answering as an attempt to persuade people. When someone asks you a question, are you sure you are answering the question asked? What did the student mean by, "I've got a biology test tomorrow"? Was it that it would be impossible to go to town because of having to study for the test? There is a lot of inferential material in the reply to the first question.

2   Deliberately fuzzy answers to questions are used to avoid giving real answers. When students are asked questions by the teacher and do not know the answer, what do they tend to do? To say "I don't know"? To stall and hope an answer comes to mind? To answer some other question that they do have an answer to, hoping the teacher won't notice? (For instance, "What were some of the causes of the American Colonies' grievances against the King of England?" "Well, uh, uh, the King of England had been doing things which had made the colonists upset—and they wrote the Declaration of Independence and based their statements on inherent human rights.") Be careful not to settle for answers to other questions than the ones which were asked—in the answer about the American Colonies, the "causes" were never brought up, but a smoke screen of other material was poured out.

3   "Rhetorical questions" are a class of questions used to *make statements*

rather than to get answers. For instance, think about the father who asks his child, "What did you do that for?" or the teacher who asks her students, "Why is it that you never read the assignment?" How about the politician who asks, "Do you want a government with such vast, centralized powers that you will live in a dictatorship?" These do not require answers; rather, they are speaking devices to gain attention or to make a point.

4   See how often during the day you ask questions and get *answers to other questions*. Develop a habit of checking (at least mentally, if not out loud), "Did that really answer the question I asked?" If it did not, ask the question again. Try to find a variety of ways of saying, "That was the answer to another question. Now let me repeat what I asked before. . . ."

The Seven Propaganda Devices

Over the years since they were first listed by the Institute for Propaganda Analysis, these propaganda devices have been used as an aid in recognizing influence attempts. A group of American journalists made this list, and their analysis has become a standard in teaching listeners, as well as readers, how to avoid being taken in by propaganda devices. We want to make two points about these devices: First, as an ethical speaker, avoid using them yourself; and second, learn to spot them when they are being used on you and help others become aware of their use as questionable techniques.

NAME CALLING

If you don't want an audience to listen to someone, call that person a name like "Communist," "hippie," "warmonger," "racist," or "male chauvinist pig." If you can pin a hateful label on others, you don't have to argue their points with them or tolerate their views.

GLITTERING GENERALITIES

Here you draw conclusions from evidence that either is too meager to mean anything or does not apply in the situation. This is an "allness" symptom, where you make it sound as if "everyone is dishonest," "all the kids are doing it," or "politicians can't be trusted."

TRANSFER

This involves applying the qualities of one thing to another (or transferring them) for the purpose of investing the second thing with the good or bad qualities of the first one. You want to make a new idea acceptable, and so you find a way to tie it to something your audience already admires. You may want them to hate a new thing, and so you scare them by showing how it is like something they already hate. "Flying in the 747 is just like being in your own living room." "Birth control is murder." "Our candidate will bring to this office great skill as a prosecutor to help rid the state of crime."

TESTIMONIALS

This is the endorsement of a product, a person, an event, or an activity by some person of prominence. Athletes telling you to buy certain cosmetics or styles of sports clothes are giving classic examples of testimonials. More recently we have seen political candidates backed by testimonials from movie stars, as well as from economic, social, and political leaders. Causes are often furthered by having famous people appear at rallies or listing their names on letterheads of organizations. Some endorsements are very subtle; a testimonial does not have to carry an actual spoken message in order to influence us. A major comedian appearing at a White House function indicates covertly that the performer is on that political team. Failing to speak out for a particular issue can also be interpreted as endorsing the other side—a reverse testimonial technique.

"PLAIN FOLKS"

This is an emotional appeal to the average person, or just plain folks which a speaker may attempt. The folksy speaker is trying to tell the

"Folks, I endorse Scrunchies because I eat Scrunchies. As God is my witness, I don't just say I eat them, I really and truly do eat them. In fact, folks, I never eat anything but. And if you don't believe me, I can supply documentation from my personal physician."   (The New Yorker.)

audience that "I'm just like you . . ." so that they will think the speaker has their interests at heart. This is a corruption of the "identification" technique we discussed earlier in terms of relating to an audience.

CARD STACKING

Here you will try to find the most absurd, outlandish examples or the most extreme instances of something and use them as if they were representative. "The mobs that stormed our campuses were those new voters we have just enfranchised." "What good does it do to spend millions on defense when our military secrets are all funneled to the Communists?" "Professor Smith is using lecture notes that are yellow—absolutely yellow—with age."

BANDWAGON

This device appeals to us because we want to go with the crowd. When someone tells us that "everybody's doing it," we are likely to join in. "The only time a banana gets eaten is when it leaves the bunch." You feel you will be left out if you don't get on the "bandwagon," which was the name used for an old circus wagon that carried a brass band to attract crowds to the circus grounds. This is an appeal to join those who are already there—the in-group, the knowledgeable ones, the jet set, the whole gang—and not to miss out. "All the kids are wearing blue jeans." "Everybody cheats on income tax." "All Texas Democrats are switching to the GOP." "Nobody on the block would sell a house to a black family." "The plant is trying for 100 percent participation in the blood drive."

PROPAGANDA: APPLICATION

THE PROPAGANDA DEVICES AROUND US
Collect from newspapers or magazines examples of the seven propaganda devices. (They are most easily found in advertisements or in the special columns or editorials.)

Be prepared to discuss the possible effect of each of these on a reader (listener) and how you might make use of the same device in your spoken communication that the publisher of the material did in written form. How do you convert a written (or printed) message of propaganda into oral form? What differences are there? Is the oral form generally more difficult or more simple? What does the spoken message add to the written one? What does the spoken message lack?

SUMMARY

In this chapter we have discussed "message strategies"—ways to make your message more effective. Rhetoricians of ancient Greece developed the art of speechmaking primarily for the purposes of oral persuasion, but they were so successful that they developed "oratory" as an art form to be enjoyed simply for its own sake.

We are not too different today. Although we may find ourselves involved in many situations in which we want to persuade another person to do or believe something (buy this book, go to the movies, help with a problem, vote for a candidate, etc.), we also find ourselves in other kinds of speaking situations. Messages we construct for the particular audience we are facing, on the basis of the situation we are in (including the occasion and setting), will influence the outcome of our communication. In this chapter we developed some methods of convincing, or appealing to, an audience. These, together with our observations on how we use the principles of reasoning and how we hear others use them against us, will make us better communicators.

■ LOOKING BACK

    I.   Audiences have certain psychological inclinations that are useful to know about whether you are the speaker or the audience.

        A. Different writers have described human motivation in terms of needs, motives, drives, etc.

            1. Maslow's hierarchy of needs moves from the physiological ones to the more abstract and personal ones.

            2. Motivation researchers have studied the forces operating on the persuasible human being and have defined some bases for persuasion.

        B. In speaking to audiences, you should make your speech purpose fit what you know about the needs of the audience.

            1. One way to be more successful with an audience is to show them that you are like them—that they can identify with you.

            2. In many speeches the use of pathos, or emotional appeal, is useful.

    II. The intellectual, or logical, approach to persuading an audience is more useful in informative and persuasive speeches than in the other categories.

        A. Correct use of reasoning will influence many audiences.

            1. Deduction is the process of reaching a conclusion by going from the general to the specific.

2. Induction is the process of reaching a conclusion by going from specific instances to more general cases.
3. Analogy may be either literal or figurative. Literal analogy is more useful in argument and instruction, and figurative analogy is more useful in entertainment and in ceremonial speaking.
4. Inferences should be used with caution so that they will not be confused with observations or statements of facts.

B. Other forms of support are useful to amplify your message and to make it more meaningful, more dramatic, more clear, and more persuasive.
1. Statistics, when used sparingly and clearly, are helpful as support and as evidence.
2. Definitions should be made when terms are unfamiliar or when they are used in a special way by the speaker.
3. Examples can help make your presentation more clear or lively.
4. Audio-visual aids are available in many forms.
5. Quotations and expert testimony may be used for different kinds of speeches, depending on the tone of the quotation and the expertness of the witness.

III. As both a consumer and a producer of messages, you should be aware of the potential misuses of thinking and reasoning and of the techniques of propagandists.
A. Reasoning fallacies include:
1. Hasty generalizations
2. *Ad hominem* reasoning
3. *Ad populum* reasoning
4. Circular reasoning
5. Red-herring reasoning
6. Straw-man reasoning
7. Reasoning from sign
8. Polar reasoning
9. Force or intimidation
10. Some miscellaneous abuses of cause-and-effect relationships and faulty analyses.
B. Seven questionable propaganda devices are often used by persuaders:
1. Name calling
2. Glittering generalities
3. Transfer
4. Testimonials
5. "Plain folks"
6. Card stacking
7. Bandwagon

CHAPTER 9
DELIVERING YOUR SPEECH

The young men of this land are not, as they are often called, a "lost" race — they are a race that never yet has been discovered. And the whole secret, power, and knowledge of their own discovery is locked within them — they know it, feel it, have the whole thing in them — and they cannot utter it.

— Thomas Wolfe

"Okie use'ta mean you was from Oklahoma. Now it means you're scum. Don't mean nothing itself, it's the way they say it."

— John Steinbeck

He who whispers down a well
About the goods he has to sell,
Will never reap the golden dollars
Like him who shows them round and hollers.

— Anonymous

☐ INTRODUCTION

Having wonderful things to say and nobody to hear you say them may be one of the most frustrating experiences of a communicator. After you have decided what to talk about, have mustered your message into an organized form, and have assured yourself you know your audience and the setting, then at some time you actually *speak*.

What has been called "delivery" of a communication message is the stage at which your other work pays off. Getting the message out to the audience is what you are after. In small groups you wait your turn, break in, or somehow manage to get the attention of others so that you can talk. There is a general tendency among friends to take turns talking (your turn is "delivery of the message"). At some time in your life you will probably have to get to your feet and make a speech—again, the delivery stage.

The physical act of speaking seems to most of us to be what communication is about. All the things you learn about language, about audiences, about symbols, about topics, about gathering data, and so on, seem to come to focus when you deliver. There are some special problems with delivery that are beyond the scope of this book. For example, this is not a text on *voice and diction* (the training of your speaking voice), however important that factor may be to the delivery of a speech or an informal communication. We shall refer only in passing to the considerations of voice and diction, but we recommend that the serious speech student become involved in such a study as early as possible. We also shall not be specific about the analysis of speech by phonetic means—for example, by using phonemic transcriptions. The whole field of phonetics is a rapidly growing one and should also be of interest to speech students who intend to analyze their own speaking and the speech of others. Further, we do not intend to go into the pathologies of speech such as aphasia, stuttering, lisping, and nasalities; these are studied and treated in the speech sciences. That area of speech education is a highly specialized one involving the diagnosis and treatment of speech disorders, and it represents an area of social service that is very attractive to the scientifically oriented student of speech.

This chapter will, however, treat speaking—delivery—as a communicative action you as the speaker will engage in during the normal course of your daily life and also in those assigned and formal situations when you must face an audience, open your mouth, and say something.

☐ SPEAKING SITUATIONS

You have already been doing some speaking. This course has covered occasions when you have talked to one another about something—the assignments, the Applications sections, and the speaking questions. You may have already found yourself "elected a speaker" for some kind of assignment.

In this chapter we want to take you through some of the more likely times and places for a speech so that we can develop suggestions about your performance.

One of the most common (and probably most mistaken) criticisms of college courses in public speaking is that the student will never make another speech after getting out of that class. In the first place, more students in today's colleges and universities than ever before will find themselves in situations we could call "public" speaking. There are more times when people will be called on to give reports, make public statements, have interviews, recite in class, address a group of visitors at the factory or office, talk to the Scouts, help organize a Brownie troop, work for a political candidate in a neighborhood campaign, lecture to a class, conduct a discussion in a service club, or "say a few words" to a bereaved friend, an awaiting crowd, or guests at a formal dinner party.

You have probably noticed that even sports figures, long admired for being so tight-lipped, are now acutely aware of the effectiveness of speaking in public places and giving interviews to encourage fans. The athletic coach has been characterized both as tough and silent and as an eloquent spellbinder who can put a team into orbit with his half-time pep talks and thrill fan clubs during the off-season.

In large offices, the ability to speak intelligently on the operations of some phase of the business (however insignificant it may seem) has made a great difference in terms of promotions and recognition. You may get that special job if you are able to speak for a few minutes on a topic as personal as yourself in an interview with a prospective employer. With a group that you are trying to convince to support your cause—whether it is selling goods in a store or fighting a social injustice—you must be effective as a speaker.

Many people will find themselves in formal speaking situations at some time or another. Teaching involves elements of public speaking, of leading discussion, of informing, and even of persuading and entertaining—the teacher without some ability in public speaking will probably have difficulty communicating with students or exciting them about learning. Other professions such as medicine or religion require communication of a very specific and highly developed form. Politics and public service require that a speaker have some ability in order to move ideas forward, to convince voters, or to promote civic programs or human welfare proposals.

There are obvious applications of public speaking in the work of media practitioners such as newspaper reporters, who must be skilled interviewers, and radio and television newspeople, who must write and often deliver speeches over the air. The field of business and sales is full of opportunities to make public appearances to groups of all sizes, from a small office force to a large industrial gathering where you demonstrate the effectiveness of your service or your product. Outside the job, many people participate in some kind of community work that requires them to communicate with others. Voluntary work of many kinds brings you to a public platform or in front of groups. It is not true anymore, if it ever was, that you will make your last speech in your speech class.

In addition to the fact that there are more opportunities than we imagine to communicate as a public speaker, there is another important reason to concentrate on the act of speaking—or delivery. The principles of delivery in public speaking are so much the same as those in our personal communication encounters that we can perhaps see better what we do individually if we can study these principles formally. We forget what kind of impact our delivery has on our day-to-day communication with our best friend, and that it can be studied, analyzed, and improved. In our interdependent world, we cannot cut off our lives from others. We go into the world to earn a living, to get food, to make acquaintances, and to accomplish many things. Speaking is a very ordinary, simple, and common occurrence. The principles of delivery we shall study here are just as relevant to those everyday encounters as they are to the situations which we normally think of as needing the art of delivery.

☐ KINDS OF DELIVERY

You are sitting in a group listening to a discussion. At some point you decide to say something. That's delivery.

You want to buy a special kind of film. You walk into the store and begin to explain your needs to the salesperson. That's delivery.

You are sitting in class. The instructor calls on you to explain some items from the textbook. When you answer, that's delivery.

You are the secretary of your club. You have written the minutes of the meeting and are called on to read them to the club. That's delivery. So is making a motion to the club. So is arguing the validity of the motion. So is chairing the meeting. So is the call for a vote.

It is possible to analyze delivery—or, rather, deliveries—from several points of view. You can talk about formal or informal settings, different kinds of audiences, different sizes of groups to talk to, standing up, sitting down, etc. One convenient way to study kinds of delivery has been to divide them into four categories on the basis of the degree of formality and the amount of preparation required. It is possible to have a mixture of these kinds of delivery even within the same message setting, but for the sake of *talking about* your delivery, we shall break them into separate categories. Remember that the distinctions between these categories become blurred in real life, and that the process of communication cannot always be divided up so neatly, *except* when we want to take one aspect, like delivery, and study it separately.

Impromptu

In its purest form, the impromptu speech is a response to a situation that you didn't know was coming. This is what you do most of the time when you talk with others in informal settings. You never know when somebody is going to ask you how to get to the post office or when a friend will ask you how to do an assignment. To respond to such requests, you muster up the information you have, organize it in some fashion that seems appropriate for the audience and the occasion, and then deliver your impromptu speech.

Imagine that someone asks the way to the post office. You think for a minute about what the questioner (the audience) already knows about streets, compass directions, right and left, and so on. Then you pull together what you know about the streets and distances and decide on the best organization for that speech—geographic or sequential, for example. "First you do this, then you turn there, then you follow . . . ."

Being called on in class provides another setting for informal and impromptu speeches. You may know the answer or you may not, but the point is that you have not prepared your material, as you would have if you had been assigned a report, and you did not know you would be asked to give a speech at that moment, however short it may be. Again in a brief moment you need to organize your answer, decide what items are useful to include, and then deliver.

The classroom provides a setting for informal and impromptu speeches. *(Rohn Engh/Photo Researchers, Inc.)*

In more formal situations, the coach, for example, may be called on to speak to the student body before a game, and may have had little chance to prepare a message. The politician who drops by the rally unexpectedly will make impromptu remarks. Press conferences with important people are examples of impromptu speaking; reporters ask the interviewee for opinions, explanations, comments, etc.

An important aspect of the impromptu speech is its spontaneity and lack of polish. An audience should not expect a finished rhetorical gem when the speaker has not had time to prepare. You as the speaker, on the other hand, must be quick to rely on your own experience. You have been preparing all your life for this event. You must make a rapid judgment of what the occasion calls for and adjust to the speaking situation. You may begin to speak almost as soon as you have begun to think of what you want to say.

Extemporaneous

This is not the same as the impromptu speech because you have had time to prepare; however, you are likely to use very few notes (if any), and you will rely on spontaneity and good contact with your audience to add enthusiasm to your delivery. The coach responding to a request to speak at a pep rally may have spent the last free period thinking up what to say, looking up the names of certain opposing players to mention, and generally getting ready to be "suddenly called on to say a few words." The important feature of this kind of delivery is that the speakers appear to be speaking without preparation because they do not have an outline, a manuscript, or an obvious set of notes, and it is most effective when they have close contact with the audience.

Manuscript

When your material is complex or when you must be very careful to give precise explanations, you need to use a manuscript. You may have written it out completely so that it can be reprinted, and perhaps even copies of it provided to reporters or others present. The manuscript might be an extensive outline of the points to be made, with suggested sentences included for clarity. For the television speaker, a manuscript may be provided in the form of a comprehensive TelePrompTer script, a reminder of points, or an outline of the speech. Often when you watch a television speechmaker looking straight into the camera, the speaker is really reading a manuscript from a sheet right next to the camera lens. Even a brief outline of the points can serve as a guide for you and helps you stay on the topic, within the time limits, and within your chosen organization. When working from a manuscript, you need to be especially careful to maintain contact with the audience and not just with your written material. You need to inject spontaneity into the message.

Memorized

You will often hear memorized speeches delivered by certain kinds of salespeople—the person selling encyclopedias or the carnival spieler selling "a thousand and one tools in this little package—it shreds carrots, peels potatoes, dices onions. . . ."

In the case of most memorized speeches, the speaker is depending on the force and flow of rhetoric to carry the selling message; the speaker is overwhelming the potential buyer with words. It is difficult to break into the sales pitch—and if you do, the salesperson needs to return to a prepared script in order to get momentum going again.

Oratory contests represent another kind of memorized speech situation. So do those political occasions when candidates have material so well in mind that they can stand up and pretend to be speaking off the cuff, although you would find if you followed that candidate from one occasion to another that the message would be almost identical. Some comics memorize their material and then make some local references to the particular audience, town, or club just to keep the message fresh.

Because of the speaking aids used by many television performers and by many political speakers on television, there are not as many public appearances that depend entirely on memorization as there once were. Instead of memorizing a speech, the candidate may make use of the rolling manuscript next to the camera or the TelePrompTer cards, thus turning a manuscript speech into what appears to be a memorized one.

Some difficulties with a memorized speech are that the speaker may have to exert so much effort to remember the correct words that contact with the audience is lost, contact with the place in the message is lost, or the delivery will sound "canned" or too rehearsed. A speaker who delivers a memorized speech must work extra hard to make it sound spontaneous because the speech has been worked over so many times. One advantage, however, is that because there are no papers or notes to get in the way, a speaker can attend completely to the audience.

☐ WHAT AFFECTS YOUR DELIVERY?

Certain things you do will help your speaking; other things will hinder you. Organization of your message helps the audience follow what you are saying. Your selection and treatment of your topic will make a difference in how well your communication is accepted. Your delivery will also affect your success with an audience.

In this chapter we shall discuss some of the factors that make a difference to those listening to you or watching you. This is not intended to be a lesson in how to make your voice better (if you think your voice quality affects your delivery). It is also not a lesson in how to wave your arms more meaningfully (if you think that your gestures may be getting

KINDS OF DELIVERY: APPLICATION

Think back over the past few weeks. Which of these kinds of delivery did you find yourself involved in? How often? Can you give one example of each that you have been involved in at some time (either awhile ago or recently)?

Kind of Communicative Delivery	Frequency of this kind of delivery in my own speaking		
	Never	Seldom	Often
Impromptu (write an example below)	____	____	____
_____	____	____	____
Extemporaneous (write an example below)	____	____	____
_____	____	____	____
Manuscript (write an example below)	____	____	____
_____	____	____	____
Memorized (write an example below)	____	____	____
_____	____	____	____

in the way of your delivery effectiveness). Rather, we shall describe those things which are a part of your communication delivery and which affect some listeners in some situations.

Mechanical Factors

In order to be a communicator, you must produce noises or movements, or a combination of these, in a way that will make sense to an audience. Without a delivery phase, your audience will never find out what it is you have to share with them. If faulty mechanical factors interfere with your delivery, your communication will not be effective. If, however, you can strengthen and capitalize on the positive factors, it will improve your effectiveness.

VOICE

Your voice is one of the first things to check. You need to be able to produce and sustain a sound with enough clarity and intensity to reach your audience. Public-address systems have extended our power to reach larger audiences and are a wonderful aid to the human voice. In less formal settings, you may need to talk loudly to a friend in a restaurant, for example, when the noise of clattering dishes interferes with your message. Whatever other characteristics of your voice you may want to develop, the first step is to make sure you can be heard. Remember that it is both necessary and courteous to speak loudly enough to be heard.

VOCAL TONE

You can probably think of speakers whose voices you like and some whose voices you can't stand. A distinctively irritating voice (too whining or too guttural, for example) may make a speaker seem unpleasant to the audience, and they will pay attention only to that characteristic. Some aspects of vocal tone can be developed by practice or professional training; however, individual physical limitations may have a great influence on vocal tone.

Voice Pitch   This is highness or lowness of your voice. Sounds are produced by the vibration of the vocal cords, you can learn something about pitch if you compare your vocal apparatus to a stretched rubber band or guitar string—the tighter it is stretched, the higher it sounds, because the speed of vibration increases. Similarly, the thickness and length of your vocal cords and the tension applied to them will affect the pitch of your voice.

Voice Volume   This is the loudness or softness of your voice. The intensity with which you project your voice should be appropriate to the situation you are in. You can whisper when you are telling a secret to someone very close to you, but you need more volume to address a group of people in a large room. Having enough force behind the air you are using to speak with is only a start on your volume control; you need a reserve of pressure, and you need the additional strength of the resonating part of your body to reinforce the air waves you are sending out. Training in voice projection can change your ability to control your voice volume most effectively for particular circumstances.

Voice Quality   You have heard about "voice prints," or visual representations of the speaking voice—wiggly lines that represent the waves created by a speaker. Those pictures of sound energy are as distinctive for each individual as fingerprints. The sound of your voice is a personal thing. It is a product of the relationship between the various parts of the speaking apparatus—the vocal cords; the resonating cavities; and the teeth, palate, and tongue—and factors such as physical and mental condition, fatigue, and posture. Your own individual way of producing speech sounds makes your voice distinctive enough so that it can be recognized even over a telephone, where much of the quality is filtered out. We all, however, hear our own voice resonating within our own head, and thus it sounds different to us from the way it does to others. That's the reason we are usually surprised when we first hear our voice on a tape recording—"That doesn't sound like me."

Tonal Duration   This is the stretching out or shortening of sound and is related to the rate at which you speak. You may extend the sounds you make, or you may clip them off. A drawling speaker will not reach the "normal" 150 words per minute, while a rapid-fire auctioneer, who doesn't spend so much time mouthing each syllable, will exceed that number by quite a few words. Studies of tape-recorded and "compressed speech" show that we can understand speeded-up speech nearly as well as speech delivered at normal rates.

Resonance   The parts of your speaking mechanism that produce this quality are the back of the mouth area, the heightened area of the hard palate, and the pharynx. These areas amplify sounds the way a sound box in a hi-fi speaker does. If you have something in your mouth and try to talk, your speech is pretty badly muffled. This is due to the obstruction of the original sound and also to the fact that the resonating areas are not being used. ("He talks as if he had a mouthful of mush.") A dull voice may result when the resonating areas are not left free and open to help the voice quality.

DICTION

Quality of diction depends partly on mechanical or physical factors and partly on intellectual ones. Standards of diction tend to change according to your age group, the part of the country you live in, the groups you want to impress, and your own desire to speak differently. Standards for pronunciation or articulation in the United States seem to be less rigid than those in some other countries because of the more diversified nature of our population's linguistic origins—so many of our citizens have other language backgrounds. Standards for *vocal* accuracy are also less rigid than those for *written* accuracy; we tend to overlook slight mispronunciations or bad articulation, but will notice misspellings or sloppy punctuation.

Major American Dialects   Speech scholars have designated three major dialects in the United States—Eastern, which is spoken by slightly more than 10 percent of the population; Southern, which is spoken by about 25 percent of the population; and General American Speech, which is spoken by the largest number of United States residents—about 65 percent.

This list does not take into account the many local dialects (those which are spoken on "speech islands") or the characteristic speech of certain ethnic groups or of those from special linguistic backgrounds. For instance, how do you account for the dialect of those who cannot pronounce certain typical American-English sounds, such as the Norwegian in Minnesota who says "yob" instead of "job"? Within the three major speech areas there are literally hundreds of speech islands.

Articulation and Enunciation   These are the mechanical factors that we depend on to make sounds that can be understood by someone else. The most basic unit studied in oral communication is not the word, but the *phoneme.* A phoneme is an identifiable sound. In some cases (such as "a" and "oh") a phoneme may also be a word, but it is more often only part of a word. For example, in "she" we have a consonant sound ("sh") followed by a vowel sound ("e"). *Articulation* is the way we say consonants; *enunciation* is the way we say vowels.

In order to more accurately relate the sounds (or phonemes) we make to the letters and combinations of letters in our language, a special alphabet, called the *phonetic alphabet,* is used. Although we can write and read all the words in the English language using only twenty-six letters, we need more than this to represent all the sounds we make in our spoken language—for instance, the letter "a" in "father" is not pronounced the same as the letter "a" in "name." The sounds of consonants also differ; the "c" in "city" is not pronounced like "c" in "cat."

Scholars and teachers of linguistics constructed the International Phonetic Alphabet (I.P.A.), which consists of forty-nine symbols. Other means for distinguishing sounds from orthographic (or written) letters have been developed by dictionary makers, but the I.P.A. is in most general use. Excellent texts are available for students who are interested in the study of phonetics and linguistics.

For the study of delivery, it is important to know that articulation of the consonants and enunciation of the vowels make up what we call *diction.* Diction also includes the factors related to vocal utterances discussed above. In its broadest sense, it also includes the choice and usage of words, which we shall discuss later in the section on intellectual factors.

WHAT AFFECTS DELIVERY: APPLICATION

THE BOSS SPEAKS

A small savings and loan company had been having some difficulty in getting employees working together for the local boss. He had been receiving some complaints about who got the tough assignments, who was told to do what, who should be the ones to produce the work, and just what each person's real job was. The boss suspected he should do something about the situation, and so he called the group together—fewer than a dozen employees—and read this prepared speech to them:

This is a chance for me to ask you to understand the boss better. Our company operates under a system of 'asking' people to do things, not telling them. We really don't like to give orders here. Any instructions I have will be forwarded in the form of a request. But I want to make it clear that a request means to do it, and do it now, unless that request is qualified by me.

One of the worst diseases our company can have is buck passing. When you are asked to do something, do it, and don't involve anyone else unless matters can be speeded up by getting help. Remember, if I had wanted someone else to do the job, I would have asked someone else.

No one is expected to do more than his share. Helping the other guy if it helps the office is OK and necessary, but remember you are being judged on your own performance and not on how well someone else does it for you. We still need Indians here as well as chiefs.

Sometimes you may disagree about the priority given some tasks and even about the jobs themselves. You are always welcome to argue your position. Once a final decision is made, however, you must cooperate. Everyone else is depending on you.

Finally, when you really disagree, hesitate before you call the boss stupid. After all, he did have brains enough to hire you. Is anybody any smarter than that?

Any questions?

1 Have a class member read this out loud as if it were being given as a speech to employees—they could be employees in a record shop, a grocery store, a lawyer's office, a radio station, or any kind of company. (This is an actual message from a boss to his employees.)
2 Ask the class members for their reactions to the tone of the talk and guess how much actual cooperation the boss will get as a result of it.
3 Have another member of the class read the message in another way. Is it possible to make these words more threatening? Less threatening? More autocratic? Less autocratic? What did the different speakers do that made the message effect different?
4 Let any members of the class try reading this speech to see how attitudes of the "employees" or other class members may change as a result of the tone of the speaker's delivery.

PHYSICAL MANNERISMS

A reminder here concerning physical appearance and mannerisms is necessary. What we covered in Chapter 3, on nonverbal communication, body language, and general visual messages, must be listed as relevant factors among the mechanical limitations to your delivery.

Gestures are commonly thought of as physical speechmaking components, complementing the voice as the oral apparatus. If you want to use all the available speaking tools, you need to develop your entire body. Gestures, however, are more than arm and hand movements. They should be thought of as all the ways in which a speaker can move any part of the body while attempting to communicate. Certain gestures will be acceptable to certain audiences, and if you know which kinds of moves to make, your communication will be more effective.

The following is a list of categories of gestures that you may want to refer to when you intend to use gestures in a speech:

Imperative—those gestures which will catch someone's attention or maintain contact so that you can make an additional point or continue a discourse without losing your audience.

Characteristic—those gestures which will label you as a certain kind of person or as a member of a particular group or which are simply characteristic of you as an individual

Locative—those gestures which indicate a direction, point to an area, or lead attention toward or away from a location

Descriptive—those gestures which show how tall, how wide, how full, etc., something is

Symbolic—those gestures which communicate definite meanings but are abstract rather than concrete (gestures describing the flight of birds or the motion of waves, for example)

Emphatic—those gestures which are used to emphasize a point being made orally—slamming one's fist into the other or hitting the lectern, for example

Summary of Mechanical Factors

The sounds you make and the physical impression you create constitute your communication delivery. Making appropriate use of your vocal mechanism will help you clearly articulate and enunciate your words and thus establish contact with your audience and arouse their interest.

Your eyes help establish and maintain that contact. The habit of looking at an audience will not be difficult to develop if you decide on a strategy for maintaining eye contact. In an informal conversation with one person you are permitted to look away occasionally; similarly, you are not expected to maintain constant eye contact with each individual in a large audience. You can, however, maintain good face-to-face contact with an audience even from a distance. One way of keeping in touch with your audience is to divide them mentally into three or four groups; select a person near the center of each group and then make sure that every few minutes you locate that person with your eyes. During a long speech you

Gestures can be imperative, characteristic, locative, descriptive, symbolic, or emphatic; they all help you establish contact.

(David Tenenbaum/Editorial Photocolor Archives.)

(Lee Greathouse/Editorial Photocolor Archives.)

(Pictorial Parade, Inc./Editorial Photocolor Archives.)

would need to "contact" different people in each group, but the audience will have the impression that you are being attentive to the entire room. Your gaze should move easily across those segments of your audience because glancing up and down, back and forth, in a jerky manner is distracting.

SEVEN SUGGESTIONS FOR USING GESTURES

1 Use gestures to support your delivery, not overwhelm it.
2 Use gestures to emphasize points. Thus use them sparingly—only when needed.
3 Use gestures that are visible to the audience; relate the extent of your gesture to the size of your audience and your distance from them. Big audiences need big gestures.

(Don Koblitz/Editorial Photocolor Archives.)

4 Use gestures that flow naturally from you and are related to the message you are delivering.

5 Use gestures that spring spontaneously from your delivery, not ones that will seem contrived or stilted.

6 Use a variety of gestures; avoid those which seem hackneyed.

7 Don't use gestures that will interfere with the audience's listening to you.

Intellectual Factors

Your delivery depends on what is happening inside your head as well as on your voice and your physical activity. Your intellectual capabilities will determine your use of words, your choice of words, and the organization and orderliness of the things you say.

(Andrew Sacks/Editorial Photocolor Archives.)

KNOWLEDGE OF YOUR SUBJECT

If you don't know what you're talking about, you won't do very well in delivery. Whatever content there is in the message you are delivering will depend on your preparation.

Not all our communication time is spent telling others about the complexity of photosynthesis or the principles of the Federal Reserve Act. Such subjects require considerable knowledge and much organization on the part of the speaker. Much of our delivery time is spent talking about relatively insignificant things. For example, how much time do you spend arguing with a friend about the merits of a recent movie, trying to convince another person to go to a particular restaurant, or discussing the outcome of a football game?

Although you may be able to bluff your friends and get by without having much information about your subject in some informal situations, you can't expect to be as successful in a public-speaking situation. For one thing, there is more chance that a member of a large audience will know something about your subject. For another thing, you are more likely to be dealing with a more complicated subject, and hence you will have to have more background than for your everyday conversations.

Earlier we said that lack of knowledge about your subject can be one of the major causes of stage fright. If you are not prepared to deliver

"Desmond always weighs his words very carefully ever since someone popped him one for making an ill-considered remark."

The speaker must choose the most effective words for his or her audience. *(The New Yorker.)*

your speech, you will very likely experience those familar symptoms of sweating, shaking, dry mouth, and "butterflies" in the stomach, and you may become so preoccupied with these sensations that you'll lose most of the poise you have been trying to develop.

Feelings of inadequacy and all the accompanying bad physical and emotional reactions can sometimes be overcome if you prepare yourself well. Being prepared will make you feel that you know at least as much as your audience does about your subject and that you're ready to give a good speech.

LANGUAGE TOOLS AVAILABLE AND READY

The speaker must have a command of words; that is, he or she must know the meanings of words, choose the most effective ones for the audience, and make them relate to one another with logic and style.

Notice we did not say "a large vocabulary." You do not need to use long words or a whole string of synonyms to demonstrate that you have command of the language. A few crisp, well-chosen words will have more meaning for an audience than a flood of multisyllabic, obscure ones.

William G. McAdoo, a member of President Woodrow Wilson's Cabinet, wrote this about the then Senator (and later President) Warren G. Harding:

> He was a speechmaker; he spoke on every convenient occasion in a big, bow-wow style of oratory. He would use rolling words which had no application to the topic at hand, and his speeches left the impression of an army of pompous phrases moving over the landscape in search of an idea. Sometimes these meandering words would actually capture a straggling thought and bear it triumphantly, a prisoner in their midst, until it died of servitude and overwork.

Another writer commenting on the same speaker was the *Baltimore Sun* columnist and authority on American speech, H. L. Mencken, who wrote:

> [The prose style of Harding] reminds me of tattered washing on the line; it reminds me of stale bean-soup, of college yells, of dogs barking idiotically through endless nights. It is so bad that sort of grandeur creeps into it. It drags itself out of the dark abyss of pish, and crawls insanely up to the topmost pinnacle of tosh.

In spite of such criticisms, however, this person was elected President of the United States. You know of other speechmakers whose oratory was a great rolling wave of rhetoric and who were therefore considered both very wise and very great by some elements of this society.

Wisdom is equated, by some listeners, with flowery words and eloquent phrases. We are still subjected daily to communication involving long words and empty rhetoric—whether it is that of a long-winded friend with a big vocabulary, a television announcer who shouts that this is our last chance to buy, or a politician who pontificates on the glories of God, motherhood, and the flag. We are tempted to believe the flowing delivery of such speakers. They are successful just often enough so that we may believe that is the way to real power. It is unfortunate that a segment of our society can be persuaded by empty words and slogans when the real meanings of our messages can be delivered with more clarity using simple words and nonemotional appeals.

If, as we mentioned in Chapter 3, meanings are in people and not in words, then it is possible to move people who share meanings in common with ours. The more difficult you make it for words to do their job—by using obscure terms, jargon, unfamiliar slang, obsolete words, offensive references, or ambiguous phrases—the harder it will be to call up the appropriate meanings in others and the less effective you will be

TABLE 9-1 Guide to Our Use of Spoken and Written Language

General Category	Formal		Informal		Popular		
Specific type	Technical	Academic Formal	Standard informal	Familiar informal	Common slang	Profanity	Obscenity
Mode of presentation	Written primarily		Written and spoken		Spoken primarily		
Source (where found)	Technical journals, at technical meetings, in professional reports, on diagrams and flow charts, legislative acts, legal opinions	Academic writing and speaking, ministers, scientists, teachers, business letters, many textbooks	Political appeals, mass media (radio, newspapers, magazines, TV)	Advertising, conversation, family talk, chatter with friends, gatherings of mixed sexes	Close friends, meetings of same sex, teams		
Language and construction	Highly organized, well-structured, extensive and esoteric vocabulary, precise expressions and usage, footnotes, jargon and catchwords, literary references, classical terms		Less rigorous construction, recognizable but not standard forms, language varied from common to specialized, repetitious		Careless construction, geographical variation, limited vocabulary, fad words, specialized terms, cliches, metaphors, rich images of physical acts and functions		
How learned	In schools, formal classes, lessons, rule books and style manuals, imitation of professional stylists		In early schooling, at home, listening to others, radio, TV, movies, peers		Among friends, peers, street talk, imitation of popular neighborhood heroes		
Word examples	*sibling* *fatigued* *renovate* *paroxysm*		*brother, sister* *tired, worn out* *repair* *seizure*		*bud, sis* *pooped* *fix* *fit*		

as a speaker. If you can keep your words simple and direct, you will gain in objective understanding.

WRITTEN AND SPOKEN LANGUAGE

Language is probably our most important means of communication. The way we use language will identify us with certain groups and may prevent our joining other groups. George Bernard Shaw's *Pygmalion*, which was later made into the successful musical *My Fair Lady*, deals with the transformation of a slum girl into an elegant lady, a transformation based mainly on language. Much of our business and social success depends on our language usage, and thus many "personal improvement" courses or programs have been designed to help people become successful in these areas by increasing their communication skills. Some of these will promise instant social success or almost immediate advancement in your career. You should look at any course that promises such things with suspicion, because only you, as a person, can make changes in your communication. There are ways you may be guided, motivated, or inspired to develop the skills and knowledge you want, but you must develop them yourself. You must first understand what you are trying to achieve and then practice to make the new behaviors an integral part of your life.

A good way to start is to analyze the levels of speaking you are likely to find in the world around you. One level is useful for one purpose, and other levels for other purposes. You are free to choose. You should understand, however, that people put you in certain categories according to the way you write and speak—and it is up to you to decide which one you want to be placed in. Reactions to patterns of speech and writing vary in different parts of the country and also among people of different occupations or social classes.

WHAT AFFECTS DELIVERY: APPLICATION

VOICE AND PERSONALITY

Studies have been conducted at many universities on the relationship between a speaker's voice (and other delivery features) and that speaker's personality. For many years, evaluations of voice quality, pitch, rate of speaking, and intonations and inflections have been the basis for determining certain qualities in the person doing the speaking.

If you were to set up categories of *loudness* and *rate*, you could have these four groups: (1) loud/fast, (2) loud/slow, (3) soft/fast, and (4) soft/slow. Can you think of speakers who hold public office who fall into these categories?

Voice quality as it relates to personality has been evaluated in terms of the continuum from a highly inflected, melodic, varied pitch to monotonous, dull pitch and inflection. In some studies, speakers toward the highly inflected end of the scale were judged to be more kind, generous, and sympathetic, while those toward the other end were judged to be more selfish and lacking in goodwill.

1 Ask some members of the class to demonstrate the qualities of voice in the categories of loud/fast, loud/slow, etc. Ask the class to give their own personal impressions of the kind of people such speakers appear to be. Are there any differences in opinion about what kind of person has a particular kind of voice? Do people always agree on factors such as rate and loudness? Could such preferences be a result of a person's own speech habits and speech environments? What do we usually think about a fast-talking person? Consider the stereotypes about carnival spielers and high-pressure salespeople. Are such judgments always accurate?

2 Do you agree with the findings mentioned above concerning people who speak in a monotone as against those who use a lot of inflection? Do you think the person whose speech is overly inflected is showing off, being "theatrical," or being overly emotional? How much inflection and pitch variation is "just right"? Does this depend on the situation and the audience?

3 Find a statement or brief speech (less than two minutes in length) and have various members of the class say it or read it, first with great pitch variations and then with no inflections—in a monotone. Ask groups in the class to discuss their reaction to these different types of delivery. Is there a tendency to judge people by how much emphasis they put into their communication? How does this relate to loudness and speed variations? Do we judge others on these bases too? Should we? What other factors should be considered in judging a speaker?

Psychological or Emotional Factors

Most of the problems in delivery that end up in this category start somewhere else. We may get stage fright because we haven't prepared well. We become embarrassed by an audience reaction and decide not to try to communicate again with that group. A mispronounced word leads to a strong desire not to use any more difficult words at all. Not understanding feedback from an audience may cause us to do something foolish in our speechmaking and to brood about it later.

THE DESIRE TO SPEAK

Unless you have an inclination to talk to others, your delivery will be pretty weak. If you have no desire to get up in front of an audience, it is quite likely that your attitude will become apparent as soon as you start to talk. We said at the beginning of this book that your attitude about speaking will determine in many ways how well you communicate. If you are not interested in communicating with others, you must look within yourself for the reasons.

INTEREST IN YOUR AUDIENCE

If you have a desire to speak, you must assume certain responsibilities. Once you are in front of that audience—whether it is a group of friends or a huge auditorium full of strangers—you assume the responsibility for the success of your communication. Maybe you don't care whether you succeed or not; if you don't, the best bet is that you will *not* succeed.

On the other hand, you may feel you'd like to get the attention of the audience, motivate them to do something (laugh at your jokes, join the Red Cross, believe in God, or get together again for a party), and watch their reactions for feedback. You as speaker have a choice about how hard to work at this.

Once you've assessed mechanical, intellectual, and emotional factors, you can deliver a message effectively to any audience. *(Editorial Photocolor Archives.)*

In an informal setting, you can experience all the excitement of making a few friends pay attention to you and then getting them to work together on some project. In a more formal setting, you have a bigger challenge, but the principle is the same: an interest in doing the job is essential to the success of your delivery.

WHAT AFFECTS DELIVERY: APPLICATION

SELF-TEST ON FACTORS

In a critical evaluation of your delivery, certain factors have been pointed out to you by others, or you have noticed them yourself. List factors in the left-hand column and indicate the degree of difficulty you would have in correcting or improving them in the column at the right.

| | *Possibility of Changing* | | |
| | *Impossible* | *Difficult* | *Easy* |

A. Mechanical factors I noticed
   or had pointed out to me

B. Intellectual factors I noticed
   or had pointed out to me

C. Psychological factors I noticed
   or had pointed out to me

■ LOOKING BACK

I. You have been a speaker for a long time in informal settings and probably in some formal ones.

II. Each of the basic kinds of delivery has some advantages of its own.

   A. Impromptu speaking has a spontaneity about it not matched in other types, but is difficult for the inexperienced speaker to pull thoughts together fast enough for effective speaking without planning.

B. Extemporaneous speaking has the advantage of being fairly spontaneous but also of your having time to prepare.

C. Manuscript speaking is very precise when accuracy is more important than spontaneity.

D. Memorized speeches, when well delivered, can sound spontaneous although the speaker plans exactly what to say at every point in the speech and has the advantage of long preparation and practice.

III. Different kinds of things will affect your delivery.

A. Mechanical factors include your voice and its qualities, your diction, dialect, articulation, and physical mannerisms.

B. Intellectual factors include your knowledge of the subject, and the language tools you can use.

C. Psychological factors include your desire to speak and your interest in impressing the audience—in other words, a basic attitude about speaking and about that particular speaking assignment.

CHAPTER 10
YOU AS A COMMUNICATION CONSUMER

The world cannot continue to wage war like physical giants and to seek peace like intellectual pygmies.

— Basil O'Connor

You can tell the ideals of a nation by its advertisements.

— Norman Douglas

Perhaps of all the creations of man language is the most astonishing.

— Lytton Strachey

Slogans are both exciting and comforting, but they are also powerful opiates for the conscience . . . Some of mankind's most terrible misdeeds have been committed under the spell of certain magic words or phrases.

— James Bryant Conant

☐ INTRODUCTION

Up to now in this book we have tried to present a balance between two roles our communication can play. (1) Communication can help us get others to believe or to act in ways we want them to or add to their information; and (2) communication can help us find out how we ourselves should believe or act or work with the information we receive. In this final chapter we openly emphasize the *consumer* role of humans as communicators.

We have said many times in the previous sections on persuasion and audience that you are a receiver of persuasion. Persuasion rules, strengths, weaknesses, abuses, ethics, tricks, and excesses are as important for persuasive **listening** as they are for persuasive **speaking**.

Consumer roles in persuasion are often subtle. Mass media, however, represent perhaps the most obvious and demonstrable way we consume information and persuasion. Whether we listen to a single speaker-persuader or we "tune in" some mass medium, the principles are the same. We will act wisely or foolishly partly because of the messages we get. We will be effective in our lives partly because we understand how the persuaders, individual and mass, operate their communication and how we operate ours.

If you take a serious look at your communication, you will find that you spend more time receiving communication than sending it. Talking, writing, or signaling to others takes only a small fraction of the time you spend in communication with your environment. You listen to others give information or directions, read magazines and newspapers, listen to the radio and watch television, read the labels on food packages, go to the movies, attend lectures, and see ads on subway walls or buildings. You are a consumer of communication.

In our economy, millions of dollars are spent every year by advertisers who want you to be a consumer of their goods. First you receive their messages, and then—they hope—you buy their products. One of the ways a seller can influence you to buy is through the mass media. You are exposed to ads on television, on radio, and in newspapers, and your buying decisions can also be influenced by movies or lectures.

Detergents are not the only things for sale. Ideas must also be sold—like a political candidate, support of the United Fund, and safe driving. Although these are not tangible items, the goal is the same—to influence you, the consumer, to accept them.

Rules of the game of influence are not always clear. Each kind of mass medium has certain responsibilities, just as each has certain opportunities to reach a public. The mass media have enormous influence, and this chapter will develop some understandings of how they work and affect our lives.

☐ SAFEGUARDS: WHO HELPS PROTECT US?

Individuals sometimes need protection from others in their society. Often we can protect ourselves, but in certain situations we need outside help. If there were no laws regarding stop signs, we would be in more danger than we already are when we drive. Even if no police officer is standing at the corner, most drivers will obey the sign and stop their cars. We depend on others to do the "right thing." We depend on a symbol rather than a person with a badge to protect us when we move through traffic. The referee of a boxing match makes sure that each fighter conducts himself according to the rules of the ring. An official at a football game is there to see that the policies and procedures of the sport are followed. A teacher may sit in class during an examination to ensure that everyone honors the rules, and thus protects the students against those who might cheat.

Some Public Controls

Over the years the federal government has become responsible for protecting citizens against many kinds of abuses. The Food and Drug Administration sees that labels on packaged goods are accurate, while the Federal Trade Commission protects against fraudulent or misleading advertising or misrepresentations. Broadcasting practices are governed by the Federal Communications Commission, and the Postal Service enforces our laws concerning the mailing of obscene or socially unacceptable printed material. More recently the government established the Consumer Protection Agency, which is concerned with our welfare as purchasers, and we have a variety of agencies interested in the environment and the pollution of our water, food, and air.

An example of communication control that you may not ordinarily think of is the work of the Food and Drug Administration. One of its tasks is to assure the purity of drugs sold to the public. It also makes sure that the *words* used on labels are not misleading and that the drug will do what the label says it will. The government carefully watches labels on such items as packages, cans, prescriptions, and clothing. The manufacturer must tell what a bottle or box contains and what material your suit or dress is made of. Thus the federal government is watching over *what is said* about various products as much as it is looking critically at their *contents*. Communication has therefore become an important part of federal control.

In addition to the federal agencies, many state licensing and testing agencies have similar powers to inspect and pass on not only the contents of what is sold but also what the seller says about it and what a normally prudent buyer expects to get.

Still another level of control is the quasi-government agency. In local areas, for example, a Better Business Bureau helps protect consumers from fraudulent practices. In some communities a chamber of commerce, a retail merchants association, or some similar public group will enforce local regulations or customs relating to consumer affairs.

Perhaps more obviously connected with the protection of our communication are such groups as the National Association of Broadcasters (which watches over radio and television practices), the Motion Picture Code Board (which helps regulate the output of the film industry), and the Association of Newspaper Editors (one group among many concerned with printed materials). Other kinds of self-regulating groups have been formed by professional people, including doctors and lawyers, whose activities are regulated to some degree both by their own organizations and by national, regional, state, or local groups. In all these cases, there is a strong emphasis on *what is said* to clients (the messages these professionals send out) as well as on the quality of the service provided by the broadcasters, film producers, newspapers, or doctors and lawyers.

When you go to a store, you want reliable service and good products. You also want the salesperson, the dealer, or the serviceperson to communicate honestly with you about what is being sold or repaired. Being treated fairly in a business transaction involves *what is said to you* as much as what you are getting. Much of the time we buy the language about a product even more confidently than we buy the product; therefore we need consumer protection against false or misleading language as much as we need protection against shoddy or low-quality merchandise.

PUBLIC CONTROLS: APPLICATIONS

COUNT YOUR CALORIES; MEASURE YOUR WORDS

In 1964 the federal government charged that the author of a bestselling book on weight loss, *Calories Don't Count*, was part of a fraudulent weight-reducing scheme involving the sale of CDC (Calories Don't Count) capsules, which were to be used in weight reduction according to instructions in the book.

The Attorney General's office alleged that the Food, Drug, and Cosmetics Act was violated. In an earlier action, the Food and Drug Administration had seized safflower-oil capsules, which had been distributed as part of the promotion of the book. Copies of the book also were held in evidence.

About six months earlier another federal agency, the Federal Trade Commission, had charged that the author of the book, the manufacturers of the pills, and the publisher of the book made false weight-control claims both in the promotion of the book and in the book itself.

Besides asserting their usefulness in weight reduction, the book claimed that the capsules were effective in the treatment and prevention of heartburn, arteriosclerosis, diabetes, heart disease, and cancer, and that they improved the complexion, promoted general health, and increased sexual drive.

1 How much of this alleged fraud stemmed from the difference between the world of words and the world of real things? Did the government charge that the capsules were harmful, or did it say that the claims made for them were not accurate?
2 The Food and Drug Administration can stop the manufacture of products whose labels do not give clear instructions for their use and which do not produce the effects claimed for them on the labels. The Federal Trade Commission is interested in how the products are promoted and in how a citizen might be misled by the claims made in advertising and promotional literature. Are both these watchdog systems based on communication?
3 Who decides what is the liability of the author of a book containing allegedly misleading material? Of the publisher who sells it? Of the bookstores that handle and promote it? Of those who pass it around to friends and endorse it?

PLAYBOY PRIVACY

The wife of a postman in a large city wrote to the local newspaper criticizing the school superintendent for reading *Playboy* magazine. She said a man who read such magazines should not have a position in the schools. The postman had approved her letter, the wife said, and it was as though he had sent it himself. It was he who had told his wife that he delivered *Playboy* to the home of the school superintendent every month.

The local postmaster ordered an investigation, saying that the postman had violated "several sections" of the code of ethics that prohibit mail carriers from telling anything about the mail they deliver. As a result of the investigation, the mailman was barred forever from delivering mail and was reassigned to the vehicle-maintenance department.

The school superintendent said that he thought the real issue was not what he liked to read, but rather his right to privacy. He added that he felt sorry for people who must spy and snoop, but he did not intend to file legal charges.

1 What is the issue here? Does a mailcarrier, or any person who has information about another, have a duty or a right to make the information known if he believes this will be in the public good? If a reporter stated in a newspaper story that the superintendent subscribed to *Playboy* magazine, would this constitute an invasion of privacy?
2 Are there absolute rules governing what one citizen can make public about another? Generally speaking, libel is the act of defaming with printed words, and slander is the act of defaming with spoken words. Would you have taken this case to court if you had been the superintendent?

3 Had you been the mailman, how would you have reacted to your wife's asking your help in making the disclosure public? (She read the letter to him before sending it to the paper.) Would you expect the postmaster to take some action against you?

LICENSE TO OPERATE

Station WXXX-TV is due for a renewal of its license by the Federal Communications Commission. A local organization representing Vida Unida (a Spanish-speaking minority group in the community) has protested to the FCC that the station does not give adequate air time to minority-group persons, that the hiring practices of the station are discriminatory, since only two office workers and one weather reporter belong to that minority group; and that reports of crime and legal affairs accent the minority involvement unfairly. The channel frequency now being used by WXXX-TV would not be picked up by another network because each now has a station in this city, and there is also a Spanish-language TV station.

1 Imagine you are the moderator for a hearing involving the station management and the leaders of Vida Unida. What arguments would you be prepared for? Could you keep the two opposing forces from blaming each other before they got down to the business of offering evidence?
2 Suppose you are the manager of the station and believe you have made many efforts to recruit minority-group technicians and reporters; in fact, three blacks and one American Indian hold very good positions at the studio. Would you use this to argue that you have an antidiscrimination policy? What response are you likely to get from Vida Unida members?
3 Suppose you are the leader of the Vida Unida and were turned down for employment at the station last year because you did not have the "kinds of skills the station is seeking." Would you make this personal case a part of your general argument?
4 Would you support the station in its renewal negotiations or oppose it? Role-play this incident for a few minutes to articulate the various concerns. Then have the actors change sides and try to develop the rest of the negotiation as members of the opposing group.

   Thus many different groups and agencies, all trying to help us be better consumers, are watching over communication, supplementing our own good judgment in selecting honest dealers and professionals. However, we can still be the victims of sharp practices on the part of communicators who may know more about how our communication works than we do. This is only one reason to learn more about what goes on in communication and speaking situations.

No agency is ready to help us unsnarl an argument with friends; but they give us feedback. *(Abigail Heyman/Magnum.)*

Some Interpersonal Controls

Just as there are agencies to watch over public communication activities (as well as the manufacturing, distributing, and consumption of goods), there are ways to govern our dealings with one another as individuals. Civil courts stand ready to hear cases of slander involving private citizens, just as they hear cases of public libel. Malicious gossip becomes a matter for court action when a person can demonstrate that he or she has been damaged by what someone else has said. The telephone company can assist a subscriber who receives threatening or obscene phone calls and will even help prosecute the offender. Verbal agreements and signed contracts are communication acts that relate to our laws, and two people in contact with each other may seek assistance from someone else.

However, much of the damage we inflict on one another with our communications is not clear-cut enough to require a slander suit or a breach-of-contract action. Mostly we harm one another interpersonally by giving bad information, by making another person angry, by spreading confusion, by increasing personal conflict, or by isolating ourselves as a result of inappropriate talking or listening behavior. And no one helps us control communication on this level except our friends and enemies who give us feedback.

No agency is ready to help us unsnarl an argument with a friend or untangle a set of directions for finding the post office in a strange city. While we have laws regarding discrimination against others because of their race, sex, or religion, a minority-group member finds little protection in society against interpersonal bias in the form of degrading remarks, jokes, name calling, or stereotyped attitudes. Such common person-to-person expressions of individual discrimination are seldom taken to court or acted on overtly, and yet in some ways they are as powerful a discriminatory force as housing covenants or job restrictions.

Some Intrapersonal Controls

The idea of thought control is hateful to Americans, brought up as we have been with a tradition of freedom. The concept that we are not free to think what we like, even if we do not express our thoughts, has been the subject of many books (George Orwell's 1984, for example), articles, and political arguments. No matter how many laws may inhibit our speech and actions or how much our friends may influence our speaking out, we feel that one area is exclusively and completely ours—our thinking.

"Nobody can tell me what to think," we say, secure that deep down inside we are free.

In reality, however, a great many people tell us what to think, and the idea that we are freethinking persons becomes questionable when we consider the influences on our intrapersonal communication. Our values and attitudes often stem from persons we admire. They probably shaped our opinions about dogs and cats, men with beards, tall people, fat people, black skin, white skin, yellow skin, brown skin, church ritual, and various kinds of food. Although we may change our minds as a result of personal experience—switch to mashed potatoes if french fries give us indigestion, for example—we are influenced by the opinions of others in almost everything we do.

We usually borrow our beliefs from someone else—what we read and what we see others doing and hear them saying. Stereotypes develop when we assume that everyone or everything in a particular group is identical—that all Texans are rich and wear big hats, that all apples are red when they are ripe, and that all dogs are friendly, for example. You are rewarded by your friends if you believe the same things they do. You are probably more comfortable with yourself if you can depend on some ideas without having to think too much about every little item in your world. In many ways we become dependent on others for our ideas. It is very difficult to tell which ideas and attitudes you have developed for yourself and which you have simply borrowed from others you trust and admire.

Intrapersonal communication—what goes on inside us—is the closest we come to freedom of thought. There are three kinds of controls we can exert over our intrapersonal communication that help keep us free: (1) control over our judgment of our sources of information—whether to believe them or not believe them; (2) control over what we do about the messages we receive; and (3) control over how we make use of the feedback we receive from others as a result of the messages we impart to them.

The first kind of control gives us the freedom to listen critically to others. We may regard our parents' ideas as realistic and reasonable, or we may reject them. We may decide to believe that a friend is giving us accurate information about what classes we take, what clothes to buy, and what movies to see, or we may put that information in perspective with other information we have and decide against the advice.

The second kind of control lets us plan to act or not to act. We may work out how we will sign up for a class, buy some new clothes, pay for a movie, get to work early the next day, or study for an exam. When we choose to take a course of action, we think about consequences, balancing risk and safety, and we speculate about what good or bad results will follow if a certain course is taken. Even when we assume that other pressures are so great that we are not free to determine the action we want to take, that in itself is a kind of planning and decision. We decide on future actions by talking to ourselves.

The third kind of control involves feedback. Each time we are in communication with another person, a whole range of things happens. We speak. Another person answers—or is silent. Either way, we receive some data as a result of our first message—and that becomes part of what we think the other person's reaction is. That is feedback. We can choose to ignore feedback or to use it. If you start telling a joke and your friends all groan, will you continue, or will you stop? If you say "Hi" to a friend and get no answer, what assumptions do you make? If you finish the joke and nobody laughs, what do you think? If you greet your friend and get a big hug and a kiss, what is your possible range of actions? Feedback helps us adjust our behavior in accordance with others' responses, in the form of signals, statements, moves, signs, gestures, noises, or acts. Until we are affected internally by feedback, we are not ready to do anything about it. We are still free to determine whether to change or adjust our communication as a result of the new information.

INTERPERSONAL CONTROLS: APPLICATIONS

POLICE METHODS

Burglary victims usually cooperate with the police by giving them a description of the items stolen. Mr. and Mrs. Joseph Smith told the police that their

$40 radio had been stolen while they were visiting friends. However, since both were blind, they were unable to describe the radio.

1 Does our society assume that we all have similar abilities? Does the law require Braille labels on medicines for the blind? (In some places druggists must read aloud to purchasers the instructions for taking medication in case the person cannot read them or will forget to.
2 How would you interview Mr. and Mrs. Smith if you were the investigating officer? Simulate a conversation between the police and these sightless victims.

TALK TO THE MANAGER

Go to a local store where you are not known. Think of a good reason to ask to see the manager—for example, to ask about a new product, to compliment the quality of the goods or service, or to inquire about the store's hiring policies.

Observe the reactions of the people around you when you ask to see the manager. If you ask a clerk, what is that clerk's reaction? If your message to the manager is not a negative one, how does the manager respond?

A Summary of Communication Controls

Both external and internal controls over our communication affect our lives. Controls make some behaviors illegal and therefore risky. They subject us to judgment by friends and others if we do not follow the laws, customs, norms, and values of the society we live in.

External controls are maintained over the mass communication media of our world (including point-of-purchase advertising and the labels on the goods we buy). Controls are also imposed on some interpersonal relationships by means of laws concerning libel and slander and statutes covering individuals who might defraud others.

For much of our interpersonal and most of our intrapersonal communication, however, we are our own control agencies. How we see ourselves in relation to others will provide guidelines for what to say and how and when to say it. But the final decision is ours, as are the consequences. Although we may not be hauled into court for making an erroneous assumption, we may act on that assumption in a way that gets us in trouble. A teacher would not be expelled from the American Association of University Professors for telling students they are dumb, but the relationship between the teacher and the students would suffer as a result. If you lie to a friend about a personal matter, the case will probably not end up in a civil court, but your friendship may be damaged.

In brief, we are our own police and enforcement agency of our communication.

☐ MASS MEDIA OF COMMUNICATION

The term "mass media" comes up so often that we assume we know what it means. Generally it refers to newspapers, magazines, books, radio, television, and movies. It is also possible to consider public lectures, rallies, church services, parades, club meetings, and even museums and zoos as mass media.

Folk singers whose ballads carried stories from one town to the next and immortalized the exciting activities of kings, thieves, knights, and ill-fated lovers were an early form of mass media. The invention of movable type made possible another mass medium—books. Prior to that, few books were produced, since they had to be copied painstakingly by hand. Once books became available in great quantities, the desire to read and to learn from them expanded. Printing was considered by some to be the work of the Devil and was protested by some who set themselves up as guardians of the public good. Too much learning was harmful, they claimed, and this new device would surely mean the end of society.

It appears that some of the same claims are being made today about television. Some argue that "bad" media of communication will drive out the "good" media. Many critics of television may be in the same position as the first critics of books. They predict that this new means of mass communication will bring an end to our society as we know it.

Some Public Myths about Mass Media

From the time the first speaker stood up to talk to an assemblage of people, we have been concerned with a mass audience. It is shortsighted of us to consider only the modern electronic media as mass media. *Language* began as a "mass" medium because it can reach a large group of people at one time.

MYTH: MASS MEDIA ARE NEW

Mass media have not just been invented. Movable type and printed books made information available to a greater mass of people. Although people were already familiar with spoken language as a mass medium, its use in this way was limited; the printed word meant that the speaker need not be physically present to influence a listener—or the reader.

Printing made it possible to record history and to preserve the tales and legends of a nation. The singing troubador was replaced by books and then by newssheets that could be passed around and posted for all to see. These were the forerunners of our newspapers, which today are one printed form of mass media. More recent electronic forms are radio, television, and motion pictures. Technology has changed our mass media—from the invention of movable type to the developments in

New technologies do not automatically make earlier forms obsolete. *(Charles Gatewood.)*

movies, TV, and radio. Modern technology has also given us a way to extend face-to-face communication; a speaker can address an audience in Los Angeles at noon, for example, and talk to a different audience—in person—that night in New York by making use of the technology of air travel.

New technologies, however, do not automatically make earlier forms obsolete, as some have feared. Newspaper reporters were afraid that radio would wipe them out. Some newspapers in the 1930s and 1940s refused to print radio program schedules because they considered radio to be a keen competitor. Later, motion picture producers were afraid that movies would disappear when television came in. While it is true that some motion picture studios and theaters have closed, more films are produced today than in the years before television. Newspapers and radio have not disappeared either. Some critics of television have predicted that it will bring an end to conversation, but it is unlikely that our communication difficulties can be blamed only on this medium. In fact, some have noted that we now have more to talk about because what we see on television provides topics for casual conversation: "Did you see the Carson show last night?" "The NBC Special was spectacular." "The congressional hearings weren't on this week, but I'll be glad when they're back." "Summer reruns sure are a bore." "Did you catch the President's talk last night?"

Predictions that the newest popular medium, television, would finish off all other means of communication—speaking, reading, movie-going, and radio and record listening have simply not come true. There are more books published today, more movies made, more radio programs produced, more records sold, and about as much conversation and public speaking going on as ever before.

MYTH: MASS MEDIA ARE ALL-POWERFUL

We exaggerate the power of the mass media, by themselves, to influence the public. When mass media operate with supporting influence, they *can* move great masses of people. But by themselves, the media do not have that same kind of power. The rise of the Nazi party in Germany in the 1930s was trumpeted by placards, radio programs, rallies, newspapers, and motion pictures; and all those media contributed to the public acceptance of Hitler. The media reported hate messages filled with threats and patriotic appeals promising rewards. Thus the media were only the *messengers* of the fears and hopes that caused the German people to follow the Fuehrer in his search for world conquest. The media did not create Hitler—they supported his drive for power, made known the consequences of opposing him, and told of the glories of his cause. However, they could not have placed him in power without armies, storm troopers, concentration camps, munitions, and control over what the population was permitted to read and hear.

In the United States in 1948, nearly every newspaper and most radio stations opposed Harry Truman's bid for election and supported the Republican candidate, Thomas Dewey. The morning after the election, the *Chicago Tribune* came out with the headline "DEWEY DEFEATS TRUMAN" while votes were still being counted in the close race, in which Truman turned out to be the winner. If the "power of the press" were as great as we sometimes imagine, the media would have been able to put Dewey into office on the strength of their editorial opinions.

Studies of television programming indicate some relationship between violence on TV programs and the actions of viewers. No investigators have yet been able to say definitely that television programs *cause* violent behavior, although many studies have shown that people will act out violence they have seen in a movie or on a television screen if they already have aggressive tendencies. However, others feel that the viewer gets the aggressive urge out of his system by watching violence on television or in a movie. It can be demonstrated only that what a person sees on a mass medium will influence his already-present inclinations. Research continues in these areas, and the effects of mass media on consumers are still not perfectly understood. It is accurate to say, however, that the mass media can exert some influences on listeners, viewers, and readers, and that these operate in conjunction with other concurrent or pre-disposing forces.

Mass media can influence us as consumers in many ways: we buy cars, soap, food, and so on, largely as a result of mass media advertising influence. Our decisions to vote for a candidate, give to the United Fund, picket the bus company, stop smoking, oppose a war, join the Army, write to a congressman, or file suit in court are all affected by mass media.

However, mass media operate only through human beings. We accord status to certain people because of the way they are treated in the media. If a person is important enough to appear on radio or television or to be written about in the newspapers, we think that person is important enough to listen to. However, we probably saw or read about the celebrity in the first place because somebody working for a newspaper or a television station assumed that he or she was interesting and important to us. That kind of circular cause-and-effect relationship may explain why some candidates for office and some breakfast cereals become well known on the basis of what we are told about them, rather than because of any inherent value or inborn "greatness."

Mass media get their power from consumers who react to their information or approach. A newspaper does not sell news or papers for a living—it sells *consumers* to potential advertisers. It charges prices for advertising space on the basis of the number of people who buy the paper. A television station does not sell time or entertainment, either. It sells to an advertiser a possible number of *viewers* who will probably see the advertising message during the programs. The cost of an hour of television time will vary depending on how many people can be expected to be watching at that time. This is why so much research is carried out to determine which television programs are watched most. These "ratings" will dictate whether a program will survive. Advertisers pay for consumers. They do not pay for programs or for space in newspapers except in the hope that such programs or space will produce purchasers of a product—people.

MYTHS OF MASS MEDIA: APPLICATION

On December 19, 1968, the official Soviet press reported the starting of a huge power generator in Siberia, terming it the "beginning of a technological revolution," as the 500,000-kilowatt unit was added to six smaller units, each capable of generating only 150,000 kilowatts. The government newspaper, *Izvestia*, reported on its front page: "The start-up operations on the seventh generating unit of the Nazarovo station have been completed. During the night of the nineteenth, it began to feed commercial power into the Siberian electricity grid." And *Pravda*, the Communist party daily, wrote: "Within seconds the gigantic machine shuddered, and its powerful bass sound merged into the cheerful chorus of the previous six operating units."

Five years later, in 1973, the Soviet Union newspaper, *Trud*, said the story was false. The huge generator had in fact burned out at the factory even before it was sent to Nazarovo for installation. "The inauguration ceremony, together with band music and speechmaking, was, therefore, purely symbolic," *Trud* said. The report added that only the steam-driven part of the unit (and not the electric generator) went into operation during the ceremony. "But the needles of instruments indicating power output did not move. There was no current, and how could there be any since the manufacturer had not even supplied the generator? Everyone knew that it had burned out during factory testing. And therefore the ceremony was purely symbolic."

1 Are false reports such as this possible in countries where the press is not tightly controlled? Under what circumstances? Does competition among reporters for the various media (TV, radio, newspapers, newsmagazines) make such large-scale hoaxes less likely to occur?

2 What kinds of speeches do you think were probably made at the original opening of the new generating unit? Do we have similar ceremonies in this country? What is said on those occasions? Why are they held? What kind of audience attends such an event in this country?

Getting Inside People   Mass media are often believed to operate on man's subconscious in a most sinister way. The term "subception" (short for "subliminal preception") refers to the way we "see" things below our level of consciousness. In the late 1940s an attempt was made to patent a process known as "Subliminal Projection," in which messages were flashed on a movie screen faster than the normal person can see them. The messages urged moviegoers to "drink Coke" and "eat popcorn." This experiment was carried out for several months in a

New Jersey movie theater, during which time the consumption of Coke and popcorn increased significantly. Although some questions were raised about the experimental design, the inventors of the process used this evidence as strong argument to seek a patent. They were ready to make a business out of reaching the public's subconscious.

There was great opposition to the system when news of it came out. Cries of "Big Brother" and "thought control" were raised by newspapers, by scientists, and even by congressmen ("Today selling popcorn; tomorrow, communism"). No patents were issued. The business of selling the public's subconscious to advertisers did not materialize.

It was quickly discovered that subception was not a new idea, but had been known in psychological circles for many years. Studies of subception in the early 1930s seemed to demonstrate that personal factors make a great difference in susceptibility to subliminal influence. The "thresholds" of consciousness vary from person to person and also from time to time within the same person. A thirsty person will respond to a subliminal message about beer, but not to one about popcorn; a nondrinker might perceive a message about a soft drink, but not one about beer. Experiments seemed to show that we develop inclinations toward, and defenses against, seeing or hearing some things on a

"I have here, gentlemen, a personally prepared and signed statement, to be included in all our advertising, declaring that everything we claim to be true is true." (The New Yorker.)

conscious level, and it was postulated that we do the same thing on a subconscious level.

Later research also showed that another limitation to the possibility of using subliminal advertising involves simple mechanics. How can an engineer fit a single message into the phasing system of a television transmission when so many sets are not tuned well enough to receive the extremely complex configurations that such a system would require? In summary, for mechanical, technical, and personal reasons, the subception scare almost disappeared.

That does not mean our subconscious minds aren't working. Much selling is still done by appealing to subconscious needs, drives, and values. We do not buy only a hair preparation when we buy shampoo— we buy glamour, sex appeal, and—we hope—a lover. We do not buy only a mouthwash—we buy closeness to others and a feeling of belonging. We do not buy an automobile only for transportation—we buy the status associated with the particular make or model. We do not need a system of subliminal advertising to get these messages into our subconscious and to induce us to buy much more than the item itself promises. Our conscious needs may be met when a product cleans our hair or freshens our breath, but at the same time the advertiser is appealing to our subconscious needs without flashing any special words at us subliminally.

MYTH: MASS MEDIA ARE ACCURATE AND BELIEVABLE

We tend to believe what we see in print. A printed report is somehow more credible than a verbal report given us by a friend. Many studies of the accuracy and credibility of the mass media indicate that people tend to believe the media in general, even though they know there are inaccuracies in a given TV or newspaper report. A person whose name is misspelled in a news story may consider the reporter inaccurate, but continues to believe many other things that are said in the same newspaper.

Consumers may also misjudge the media by thinking that the news is slanted by reporters who are "paid off." While payoffs have been exposed in the annals of journalism, they very seldom occur. More often the slant of a news story is a product of the reporter's decision on what to include, limitations of space, and the fact that the reader's prejudices may be just as slanted in another direction. Bias usually results more from inept reporting than from design. Details in a news report that one reader may find of great significance may not seem so important to another reader or to the person who prepared the item for print or broadcast. News is gathered by human beings, written by human beings, edited and revised by other human beings, and, finally, consumed by still other human beings; knowing that sequence should cause us to modify our hopes or expectations for completely accurate reporting.

MYTHS OF MASS MEDIA: APPLICATIONS

INVASION OF NEW JERSEY

On Halloween night in 1938 the "Mercury Theater of the Air," directed by Orson Welles, presented a radio drama of H. G. Wells's fantasy *The War of the Worlds*, which told a fictional story of invaders from Mars landing in New Jersey. Panic resulted. People along the East coast barricaded their homes and sought help from the police and the National Guard, even though the radio stations had announced that the program was fictional.

In 1971 a radio station in Buffalo, New York, decided to air the same program on Halloween. Anticipating that some listeners might think it was a report of a real invasion, the station announced that the program was fictional many times during the week preceding the rebroadcast and at about ten-minute intervals during the day it was scheduled to be aired. Although the announcements emphasized that it would be only a dramatization, the program proved all too realistic, since the voices of the station's regular announcers were used. Listeners responded.

In Buffalo, the police received over 100 phones calls; news media in Boston, Washington, New York, Rochester, and Providence all received inquiries. State police received calls, as did county sheriffs. One man ran up to a sheriff's patrol car shouting about the invasion and had to be calmed down. About half the calls to state police were from people who were angry at the radio station, and about half were from those who were frightened. The panic that resulted from the original broadcast thirty-three years earlier was not duplicated in Buffalo, but listeners were considerably nervous and upset.

1 What responsibility does a broadcasting medium have to its listeners? Should it label programs as dramatizations, on-the-spot news, editorials, etc.? Do frequent notices about the nature of a program reach all potential listeners? What does this imply about listening? About broadcasting?

2 If your favorite radio station broadcasted an account of an invasion from another planet, how would you react? How would you try to determine whether the broadcast was authentic?

3 Suppose you were fooled by such a broadcast and called the police or ran to a neighbor's house for help. How would you feel about the originator of the hoax when you realized you had been taken in? What would you do about it? Role-play a group of anxious and upset citizens who call a radio station's manager after having been fooled by a program.

"DEAR DOCTOR . . ."

Letters that television performers receive give some indication of their popularity and also of the extent to which viewers are involved in the programs on which they appear. One performer who plays the part of a doctor in a television series gets considerable mail asking for medical advice. Most letters are addressed to "Doctor" or include the initials "M.D." after his name. He responds to these inquiries with a polite letter explaining that he is only an actor and that the writer should contact a physician in his own community.

A performer who plays the part of a lawyer will also get fan mail asking questions about legal matters. An actor who played the part of a tough policeman was asked by a frightened viewer whether he could arrange to drive by her house several times a night to keep prowlers away.

1 What factors would encourage a person to ask a television performer for medical advice rather than a local doctor? Is it less expensive? Does the performer seem more like a real person? More sympathetic?
2 How does a letter writer react to the information that the "doctor" is just an actor? Will the letter writer continue to have confidence in the "doctor" on the television series? How can the actor let his fans know that he has no medical training and still remain believable?
3 Discuss with others how you have been affected by a performance on television or in a movie. Have you tried to be like that performer? Have you seen others act like characters on television or in the movies? (Remember that there are good character traits to imitate as well as bad ones.)

MYTH: MASS MEDIA DESTROY GOOD TASTE

Any new medium makes us reconsider what we are and what we have been. Any new medium threatens the status quo and those who want to preserve the system as it is or used to be. Older media become the property of the conservative element, the older forces in the society that may want to resist the incursion of the new. Radio was criticized by those who considered it in poor taste and feared we would become illiterates as we tuned our ears to the radio waves instead of enjoying the printed word. Movies were criticized as escapist nonsense that would free the masses from the effort needed to read a book or listen to the radio. Now television is the center of concern among those who feel that this newest electronic means of mass information, mass entertainment, mass involvement, and mass advertising threatens to destroy public taste.

Each new medium has caused concern that the standards of good taste in society will be destroyed. Members of a culture who have been deeply influenced by one set of media are inclined to think that all is lost when a new wave of attention is started. But no medium in itself destroys good taste. Instead, a new medium provides new ways for us to explore standards of taste that may or may not be consistent with what we're used to. Until standards and critical judgments can stabilize, any new medium flounders in a copycat repetition of older media. Movies started out as an artistic medium by simply photographing acting as it had been done for years, and television at first was very much like radio with pictures.

Another conflict over taste occurs when one group assumes an elite position in defense of a medium, while looking down on the masses for enjoying some other form of communication. Some people feel that what they themselves enjoy is in good taste and that all else is in bad taste. Early composers had patrons who, along with a few of their friends, constituted the audience and the critics of that day. Even now, those same composers may be enjoyed by relatively few people when compared with popular groups whose records sell in the millions. In another field, some of Shakespeare's contemporaries considered him a hack writer because his plays appealed to the masses , as well as to other levels of society. Today, Shakespeare's popularity is limited to a relatively small segment of our population, while a television series may be viewed on any one night of the week by more people than would have seen one of Shakespeare's plays during his lifetime.

Someday "The Edge of Night" or "Marcus Welby, M.D." may be considered great drama and studied only in the universities, while the rest of the population enjoys a multisensual, multimediated, immediate experience of some new and yet unimagined communication medium.

MYTHS OF MASS MEDIA: APPLICATIONS

KEEPING A LANGUAGE PURE

The following is a quotation from a manifesto concerning the safeguarding of the Castilian language. It was written by a Spanish historian, Ernesto Juan Fonfrias, president of the Augusto Malaret Institute of Hispano-American Lexicography of Puerto Rico.

In view of the irresponsible deterioration occurring in our spoken and written language, the Augusto Malaret Institute of Hispano-American Lexicography, in accordance with its duty of ordering cultural activities, publishes this manifesto as the first step of a campaign which is to use all possible communications media to try to stop the evils inflicted by our community upon the Spanish language which is the cultural heritage of our forefathers.

Without entering any kind of anthropological considerations it is true to say that a people is identified by the language it uses. This is certainly true in our case. It is thus everyone's duty, no matter what his social or professional standing may be, to safeguard at all costs this heritage, and make the needed sacrifices for it. Correct usage and language have many enemies of a grammatical, political, socio-cultural, and geographical nature, not the least of which is an economy in alien hands.

Young people should and must enrich their cultural means with other languages, but it is their duty to keep the basic structures and ideas of the language of our parents clean and clear. We must check present methods of teaching Spanish at all levels and instruct those whose job it is to print the language how to use it properly, while still keeping up the teaching of the English language. We must make sure that mass communications media (press, television, radio) understand the problem and help to solve it. The survival of our cultural entity, which is one of our raisons d'être, depends upon it.

1 What influences made this kind of statement seem necessary to the Institute? Does language change, or is it always the same? What makes language change? Is it people who change it?
2 Do you agree that "a people is identified by the language it uses"? Would you agree that it is everyone's duty to make sacrifices in order to retain the purity of a language? What kinds of sacrifices do you think are referred to here?
3 The writer singles out young people (in the third paragraph). Why do you suppose he mentions them specifically? Does the appeal to the "language of our parents" seem to carry much weight?
4 The writer also singles out the mass media. Does this mean that he believes their influence is important? He relates the media to the teaching of languages; does he do this on purpose? How do you react to his using the teaching of English as a part of his appeal to keep the Castilian language pure? How do you react to his using a French expression ("raison d'être") to make his point about the purity of the Castilian language?

WHO SETS THE TASTE FOR SOCIETY?

Pianist David Tudor once performed a composition entitled *4'33"*, by John Cage; some reviewers considered it an example of "inferential art." For four minutes and thirty-three seconds, Tudor sat silently at the piano. He changed the position of his arms three times to indicate that the composition had three movements. There was no sound from the piano.

1 John Cage is trying to tell us that music played by performers is not necessarily more significant than the casual noises in a concert hall (one interpretation of the composition). How large an audience was this composition intended to reach? Would you consider this a "mass" production? If not, is this presentation a part of mass media?

What artistic expressions seem to ignore mass audiences? What experiences have made you think that those who produce art or music or literature either care for a mass audience or do not care for a mass audience? (Avoid condemning or supporting creative artists; consider them objectively in relation to their expectations of audiences.)

MYTH: MASS MEDIA CREATE A MASS MIND

It is important to have an understanding of what we have come to call the "masses." This term doesn't refer to a vague blob of humanity with a single mind and a single reading or listening level. Newspapers, for instance, may be written on an eighth-grade reading level, but this doesn't mean that everyone in the country reads at this level. Advertisers, too, know that they don't deliver messages to a homogeneous mass. The mass audience is composed of millions of individuals, all with their own interests, economic standing, social inclinations, religion, values, attitudes, and attention span. However, the fact that these are certain common human needs and interests makes it possible to appeal to a large number of people at one time.

Making a medium mass: Does it extend communication beyond face-to-face relationships? Does it multiply one person's message? Does it communicate a message that many people participate in?

(David Margolin/Black Star.)

(W. Leon Riegler/Frederic Lewis.)

(Laima Turnley/Editorial Photocolor Archives.)

In calling these "mass" media, we may be misled into thinking that a single audience exists. But people's actions are not determined simply by the printed word or electronic persuasion; other factors like fear, greed, patriotism, love, and hope are involved in communication efforts.

It has often been said that even in the mass media, successful communicators depends on a "one-to-one" relationship with consumers. Television talk-show hosts are skilled at establishing such relationships with their viewers, and they receive gifts, invitations to dinner, as well as letters from them. Similarly, when a major character in a soap opera is sick, the network receives a flood of get-well cards.

In spite of such identification, a counterforce works against the close relationship of a communicator and a mass audience. Most mass media have no feedback function; that is, the communicator cannot tell immediately how an audience is reacting to the communication efforts and thus make adjustments. At the same time, a mass media audience cannot react as a live audience would, laughing at jokes with the performer, applauding points they approve and shaking their heads at those they don't, talking to their neighbors, falling asleep, or getting up and walking out. Turning off a radio or television program does not give the audience the same kind of satisfaction and does not deliver the same message to the communicator. In other words, in most mass media situations, speakers have no feedback to help them adjust to their audiences as they change, and the audience lacks a feedback system with which to control the speaker.

☐ WHAT MAKES A MEDIUM MASS?

Because of the dynamic nature of our communication, the media we use will be always changing. As new inventions thrust us into new relationships with one another and with our communication environment, there is no way of knowing what kinds of mass media will be written about in another century—we don't even know how long *writing* is going to survive. At this time there are three main characteristics of mass media. These are probably the most general definitions of mass media we can use at the moment.

First, to be considered "mass," a medium should represent an extension of communication potential beyond face-to-face relationships. "Extension of a medium" usually involves mechanical aids that enable one person to speak with another from a distance, as by telephone. Radio spans the world under certain conditions of transmission power and atmospherics. Television can be boosted beyond the horizon by cable or microwave. Movies made in Hollywood can be shown in Australia. Books, of course, also extend communication beyond our immediate surroundings—for example, a best seller may be distributed to thousands of readers in a matter of days. So, in the first place mass media are those which can reach large numbers of people without the originators—authors, announcers, performers, actors—being there in person.

Second, we think of mass media as those means (usually mechanical or electronic) which individuals can use to multiply their effectiveness. A simple bullhorn or a public-address system might, by this definition, be a mass medium. For most purposes this rules out the telephone and its one-to-one communication, but it includes books with their many readers. Newspapers spread the writings of a single reporter over an entire city—or further—in hours. Radio multiplies the announcer's voice by the number of sets tuned in; television multiplies on the same principle. Movies are seen by millions of people in all parts of the world and are heard in many languages. These are the multipliers of one person's messages that we usually think of as mass media.

Theater, art exhibits, concerts, public lectures, political rallies, protest marches, ceremonial parades, highway billboards, and even the Friday night bowling league all seem to have qualities of mass media. It is impossible to exclude some of these from the media influencing our lives, but their content may place them in some other category. For that reason we need to make a third point about mass media: Not only should the medium be able to extend communication beyond the face-to-face contact and reach many recipients, but it should also communicate messages that many people tune in to and also understand, enjoy, learn from, or otherwise participate in.

A MASS MEDIUM: APPLICATION

HOW MUCH DO YOU BELIEVE?

If information comes to you from one of the following media, how strongly do you believe it? Fill in the blanks below by checking the items that most nearly represent your own attitudes. When you are finished, compare your responses with those of others. Can you find reasons for the similarities or differences between your responses and others'? Can you find reasons for the similarities or differences you might discover in the way you respond to the various media as compared with the way another person does?

Information about	Appearing in	Strength of Belief		
		Strong	Moderate	Disbelief
A political candidate	News magazine	____	____	____
	Magazine advertising	____	____	____
	Television news	____	____	____
	Television advertising	____	____	____
	Newspaper	____	____	____
	Newspaper advertising	____	____	____

	Radio news	___	___	___
	Radio advertising	___	___	___
	Conversation (personal)	___	___	___
A scientific	News magazine	___	___	___
invention	Magazine advertising	___	___	___
	Television news	___	___	___
	Television advertising	___	___	___
	Newspaper	___	___	___
	Newspaper advertising	___	___	___
	Radio news	___	___	___
	Radio advertising	___	___	___
	Conversation (personal)	___	___	___
A land	News magazine	___	___	___
investment	Magazine advertising	___	___	___
	Television news	___	___	___
	Television advertising	___	___	___
	Newspaper	___	___	___
	Newspaper advertising	___	___	___
	Radio news	___	___	___
	Radio advertising	___	___	___
	Conversation (personal)	___	___	___

Effects of Mass Media on People

In order to determine which communication media can be considered "mass," we must take into account two effects that media have on their participants.

First, mass media bestow social status and public influence. This is a circular process, mentioned earlier, in which the person whose name is in the paper or who speaks on radio or television is assumed to be important because we consider these media important. If these media pay attention only to important people, then the people who appear there must be important.

In the days of its greatest popularity the now-defunct *Life* magazine had a feature called "*Life* Goes to a Party." Because of the tremendous influence of the magazine, its photographers and reporters were admitted to every kind of event in the world—coronations, jet-set soirees, underworld gatherings, high-society weddings, and small-town family reunions. Of course, the *Life* coverage also made the party appear very important. *Time* magazine's "Man of the Year" award also bestows prestige on the recipient, and *Time* receives thousands of suggestions both before and after the selection is made. While most of us will not make the cover of *Time*, we do like to see our names in print or to be mentioned on television or radio. Recognition is important to us, and recognition by the mass media adds greatly to our stature.

Favorable attention in the mass media also gives stature to public movements, organizations, and events. If an event we attend or an organization we belong to is mentioned in the newspaper or is covered on TV or radio, we believe it enhances our own prestige.

People or organizations of some stature gain additional importance if treated well by the mass media. This has been called the "legitimizing" of status. If you already have status and receive further recognition, you prove what we suspected all along: you are important.

Media also affect people in that they help protect social norms. For example, illegal acts committed privately are seldom punished. If your neighbors don't know that you cheat on your income tax, beat your children, or threaten to shoot the President, then nobody will come to question you or arrest you. However, a person who suddenly gains public recognition—by cutting a hit record or being elected to office, for example—finds that he or she is now less able to keep affairs private and may be condemned or punished by society for acts that would go unnoticed if committed by a less prominent person. Thus media help protect the norms of the society. They may help protect the legal rights of the accused, or they may help bring a culprit to trial. Media pose the threat of exposure to those who are potentially immoral, dishonest, perverted, self-serving, or deviant.

EFFECTS OF MASS MEDIA: APPLICATIONS

MEDIA INFLUENCE OUR NORMS

A few years ago in the Midwest, the parents of a thirteen-year-old girl sold her as a wife to a wealthy man (according to allegations by police). After public disclosure of their action, the girl's parents admitted that it was a terrible thing to do, and the man was indicted on several counts. However, before the case became public, as a result of neighbors' reporting it to the police and to newspaper reporters, the girl's parents felt sufficiently sure about the morality of their act to have spent most of the money paid to them.

1 How was the morality of the parents' act changed by its being made public?

2 If the neighbors had not complained, would it have been all right for this transaction to have taken place? What do you think about neighbors who make this kind of thing their business? Is the gossip of neighbors justified if their suspicions are proved true?

3 Is this the kind of story that newspapers should devote a lot of space to? Did the newspapers publish this story out of a sense of moral responsibility or to sell newspapers? For both reasons? Do news media generally crusade for causes that also serve their own self-interests?

Most television stations offered live coverage of the Senate hearings on the electronic bugging of the Democratic headquarters at the Watergate Hotel during the 1972 presidential campaign. Regular network programs were preempted. Faithful viewers of daily quiz shows or soap operas had only the Watergate hearings to watch on national network television channels.

The switchboards at network and station offices were busy with calls from people who complained that their time was being wasted with "this dull stuff." "Give me back my program and keep that small-time cops-and-robbers story off the air," the demand went.

The Public Broadcasting System (PBS) aired the Watergate hearings in full during prime evening hours so that people who were unable to watch them live could see them at night.

1   The networks lost money on this project; they had to cover much of the cost of the hearings themselves while at the same time losing revenue from advertisers on their regular shows. Were the networks right in preempting regular programming for the Watergate hearings? Why do you suppose they thought it was important to give viewers a look at history in the making?

2   Did the fact that the national networks compete with one another make it important for *all* to broadcast the hearings simultaneously? Later they pooled their coverage and took turns broadcasting the hearings. Was this a more useful system? Are programs such as this more appropriately aired over the Public Broadcasting System? Who supports the PBS?

The Two-Step Process

We noted earlier that the mass media operate with the support of people. The influence of the press is basically a two-step process in which the news and opinions are reinforced by people talking about what they hear and see in the media. These "opinion leaders" are the second step in the process of attitude change or social sanction.

The first step is the publication or airing of some messages or information. These are heard by people who talk to other people. It is this second step—your friend telling you about something—which may influence your actions. Source credibility, or the reliability of what someone expresses, may be established because that source is seen to have some special "inside" information. Some people acquire a reputation for credibility because of their professional qualifications, while others may be considered experts by those with whom they have the most contact. How much you believe is related to how well acquainted you are with the source of your information. That is one reason why the two-step process of influence is effective. A stranger who broadcasts the news may not be as well believed as the local mail carrier who tells the same story. "Ask the man who owns one" was the slogan for an automobile sales campaign. Your voting behavior is affected more by what local opinion leaders tell you than by what you hear the candidates say. During World War II when housewives were lectured about the advantages of buying kidneys, brains, and other organ meats, and also when they simply read articles about it, they were not convinced. But when they listened to each other in casual conversation give the same reasons for buying such meats, they altered their habits.

If It Sells Soap, Why Not Social Harmony?

Since mass media operate within society as givers of social status and protectors of social norms, why isn't it possible to use these same media to help fight racial discrimination, drug abuse, bigotry, or intolerance? If Madison Avenue can sell soap, why can't it sell intangibles that might improve human relations?

One reason things don't work this way is that in selling soap, one brand competes with another. People are going to use soap, for example, because washing is a necessity, and it is simply a question of which kind to buy. But this is not the case with discrimination. Not all people have decided that they want to work beside, go to school with, eat in a

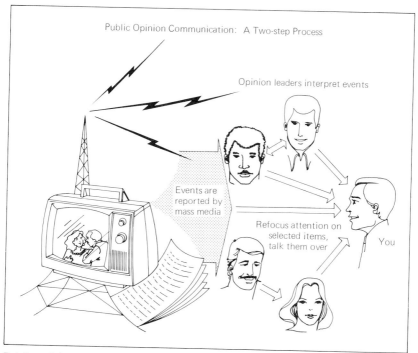

Public-opinion communication: A two-step process.

Mass media are only as powerful as the readers and listeners make them. *(Daniel S. Brody/Editorial Photocolor Archives.)*

restaurant with, or marry a person of a different racial, ethnic, or religious background. Until such a basic decision is made, trying to sell competing brands of antidiscrimination is not possible. However, in the past few years many of the media have been using the "social status" role to foster tolerant attitudes. They have also begun to acknowledge (at least publicly) that one of society's norms is to be nondiscriminatory, and today more news gatherers, news writers, news commentators, and newsmakers come from minority groups than in previous years. If media can make people appear important by legitimizing status, they can use this as one way of "selling" social goals like racial harmony.

When we ask the mass media to crusade in matters of social concern, we are putting much faith in the power of the press. But big media corporations are generally conservative and would not choose to lead the charge against all social injustices. In spite of the liberalism of many reporters, publishers, and commentators, the corporations have a very strong inclination to support the status quo. Because communication media are limited by time and space, they must carefully choose what to focus on. Until a new movement or idea has gained some popular support, it is not likely to get significant media coverage. But when it does achieve notice, it will be further legitimized because the media are interested in it.

☐ SUMMARY ON MASS MEDIA

Mass media are only as powerful as readers and listeners make them. If news or other messages meet our expectations and especially those of opinion leaders, then the media become even more powerful. If we continue to see and hear reflections of our own opinions, our own evaluations of which people and ideas are most important, then we become more confident in the media and in all they stand for.

It is imperative, therefore, to understand the myths about the mass media so we do not mistakenly assume their influence apart from human control. Mass media do not operate in a vacuum, but in the minds and will of readers and listeners. Mass media are not new, and are not likely to destroy good taste in our culture, nor to create some kind of mass mind. They are not perfectly motivated, nor perfectly honest or believable or all-powerful. They are subject to all the human error and limitations of any practitioners of communication and subject to control by your sensitive and informed responses as wise consumers.

■ LOOKING BACK

I. In society we need protection against the possibility of abuse from others.
   A. Public controls include governmental agencies that guard citizens from those who would take advantage of them.
   B. There are very few controls on our interpersonal communication that would make us more effective communicators.
   C. We have the most freedom in our intrapersonal communication.
II. The mass media of communication include all those systems which can make us more aware of what is in our world.
   A. Some myths about the mass media interfere with our understanding of them:
      1. Myth: Mass media are new. Mass media are not new; they date back to the days of the wandering troubadours and the invention of printing.
      2. Myth: Mass media are all-powerful. Mass media do not have the power, by themselves, to bring about great changes or create support for movements.
      3. Myth: Mass media are accurate and believable. Mass media are subject to the same limitations of perception and of reporting that an individual is because human beings produce the material that media transmit.
      4. Myth: Mass media destroy good taste. Mass media do not destroy good taste as much as they point up the relative differences between "mass" consumption of messages and older ways that seem to us more refined or governed by higher standards.
      5. Mass media create a mass mind. There is no "mass" audience in the sense that everyone will respond in the same

way to messages or can be counted on to follow the dictates of a message.

B. Mass media derive their importance from the fact that they extend a speaker's reach across space and time and permit contact with many audiences at once.

C. Mass media affect individuals by bestowing status, and they can affect society by reinforcing norms.

D. The influence of the media is basically a two-step process in which the news and opinions (first step) are reinforced and given strength by persons who talk to others as opinion leaders (second step).

E. Mass media can be expected only to influence people as they exist; they have no magical power to create new kinds of people.

SUGGESTED READING

An Annotated Bibliography

Note: The chapter numbers following titles below refer to chapters in this book

Adorno, Theodore W., Else Frenkel-Brunswick, Daniel J. Levinson, and R. Nevitt Sanford: *The Authoritarian Personality: Studies in Prejudice,* Harper & Row, Publishers, Incorporated, New York, 1950 (Chap. 4). An important classic research on anti-Semitism, social discrimination, and political ideologies. The book marks the first time that empirical measurements of social attitudes were made, and the basic unit of analysis was the attitude. Also new and important was the link made between social attitudes and personality. This is somewhat difficult reading for those not familiar with research in the social sciences.

Andersen, Kenneth and Theodore Celvenger, Jr.: "A Summary of Experimental Research in Ethos," *Speech Monographs,* vol. 30. pp. 59–78, 1963 (Chap. 2). One of the best summaries of the research findings on the subject of ethos and source credibility.

Applbaum, Ronald L., Edward M. Bodaken, Kenneth K. Sereno, and Karl W. E. Anatol: *The Process of Group Communication,* Science Research Associates, Chicago, 1974 (Chap. 3). This book attempts to integrate theoretical-conceptual positions in the area of group communications with applications of that information to practical problems and situations. The approach is from a general system perspective, and the authors have developed a group process model around which they have organized each part and chapter. Factors such as language variables and nonverbal communication in groups are treated at length. Exercises are included.

Asch, Solomon E.: *Social Psychology*, Prentice-Hall, Inc., Englewood Cliffs, N.J., 1952 (Chap. 4). A classic text on social psychology which has its roots in gestalt theory. The author first examines some conceptions of man—biological, sociological, and Freudian—and then presents his thesis of a blend between sociological and psychological theories necessary to fully understand social behavior. The chapters on human interaction, group theory, effects of group conditions on judgments and attitudes, and group pressures are based on pioneering research.

Barnlund, Dean C.: "A Transactional Model of Communication," in **Johnnye Akin, Alvin Goldberg, Gail E. Myers, and Joseph Stewart (eds.),** *Language Behavior: A Book of Readings*, Mouton, The Hague, 1970 (Chap. 1). In this original article, Barnlund presents his model of the communication process. Several postulates of communication are explained. Particular emphasis is placed on a meaning-centered philosophy of communication. Although somewhat complex for the beginning student, the model is well worth studying.

Barnlund, Dean C. and Franklyn S. Haiman: *The Dynamics of Discussion*, Houghton Mifflin Company, Boston, 1960 (Chap. 5). An analysis of the processes of group discussion. The book is written clearly and simply, without much jargon. Each one of the four parts deals with a major aspect of group discussion. First, the setting of discussion is described, its place in our modern society, its forms, and the goals of those who engage in it. The second part deals with problem solving, conflict resolution, and the raw materials for discussion. The third part is concerned primarily with interpersonal relations in groups and emphasizes problems of apathy, emotional conflict, and communication. The last part deals with leadership in small groups, the various functions of discussion leadership, styles of leadership, and the issue of control versus freedom. This book is one of the best introductions to small-group processes available to the interested student.

Berlo, David: *The Process of Communication*, Holt, Rinehart and Winston, Inc., New York , 1960 (Chap. 3). This book provides a description of modern communication theory and serves as a foundation for further study. The author pulls together material from the behavioral sciences, linguistics, semantics, and the philosophy of language and integrates it into his communication model. One of the best introductions to the study of the communication process.

Bettinghaus, Erwin P.: *Message Preparation: The Nature of Proof*, The Bobbs-Merrill Company, Inc., Indianapolis, 1966 (Chap. 8). In this paperback, the author combines the rhetorical and practical elements of the study of proof. He examines the formal requirements of proof and the practical requirements of persuading a given audience. The author reports on many of the most common analytical approaches to message analysis and assesses their usefulness to the communicator for predicting the behavior of his audience. The Toulmin model is particularly well described.

Bettinghaus, Erwin P.: *Persuasive Communication*, Holt, Rinehart and Winston, Inc., New York, 1968 (Chap. 4). This book deals with the ways in which people try to influence the behavior of others. It is concerned with persuasion through communication, that is, the deliberate attempts people make to change the attitudes, beliefs, values, and behaviors of those around them. The author describes the process of persuasive communication in many different situations and analyzes communication sources, messages, and channels and their influence on behavior. He is concerned with the problems facing the persuasive communicator and presents materials on audience characteristics as well as on the speaker and his techniques. The book contains an excellent chapter on reference groups.

Bormann, Ernest G. and Nancy C. Bormann: *Speech Communication*, Harper & Row, Publishers, Incorporated, New York, 1972 (Chap. 1). This text on interpersonal communication is written for a first course in speech communication. It integrates information from psycholinguistics, small-group communication, persuasion, attitude studies, rhetoric, and public speaking. The book includes an overview of communication theory and then applies it to interpersonal communication, informative speaking, persuasion, small-group communication, and public speaking.

Boulding, Kenneth: *The Image*, The University of Michigan Press, Ann Arbor, 1956 (Chap. 3). The author's theory is that the image is the sum total of our subjective knowledge at any given moment and that it is the image which provides the key to understanding human behavior. The personal image provides the social image, and, in turn, it is society which provides the messages that change the images of individuals. Well written and clear, this book makes excellent additional reading for a course in communication.

Brown, Charles T. and Charles Van Riper: *Communication in Human Relationships*, National Textbook Company, Skokie, Ill., 1973 (Chap. 3). This highly readable paperback presents in detail the many purposes served by man's speaking. The book is a good introduction to speech communication and highlights language obstacles to effective communication.

Burgoon, Michael: *Approaching Speech Communication*, Holt, Rinehart and Winston, Inc., New York, 1974 (Chap. 1). This text is designed for introductory courses in speech communication. It attempts to develop an understanding of the communication process using theoretical models and applications from real-life situations. More traditional interests such as public speaking, persuasion, and message construction are included, as well as nonverbal communication and mass communication.

Burgoon, Michael, Judee K. Heston, and James McCroskey: *Small Group Communication: A Functional Approach*, Holt, Rinehart and Winston, Inc., New York, 1974 (Chap. 5). This book represents the authors' attempt to integrate the behavioral science findings in persuasion, conflict resolution, leadership, decision making, and other communication areas into a course in small-group communication. The authors also give an overview of functions of small groups and describe how they operate. A chapter on group therapy and encounter groups provides data about a popular type of small-group experience.

Campbell, J. H. and H. W. Hepler: *Dimensions in Communication*, rev. ed., Wadsworth Publishing Company, Inc., Belmont, Calif., 1971 (Chap. 1). In this book of readings, the authors take the view that all communication is persuasive, and their selection provides information and ideas that will be useful in a careful analysis of communication situations. The section on models is excellent, and the five chapters are very readable. Section 2, on persuasion, presents some classic works from Goffman, Asch, and Hovland. The third section, on message systems, presents some interesting articles on language and nonverbal communication and includes Wendell Johnson's beautiful essay entitled "You Can't Write Writing." This collection is well worth reading by any student of communication.

Chase, Stuart: *The Power of Words*, Harcourt, Brace and World, New York, 1954 (Chap. 3). This book on language and communication reflects the author's concern with the positive as well as the negative uses of language. In his attempt to set forth broad communication principles, the author relies on many communication scholars, and in the process he clarifies many of their theories. The book is a good introduction to the field of communication with an emphasis on language.

Clevenger, Theodore, Jr.: "A Synthesis of Experimental Research in Stage Fright," *Quarterly Journal of Speech*, vol. 45, pp. 134–145, 1959 (Chap. 1). This early summary of experimental research in stage fright yields a set of eleven hypotheses about variables related to perceived stage fright, speaking ability, and personality. This is somewhat difficult reading for students not familiar with experimental procedures.

Clevenger, Theodore, Jr.: *Audience Analysis*, The Bobbs-Merrill Company, Inc., Indianapolis, 1966 (Chap. 4). This short paperback focuses on different methods for analyzing audiences. It is intended for the undergraduate who is in the process of speech communication and especially the usually silent but crucial participant in that process: the audience. The reader will gain an enlarged understanding of what audiences are like, how they respond to communication, and what factors interact to shape their responses.

Clevenger, Theodore, Jr. and Jack Matthews: *The Speech Communication Process*, Scott, Foresman and Company, Glenview, Ill., 1971 (Chap. 1). This paperback provides a comprehensive overview of the major elements of the process. Quite technical in parts, it is hard reading for the beginning student.

Cronkhite, Gary: *Persuasion: Speech and Behavioral Change*, The Bobbs-Merrill Company, Inc., Indianapolis, 1966 (Chap. 4). The author explores the nature and problems of persuasion by explaining the processes of communication research. Rather than presenting conclusions about persuasion and dealing with the nature of the speech to persuade and with the persuasive effects of messages, the author emphasizes the question of how persuasive effects can best be described and tested. He describes the major classical and modern theories of persuasion and points out where they differ. The debate is followed by a discussion of research approaches using the methodologies of psychologists and social psychologists. The chapter on audience characteristics is excellent and presents useful research findings.

De Fleur, Melvin L.: *Theories of Mass Communication*, 2d ed., David McKay Company, Inc., New York, 1970 (Chap. 10). This book provides a theoretical framework for the study of mass communication. The author explains in detail the historical development of the mass media in the United States.

Fabun, Don: *Communication: The Transfer of Meaning*, Glencoe Press, The Macmillan Company, New York, 1968 (Chap. 3). A short but highly creative and graphic introduction into the nature of the communication process. Selective perception, the differences between inferences and observations, and nonverbal communication are treated exceptionally well. The illustrations are delightful and quite entertaining. The book is an excellent additional text for a course in communication.

Fisher, B. Aubrey: *Small Group Decision Making: Communication and the Group Process*, McGraw-Hill Book Company. New York, 1974 (Chap. 5). This book emphasizes two perspectives within the group context: decision making and communication. The author considers the data gained from studying all types of groups, including training groups, therapy groups, family groups, and decision-making groups. A guide to jargon is included at the end and provides a useful glossary of terms for students.

Gardiner, James C.: "A Synthesis of Experimental Studies of Speech Communication Feedback," *The Journal of Communication*, vol. 21, pp. 17–35, 1971 (Chap. 4). This article presents detailed research findings on feedback and its effects on the communication process.

Giffin, Kim and Bobby R. Patton (eds.): *Basic Readings in Interpersonal Communication*, Harper & Row, Publishers, Incorporated, New York, 1971 (Chap. 1). In this book of readings, the authors, through their selections, present the view that people are increasingly concerned about developing meaningful and satisfying relationships with others through interpersonal communication. This new aspiration regarding interpersonal communication places special importance on the personal and interpersonal facets of the communication process. People's perceptions, orientations, needs, and response sets are analyzed in the various chapters. The opening section of the book presents an examination of the basic principles of communication. The concluding section contains specific suggestions for improving interpersonal relationships.

Goffman, Erving: *The Presentation of Self in Everyday Life*, Doubleday & Co., Anchor Books, Garden City, New York, 1959 (Chap. 2). Using a theatrical metaphor, Goffman describes how a person presents himself or herself as a kind of mask which others will acknowledge. Goffman illustrates how individuals form groups which help define and support the characterizations of self and how people manage impressions of one another.

Gulley, Halbert E.: *Discussion, Conference, and Group Process*, 2d ed., Holt, Rinehart and Winston, Inc., 1968 (Chap. 5). This book is designed for students who wish to understand the process of group functioning and the ways in which individuals can become more effective group participants and discussion leaders. The book focuses on decision making and leadership in small groups.

Hall, Edward T.: *The Silent Language*, Premier Books, Doubleday & Company, Inc., Garden City, N.Y., 1959 (Chap. 3). This book deals with cross-cultural communication in a most delightful and insightful way. Hall maintains that we are ignorant of what we communicate to other people by our own normal behavior, and he sets out to describe the effects of communication, particularly nonverbal communication, on people from other cultures. His treatment of time and space is particularly good. The book is extremely readable and, by now, is a classic.

Hall, Edward T.: *The Hidden Dimension*, Anchor Books, Doubleday & Company, Inc., Garden City, N.Y., 1969 (Chap. 3). The distance that we create between ourselves and other people or things constitutes our private space. This space or territory affects our growth, our environment, and our relationships with others. Hall deals with cross-cultural communication, distance regulations, and social behavior in animals. He explores man's perceptions of space and explains the distance zones that man has created and in which human communication takes place.

Hall, Edward T.: *Beyond Culture*, Doubleday and Co., Anchor Books, Garden City, New York, 1976 (Chap. 3). Hall examines the power of our cultural environment, the difficulties in studying its impact on human behavior because of the relationship between language and culture, and of the importance of context in developing meaning for symbols. The author presents his view on how culture and communication can be better understood.

Hayakawa, S. I.: *Language in Thought and Action*, rev. ed., Harcourt, Brace and Company, Inc., New York, 1964 (Chap. 3). This book presents a good and thorough discussion of semantics as a study of human interaction through communication.

Hovland, Carl I. and Irving L. Janis (eds.): *Personality and Persuasibility*, Yale University Press, New Haven, Conn., 1959 (Chap. 2). This book is a compilation of research studies on the demographic and personality variables that affect the persuasion process.

Hovland, Carl I., Irving L. Janis, and Harold H. Kelley: *Communication and Persuasion*, Yale University Press, New Haven, Conn., 1953, chap. 4, "Organization of Persuasive Arguments" (Chap. 6). This is a classic compilation of research studies on the effectiveness of persuasive communication. The book is divided into four parts. Part 1, "The Communicator," deals with the trustworthiness, intentions, and affiliations of the source of a communication message. Part 2, "The Content of the Communication," deals with types of motivating appeals and the organization of persausvie arguments. Part 3, "Audience Predisposition," deals with group-conformity motives and individual personality factors. Part 4, "Responses," deals with the overt expression of a new opinion and the retention of opinion change. All chapters are based on empirical and experimental data.

Huff, Darrell: *How to Lie with Statistics*, W. W. Norton & Company, Inc., New York, 1954 (Chap. 8). This is a sort of a primer in ways to use statistics to deceive. Written humorously and clearly, it is delightful reading on a quite serious matter. The author explains biased sampling, deceiving averages, deceptive graphs, and other deceptions based on the misuse of statistics. The fact that it contains no jargon makes it readable by anyone. We recommend it highly as a good book on common sense.

Johnson, Wendell: *People in Quandaries*, Harper & Row, Publishers, Incorporated, New York, 1946 (Chap. 3). This is a standard textbook in general semantics and its application to everyday living. It is a must for anyone who wants to grasp the personal and practical value of general semantics in dealing with the ordinary, common affairs of life. The same scientific approach employed in the laboratory by the scientist can also be used to deal with real-world, human problems. The author treats the major common maladjustments of our society remarkably well. The book is extremely readable and well written.

Katz, Elihu: "The Two-Step Flow of Communication: An Up-to-Date Report on a Hypothesis," *Public Opinion Quarterly*, vol. 30, pp. 61–78, 1967 (Chap. 10). This article presents a detailed discussion of Katz's theory of the two-step flow of communication. The author also describes some of the recent modifications of the theory.

Keltner, John W.: *Interpersonal Speech-Communication: Elements and Structures*, Wadsworth Publishing Company, Inc., Belmont, Calif., 1970 (Chap. 1). In this book the author attempts to help the reader understand the significance of the speech-communication process and to develop his own communication experiences. The first part deals with the elements necessary for interpersonal speech communication, language, feedback, perception, listening, decision making, etc. The second part centers on the structures in which these elements operate. It presents the various contexts for communication such as dyadic communication, small-group communication, public speaking, oral interpretation, and theater. The second part is somewhat weak and was deleted from a more recent brief edition. The book is very readable and presents a useful, if somewhat disconnected, treatment of interpersonal communication.

Klapper, Joseph T.: *The Effects of Mass Communication*, The Free Press, New York, 1960 (Chap. 10). This book is an attempt to integrate the major research findings about the social and psychological effects of mass media.

Knapp, Mark L.: *Nonverbal Communication in Human Interaction*, Holt, Rinehart and Winston, Inc., New York, 1972 (Chap. 3). A comprehensive treatment of nonverbal communication and a very readable summary of research in most areas of nonverbal communication. The author describes six variables that impinge on and affect the process of human communication. These variables, which were selected on the basis of how likely they are to occur in almost any human transaction, are body motion (kinetic behavior), touching behavior, paralanguage, proxemics (man's use of space), artifacts, and environmental factors.

Lee, Irving J.: *Language Habits in Human Affairs*, Harper & Brothers, New York, 1941 (Chap. 3). The author popularizes the writings of Korzybski, the founder of general semantics. This highly readable book focuses on language and how language affects human behavior in everyday situations.

McCroskey, James C.: "Ethos: A Dominant Factor in Persuasive Communication," in *An Introduction to Rhetorical Communication*, 2d ed., Prentice-Hall, Inc., Englewood Cliffs, N.J., 1972, pp. 63–81 (Chap. 2). This chapter presents a good discussion of the traditional concept of ethos and the more modern concept of source credibility. The author analyzes their effects on the communication process.

McGuire, William J.: "The Nature of Attitudes and Attitude Change," in **Gardner Lindzey and Elliot Aronson (eds.)**, *Handbook of Social Psychology*, 2d ed., Addition-Wesley Publishing Company, Inc., Reading, Mass., 1969, vol. III, pp. 136–314 (Chap. 4). A lengthy and rather comprehensive summary of the theoretical and research literature on attitude and attitude change. The author deals first with the nature of attitudes from a theoretical standpoint, attitude structure, functions, and the determinants of attitudes. He then presents a thorough analysis of attitude change as a social influence process and focuses particularly on the matrix of persuasive communication. This is followed by a description of the general theories of attitude change. A lengthy bibliography is provided. This is difficult reading for the person not acquainted with the language and methods of social psychology.

Mehrabian, Albert: *Silent Messages*, Wadsworth Publishing Co., Belmont, Calif., 1971 (Chap. 3). The author presents a psychological approach to the study of gestures. He develops his theory that gestures convey three dimensions of feelings and attitudes: like/dislike, status, and responsiveness. He summarizes the research in this area of nonverbal communication.

Miller, Gerald R.: "Studies on the Use of Fear Appeals: A Summary and Analysis," *Central States Speech Journal*, vol. 14, pp. 117–125, 1963 (Chap. 4).

One of the best summaries of experimental research on the use of fear appeals and their effects on persuasion.

Mills, Glen E.: *Message Preparation: The Nature of Proof*, The Bobbs-Merrill Company, Inc., Indianapolis, 1966 (Chap. 7). In this paperback the author deals with new and old theories about the selection of topics for communication, their analysis, their investigation, and their structuring. The selection of topics in relation to the types of speeches and purposes is extensively treated. The chapter on investigation is particularly useful for the beginning student. Outlining is presented in considerable detail. This is a very useful text for an introductory course in public speaking.

Minnick, Wayne: *The Art of Persuasion*, 2d ed., Houghton Mifflin Company, Boston, 1963 (Chap. 4). In this book the author formulates a theory of persuasion built on non-Aristotelian premises derived from the behavioral sciences. Perceptual and motivational theories are particularly useful because of the effects of attending and perceiving on the meaning a receiver will give a particular persuasive message. The construction and delivery of persuasive messages are thoroughly examined and handled both descriptively and prescriptively.

Monroe, Alan H. and Douglas Ehninger: *Principles and Types of Speech*, 6th brief ed., Scott, Foresman and Company, Glenview, Ill., 1967 (Chap. 1). While reflecting some awareness of current trends in the behavioral sciences, this text on public speaking remains solidly grounded in traditional rhetorical principles. Throughout the book, stress is placed on the three primary interactive components of the speech process: the speaker, the speech, and the audience. Some rewriting from previous editions brings the book more closely in line with current development in communication theory and audience analysis.

Myers, Gail E. and Michele T. Myers: *The Dynamics of Human Communication: A Laboratory Approach*, McGraw-Hill Book Company, New York, 2nd ed., 1976 (Chap. 1). Designed to develop and improve communication skills systematically by truly integrating communication principles with practice in skills, this first complete combination text and laboratory manual focuses on human interaction and human behavior rather than on the skill of platform speaking. Concerned with the identification of communication problems, the book also emphasizes language behavior in its approach to intrapersonal communication. Class activities and special projects provide for learning situations in which effective communication is facilitated by student interaction. The book is highly readable.

Nichols, Ralph G. and Leonard A. Stevens: *Are You Listening?* McGraw-Hill Book Company, New York, 1957 (Chap. 4). This is an excellent introduction to the topic of listening by two of the pioneers in the field. The book contains practical suggestions for the improvement of listening as well as some of the common reasons for poor listening.

Pace, R. Wayne and Robert R. Boren: *The Human Transaction*, Scott, Foresman and Company, Glenview, Ill., 1973 (Chap. 1). This text focuses essentially on interpersonal interaction and attempts to integrate communication theory with the analysis and practice of sound interpersonal interaction. Although much of what is written applies to the public-speaking situation, little emphasis is placed on public forms of communication. The authors view *clarification* (making clear and understandable messages and eliciting from the listener responses consistent with what the sender has in mind), *verification* (the discovery and use of evidence to confirm the authenticity of the message), and *amelioration* (the intentional improvement of human relationships by being aware of, using, and coping with feelings) as the basic functions of interpersonal communication.

Packard, Vance: *The Hidden Persuaders*, Pocket Books, New York, 1958 (Chap. 10). This is an exploration of, and an attack on, the large-scale efforts to channel our habits, purchasing decisions, and thought processes by the use of insights gleaned from the social sciences.

Public Opinion Quarterly, vol. 24, 1960 (Chap. 4). This special issue is devoted to studies in attitude change.

Rein, Irving J.: *Rudy's Red Wagon, Communication Strategies in Contemporary Society*, Scott, Foresman and Co., Glenview, Ill., 1972 (Chap. 10). In a most entertaining fashion, the author unmasks the deceptive language strategies of advertisers, politicians, educators, and others who attempt to manipulate individual behavior to achieve their goals.

Ruesch, Jurgen and Weldon Kees: *Nonverbal Communication*, University of California Press, Berkeley, 1956 (Chap. 3). In this early and pictorial book, the authors explore the principles that apply to nonverbal communication. Aided by still pictures, they explore the informal and spontaneous methods of communication which, if considered only in verbal and abstract terms, would be grossly distorted. Part 1 presents some theoretical material on communication and is followed by a section on messages through nonverbal action, a section on messages through objects, and finally a section on the language of disturbed interaction. Although the pictures are a bit outdated, they illustrate the authors' points excellently.

Scheflen, Albert E.: *How Behavior Means*, Gordon & Breach Science Publishers, New York, 1973 (Chap. 3). The author explores the ways in which people assign meaning to behavior. He discusses how gestures identify a referent and how they structure communication contexts. He develops the ideas that gestures are not necessarily a consequence of an ongoing communication sequence, that gestures are a form of metacommunication and that gestures can be used to change and manipulate situations.

Scheidel, Thomas M.: *Speech Communication and Human Interaction*, Scott, Foresman and Company, Glenview, Ill., 2nd ed., 1976 (Chap. 1). Intended for a first-level college course in speech communication, this book attempts to develop an understanding of basic concepts and principles operating in the speech-communication setting. It also provides exercises and study probes. The situation in which two persons speak with each other is suggested as the prototype of all oral communication contexts. The text progresses from interpersonal communication, to small-group communication, to speech making appropriate for public platforms and the mass media.

Watzlawick, Paul, Janet Beavin, and Don Jackson: *Pragmatics of Human Communication*, W.W. Norton & Company, New York, 1967 (Chap. 1). This book is a study of the behavioral effects of communication, with particular attention to disturbed communication or behavioral disorders. The book proceeds from a general system-theory base. It is of value to the reader who wishes to gain an understanding of the relevance of general system theory to interpersonal relations and communication. Somewhat hard to read in places. The authors' analysis of *Who is Afraid of Virginia Woolf?* is entertaining and very insightful.

Wilmot, William: *Dyadic Communication: A Transactional Perspective*, Addison-Wesley, Readings, Mass., 1975 (Chap. 2). Wilmot focuses on two-person communication systems. He shows how perception of self and of others is socially influenced and how relationships are perceived and maintained. This book serves as a highly readable overview of a transactional view of human communication.

APPLICATIONS

INDEX